BILL IVY

THE WILL TO WIN

Drawing by
David Boarer.

BILL IVY

THE WILL TO WIN

MICK WALKER

First published in Great Britain in 2009 by
The Breedon Books Publishing Company Limited
Breedon House, 3 The Parker Centre,
Derby, DE21 4SZ.

Dedication

This book has been published in memory of a truly great rider who was taken from us 40 years ago, in July 1969.

Mick Walker
2009

ISBN 978-1-85983-680-4
UPC 8 262051 0016 7

Printed and bound by TJ International Ltd, Padstow, Cornwall.

Contents

"I am privileged to have access to the Mortons Motorcycle Media Archive, which I consider to be the finest in the world and a national treasure."
MICK WALKER

Every so often a unique snapshot of times gone by is discovered in a dusty vault or in shoeboxes in an attic by an enthusiastic amateur photographer. They are living history. Each and every one of us cannot resist the temptation as we marvel at the quality of the images, to let our mind drift back to the good old days and wonder what it was really like.

We at Mortons Motorcycle Media, market-leading publishers of classic and vintage titles, own one of the largest photographic archives of its kind in the world. It is a treasure trove of millions of motorcycle and related images, many of which have never seen the light of day since they were filed away in the dark-room almost 100 years ago.

Perhaps the biggest gem of all is our collection of glass plates – almost two tons of them to be precise! They represent a largely hitherto unseen look into our motorcycling heritage from the turn of the century. Many of the plates are priceless and capture an era long gone when the pace of life was much slower and traffic jams were unheard of.

We are delighted to be associated with well known author Mick Walker in the production of this book and hope you enjoy the images from our archive.

Terry Clark,
Managing Director,
Mortons Media Group Ltd

Preface

When I wrote *John Surtees: Motorcycle Maestro* back in 2002 (published in 2003) it was as a one-off book, not a series. However, thanks to its critical success, including winning 'Book of the Week' in *The Independent* newspaper, I was given the chance by the publisher, Breedon Books, to compile an on-going series. And *Bill Ivy: The Will to Win* is the seventh title.

Throughout the series I have attempted to provide the most detailed possible story of each rider's career, recording the facts and events without in any way making it all sound more glamorous than it really was. It is also important to me to make each book an interesting read. And, finally, I have attempted to provide the reader with as many previously unpublished facts and photographs as possible, plus mini biographies of the men and machines which played a vital co-starring role in the racing careers of Surtees, Agostini, Hailwood, McIntyre, Duke, Minter and now Ivy.

Bill Ivy was certainly not only a great rider but also a unique personality. In fact, Mike Hailwood is on record as saying, in his view, Bill: 'Was the last of the great racing characters.' This was, of course, before a certain Mr Rossi came on the scene!

Besides his obvious riding talent, Bill had a great determination to succeed, an almost fearless courage, which meant he never backed away from a challenge, a love of fashion and fast cars – and, of course, he more than made up for his lack of stature by his immense upper body strength, which meant he could cope with any size of motorcycle from a 50cc Itom to a 750cc Norton-engined Matchless G15 CSR.

I would like to thank all those who have helped in some way to produce this book with either photographs or information, sometimes both. These include George Paget, David Boarer (who also did the magnificent drawing at the beginning of this book), Peter Reeve, Jasmine Rodger, Ian and Rita Welsh, Peter and Lesley Martin, Les Parker, Ray Palmer, Maggie Smart, Maurice Thomas, Pauline Tranter, Marie and Syd Rose, Sue and David Swift, my Austrian friend and former Grand Prix photographer Wolfgang Gruber, Gary Swift, Gary James, Ray Palmer, Elwyn Roberts, Ken Whorlow and most of all, Roy Francis.

Finally, my wife Sue for the many, many hours I am tied up with research and writing.

I sincerely hope that you will garner as much pleasure from *Bill Ivy: The Will to Win* as I have had in compiling it.

Mick Walker
Wisbech, Cambridgeshire

Chapter 1

The Maidstone Kid

W.D. (William David) Ivy – Bill to the wider world and simply Billy to family, friends and schoolmates – was born in the back of an ambulance at Linton crossroads, while his mother Nell was being transported to Pembrey hospital from her home in Kingswood, near Maidstone, Kent. The date was 27 August 1942 and the ambulance had got lost in thick fog – a most unusual occurrence at that time of year.

The Family

Bill's father Maurice (also known as Bill, and later, affectionately, as 'Ringo') was an engineer employed by the Noakes family's forge and agricultural business at Pye Corner, Ulcombe (see photograph).

Besides young Bill, Maurice and Nell (also known as Ethal) had two daughters, the oldest Suzette (Sue) was born on 25 May 1939, while Marie arrived on 28 January 1944.

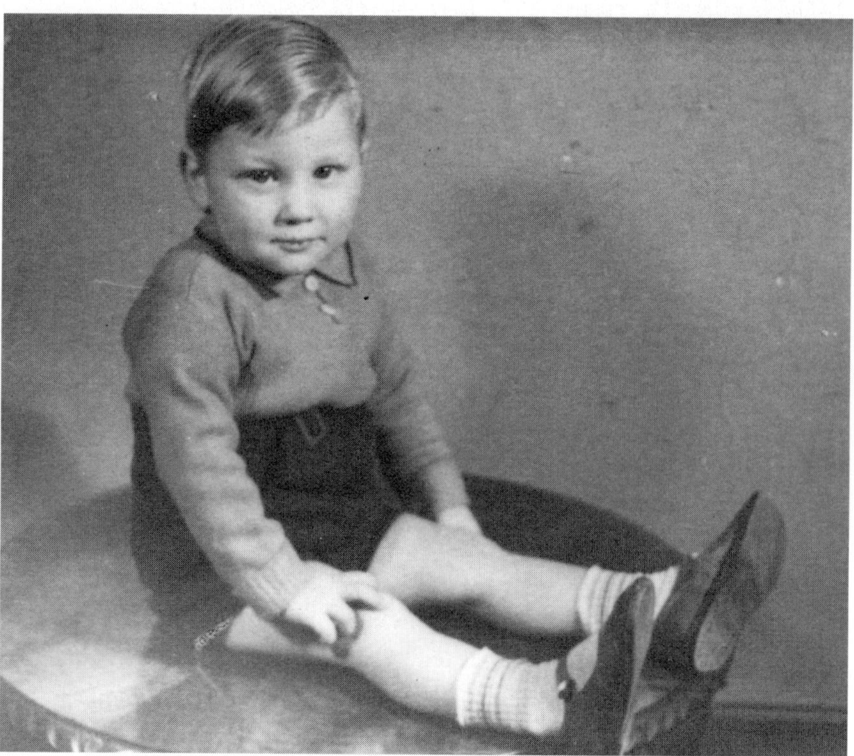

Billy aged two years and four months.

An aerial view of the Noakes forge and agricultural business at Pye Corner, Ulcombe.

From 1949 the Ivy family lived in Sutton Valence. Then, as the 1960s arrived, Nell Ivy opened a general store in Albert Street, Maidstone. These premises had living quarters above and to the rear of the shop. In the mid-1960s the family moved to Glebe Lane, Barming, near Maidstone. Finally, during 1967, Bill, by now a fully fledged works rider with Yamaha, purchased a bungalow in Ditton for his mother and father; thus showing his generous and caring nature.

Bill's Education

Bill's first school was Ulcombe Primary near his original home at Kingswood. Then came Sutton Valence Primary before, aged 11, moving to Oldborough Manor Secondary Modern at Boughton Lane in Loose, a suburb of Maidstone.

An Oldborough Manor Secondary Modern School class photograph with Bill, aged 13, third from the right on the front row.

Right from the beginning there is absolutely no doubt Bill was a bit of a rebel; he was always getting into mischief. One of his early school photographs shows Bill with other members of his class, everyone else posing in an orderly fashion for the photographer except Bill who has his tongue sticking out! But at the same time one could not help liking him and he had plenty of good traits. Typical was his love of animals from a young age. His younger sister Marie remembers Bill arriving home one day. He was wearing a parka coat and his mother thought he was hiding something underneath. At first she thought he had been scrumping apples, but on closer inspection when the coat was unzipped Bill had a kitten instead!

As Marie also recalls: 'Bill had found the tiny kitten and taken it home thinking it was lost. Mum told him to take it back as its mother would be looking for it. Amid tears he did so, but he had only wanted to make sure it was safe.'

On Two Wheels

Having a father who was an engineer had benefits for young Bill, as his dad was able to convert an old pedal cycle to having suspension at either end, with a small sprocket at the front so it could be ridden up banks and other steep inclines. This was when it was first realised that Bill possessed outstanding natural balance on two wheels. Soon he was winning slow cycle races by balancing on the pedals at the start line and became the envy of his school friends.

At school he endeared himself to teachers and pupils alike. Of the many letters Nell Ivy received after Bill's death in July 1969 were several from his various school teachers. Typical are the words from Bill's former English teacher at Oldborough Manor Secondary Modern School, Bill Green: 'He was always a lively pupil [older sister Sue describes him as a "bit of an imp"]. I shall never forget his performance on the school stage in 1955. I have rarely seen a boy so nimble and agile.' Mr Green also recalled that later, when Bill had become a star, 'I really enjoyed chatting to Billy [note the use of Billy not Bill] when he came to see us at Oldborough; he was modest, unassuming and so pleasant to talk to.'

His school friend and later fellow racer Roy Francis had this to say to the author while compiling *Bill Ivy: The Will to Win*, 'In-between riding around on pedal cycles, later motorcycles, and making a monkey of himself in the school concert dressed as a gorilla, Bill was a very accomplished boxer and represented his school [Oldborough Manor] doing very well until deciding to quit after getting fairly well beaten in an inter-school boxing match by a much bigger opponent.'

Left to right: Bill, older sister Sue and younger sister Marie; *c.*1947.

The Francis Barnett

Roy Francis went on to say 'I really got to know him better around the age of 12, after he got his first motorcycle, a 1930s Francis Barnett 250 Cruiser, which he used to ride around some old allotments at the bottom of Sutton Valence hill. He was upsetting the gardeners because he was riding the machine through the rows of runner beans and other vegetables and was eventually banned. We became friends and after he heard that my father owned Brissenden Farm at East Sutton, the Francis Barnett was transported there to be ridden. We took all the tinwork off and cut the exhaust down. Then we marked out a track around the fields and that was it – we rode around for hours. We had a small group of friends who used to all take turns riding the bike and whenever it ran out of petrol we all used to try and get a ride on Bill's tricked-up pedal cycle to make a trip to the garage for more.'

The Francis Barnett had previously belonged to Bill's father's employers, the Noakes, and during the summer it had been loaded onto the back of their combine harvester and taken to various locations; at the end of each day it was used to transport the harvester's driver to his home.

The Noakes, father Nobby and son Ned, were enthusiastic motorcyclists themselves and in fact Ned is currently president of the Tenterden & District Motorcycle Club.

A 1930s Francis Barnett 250cc Cruiser. In stripped down form, this was used on allotments and Roy Francis' father's farm by both Roy and Bill.

Brissenden Farm, East Sutton, where Bill and Roy rode the old Francis Barnett during the mid-1950s.

A Competitive Debut

Bill's competitive motorcycle debut came in 1958, when he was invited to take part in a 'closed to club' grass track meeting at Headcorn by the local Maidstone Aces Motorcycle Club. He was to ride the Tiger 80. He won a couple of events, even beating his future employers the Chisholm brothers Bill and Don, and at this early stage his natural aptitude for racing began to display itself. Roy Francis recalls Bill's result as being, 'Not bad for an ancient bike with a split in the offside [right] of the rear tyre, so as not to tear it completely as it went anti-clockwise round the track.'

It was around this time that Bill's older sister Sue began going out with Dave Swift. Soon Dave and his brother John became firm friends with Bill.

A 1958 photograph showing Roy Francis (then aged 15) with his father and Bill's Triumph Tiger 80 three-fifty.

Street Legal at Last

Shortly after the grass track debut, Bill purchased a sprung hub, alloy-engined Triumph Tiger 100 five-hundred twin. This was the first street legal motorcycle that Bill owned. As Roy Francis recalls, 'There was a crowd of us who used to go around together to different coffee bars and cafés.' Roy continues, 'Bill then exchanged the Tiger 100 for an MV Agusta 175, which blew up very quickly and was soon replaced by a red-and-white Gilera 175 Rossa Extra. He used to race around with John [Swift] who owned a standard black-and-red Gilera 175, trying to beat each other around the local Kent roads. The group of us used to frequent a café near the railway station in Staplehurst, owned by Len Johnson, and the Singing Kettle nearby. We also visited one at Cross at Hand and the Rising Sun in West Kingsdown off the A20.'

Plumstead

Bill left school in summer 1958 and began work at the giant AMC (Associated Motor Cycles) works in Plumstead, south-east London. As his sister Sue told the author, 'He stayed with our grandparents at Petts Wood near Bromley. Bill used to travel up to them on Sunday evenings. I would go to Maidstone East rail station with him to see him off and as he went, the tears used to come down his face because he had not been away from home before and he hated it. He was only 15 and had just left school, Dad knew he was unhappy with his job and went to see Chisholms and got him a job there.'

And why had young Bill quit AMC? Well, not only did he hate living away from home for the first time, but instead of being allowed to work on engines and the like as he had imagined, as many youngsters before and since have discovered to their cost, being an apprentice at the beginning meant spending his working day sweeping up or making cups of tea for the older and more experienced members of the staff! But probably worse than any of this was the fact that when Bill had swept the floor the rubbish was kicked back – which really upset him.

The Velocette Experience

During early 1959 Don Chisholm took young Bill up to Brands Hatch one Wednesday afternoon to have a ride round the famous Kent track on the former's ex-Frank Fry Velocette KTT Mark VIII. During this practice session Don Chisholm was able to realise that his young employee had real ability – and this was to impress him so much that Don promised himself that he should do something to realise the youngster's potential.

A view of the AMC (Associated Motor Cycles) factory in south-east London, where Bill worked as an apprentice during the autumn of 1958. The picture shows Bob Manns from the Competition Department where Bill was employed, with a couple of AJS 250cc machines.

So, as the following chapter reveals, being Itom agents the Chisholms took a nearly new Itom Astor Sports model from their showroom stock and eventually converted this series production, pre-mix, three-speed, hand change, air-cooled bike into a pukka racing machine. Over the next few years this was to evolve from a non-faired bike into a water-cooled, oil-pump lubricated, six-speed, footchange, fully-faired racer. All the mechanical work for this conversion was carried out in the Chisholms's small engineering workshop in the village of Boughton Monchelsea, just outside Maidstone.

And Bill most certainly did not disgrace himself even at his first-ever road race (on the Itom), at Brands Hatch on Good Friday 1959.

Personalising the Crash Helmet

Bill had talked about personalising his crash helmet and the obvious choice was to paint an ivy leaf onto the front. Unsure what they looked like, Bill and Roy Francis (both now working at Chisholm's Boughton Monchelsea workshop) went out of the back of Bill's mother's shop to an old outside toilet, and growing up the building was an ivy bush. Bill selected a suitable leaf and then drew around its outline. It is thus possible to work out what year some of the photographs are from as the design changed as it was repainted. The early years of Bill's racing career still had the stalk of the ivy leaf in place – whereas later this was discarded.

Café Racer Days

Talking to Roy Francis revealed that the local group of motorcyclists, of which Bill was one, staged runs to New Romney, sometimes via the Military Canal Road, and were a regular occurrence, stopping for a break at a small café near the railway station. Sometimes Bill was able to use a bike from Chisholm's, depending on what was available. On one occasion he lent his Gilera 175 to a friend, Brian Hemsley, while out in Staplehurst. When Brian did not return he was discovered standing at the side of the road.

A 1959 photograph of Bill with his sprung-hub Triumph Tiger 100 500cc twin, registration number MYN 107, which Bill referred to simply as Myn (Mine).

Cyril Rogers

On the outskirts of Sutton Valence village, on the Headcorn road, was a bungalow occupied by professional speedway rider Cyril Rogers. Cyril, the former lap record holder at Brands Hatch on the grass track riding 347 and 495cc AJS machines for Barham (Canterbury) entrant Tom Arter, was by the late-1950s riding speedway for New Cross and later Norwich.

Bill and Roy Francis got to know Cyril when still schoolboys and they would cycle round to his workshop to watch him prepare his machine for the next event. Unlike today's riders with different machines and engines for each track, Cyril would adapt his single bike from meeting to meeting. This would entail not only altering gearing but also the engine compression and timing to give what characteristic of performance was required. The two boys were fascinated by his removal of the cylinder head and barrel of his JAP engine to carry out work such as fitting additional gaskets to lower or higher the compression ratio.

Bill was often invited along on occasions to accompany Cyril to a meeting with everything packed into Cyril's Morris 1000 pick-up, then in vogue as a rider's transport.

Cyril Rogers not only rode in the 1948 British Speedway League's Championship-winning team, but also later as a member of the Southampton team, along with legendary New Zealander Barry Briggs, won the League again in 1962. Cyril also reached the World Speedway Finals on more than one occasion.

Unfortunately Brian had crashed into a car and although he was unhurt, the same could not be said of Bill's Gilera (which by now, in the summer of 1960, doubled up as a second racing machine to compliment the Chisholm Itom). Brian Hemsley owned a very nice, gold, swinging-arm Triumph Thunderbird six-fifty. Knowing Bill used his Gilera as his ride-to-work transport and for visiting his girlfriend Ann in Tenterden, Brian offered Bill the loan of his Triumph until the Gilera was repaired.

The Big Crash

Everything went along fine until one evening on his way home from Tenterden on the A262 after visiting Ann, when Bill crashed into a telegraph pole (now long gone) at the Woolpack Corner on the outskirts of Biddenden village, breaking his pelvis and both legs. As Roy Francis told the author, 'We later found one of his boots some distance away out in a field, thrown there due to the impact of the crash.' Bill ended up in Ashford hospital for a while, before finally returning to work with one of his legs still in plaster and on crutches. By this time the Gilera was back in a roadworthy condition and being Bill he rode the machine to work each day – being given a push off by his mother – with the crutch up and his plastered leg resting on the

The 1959 Gilera 175 Rossa Extra.

fairing stay! Homeward bound it was very much the same procedure, with a bump start from one of his work colleagues. Bill also used a walking stick to operate the clutch of his first car, which he purchased around this time.

The crash on Brian Hemsley's Triumph had not only totally destroyed the motorcycle but had also prematurely ended Bill's activities for the remainder of the 1960 road racing season; the accident having occurred in July of that year.

As the next chapter reveals, for the first four seasons of Bill's road racing career – and later with the CR93 Honda – the Chisholm brothers were to be instrumental in helping the Maidstone youngster in taking his first steps along the road to ultimately breaking into the big time and eventually winning the World Championship title. *Bill Ivy: The Will to Win* will take you on a memorable journey, a true rags to riches saga to equal any in the long history of motorcycle racing.

Chapter 2

Chisholm's

As we know, Bill's job at the giant AMC motorcycle plant in south-east London had come to an end and he had found a much more likeable job locally, with the Chisholm dealership in Maidstone.

Setting the Wheels in Motion

The Chisholm brothers, Bill and Don, were to play an important part in Bill Ivy's early racing career. And they did in fact provide Bill with his very first racing mount. This was an almost new Italian Itom 50cc machine – Chisholm's being an agent for the marque. Cyril Standing (known as 'Ginger') asked Don Chisholm why he did not use one of the pukka Competition models as the basis for the racer; Don's reply was: 'this is what we sell, so this is what we race.' The machine was a nearly new Astor Super Sports, taken from Chisholm's showroom stock.

Work began during the winter of 1958–59, and at first it was more a case of simply removing all the road equipment (lights, exhaust, mudguards etc) and fitting the optional 'racing only' open (referred to as the cowhorn)

Bill riding Don Chisholm's ex-Frank Fry Velocette Mark VIII three-fifty at Brands Hatch, 20 September 1959. It could not have been more different from his usual racing mount, the 50cc Chis Itom.

Bill (168) on the Chis Itom, leads Howard German (Sheene special) during the 50cc event at Brands Hatch on 11 October 1959. After setting a new class record lap, Bill was forced to retire on the third lap.

exhaust. This latter component certainly provided a vast amount of noise if not performance! And after a couple of Wednesday Brands Hatch test days, the Chisholm brothers and Bill were ready to enter a race meeting proper.

Debut Day

Debut day for W.D. Ivy came at the new season's first Brands Hatch meeting, on Good Friday 27 March 1959, when a huge crowd packed the 1.24 mile (2km) Kent track to watch many of the most famous names in racing – including Bob McIntyre, Derek Minter and Mike Hailwood – with weather conditions which *Motor Cycle News* described as 'dull and drizzly.'

As for Bill, he was only entered in a single event, the three-lap 50cc race. This was won by Itom-mounted C.V. Dawson, with Don Field (Special) runner-up and Bill third on the Chisholm machine. C.R. Denton, on yet another Itom, was fourth. Dawson's race time was 4 min 56.2 sec, with an average speed of 45.32mph (72.91km/h).

A rather comical footnote to Bill's debut day was that he borrowed leathers from Don Chisholm, who was not only much taller but was also considerably heavier, giving Bill what is best described as a 'saggy' look!

Brands Only

During the 1959 season Bill only rode at Brands Hatch, and, except for a solitary outing on Don Chisholm's ancient KTT Mark VIII Velocette, he rode exclusively on the Itom (a full description, including its development, can be found in a separate boxed section within this chapter).

Only three weeks after his debut, Bill was back in action on the Itom at the Kentish circuit. And once again he was to bring the Chisholm bike home in third position. However, this only came after an opening lap crash involving D.M. Field, who suffered facial abrasions. The race was won by Howard German, riding Frank Sheene's Special (an Itom-based model).

50cc Brands Hatch – 5 laps – 6.2 miles

1st	H.D. German (Sheene Special)
2nd	A.A. Stride (Itom)
3rd	W.D. Ivy (Chis Itom)
4th	D. Guy (Fruin Dartella)
5th	C.V. Dawson (Itom)

Brands Racing Committee

Bill's third outing came at Brands Racing Committee's national status meeting on Whit Monday, 18 May. And although Bill was a retirement, the race was notable as Howard German (Sheene Special) broke the lap record, with a speed of 51.50mph (82.86km/h).

A photograph from the very early days of 50cc racing at Brands Hatch, spring 1959. Number 2 is Alan Dawson (Demm).

The Chis-Itom 50

During 1959, 50cc racing was in its infancy. Small motorcycles were in fashion and supplied by Italian manufacturers.

The Chisholm brothers Don and Bill in their Upper Stone Street shop in Maidstone held the agencies for Itom, MV Agusta and Gilera.

Don had been road racing for many years on 250 and 350 Velocettes. He fancied getting involved with the new era of 50cc but he was not of ideal stature being well over 6ft tall. At this time a young lad by the name of Bill Ivy had joined the workshop staff. He was a ready-made rider, being of the ideal size and weight and keen to go racing after trying Don's 350 KTT at Brands Hatch. The Itom range included a competition model but because of the supply situation at the time Don and Bill Chisholm decided to use the Astor Sport model. This three-speed, hand change model was fitted with a suitable seat, drop handlebars and a short cow horn-shaped megaphone exhaust for young Bill to test at Brands Hatch. The Chisholm brothers soon got drawn into two-stroke tuning to improve the machine's performance, working many long hours into the night at their Boughton Monchelsea engineering section, which was in an old oasthouse-type building. The air-cooled, three-speed engine was developed by them into a water-cooled unit by welding a steel jacket around the cylinder and fitting a radiator. Big-end failure soon became an issue with the increased rpm and power output. This problem was tackled by the brothers designing and manufacturing a small oil pump to supply a direct feed to the crank pin thus increasing lubrication of the big-end bearing, giving reliability.

To test their work a form of brake tester was built on the upper floor of the workshop. This consisted of a table-like construction with the engine mounted on one side. With a chain, the engine drove via sprockets a cross paddle wheel arrangement. The paddles acted as a constant load on the engine and allowed more rpm to be sought. This was a very primitive, highly dangerous device with no guards. The exhaust of the engine vented into a packing case to deaden the sound. The vibration and noise when the

Bill Ivy with the converted Itom 50cc Astor Super Sports; Brands Hatch, 20 September 1959.

brothers were carrying out testing was horrendous and only very short runs were possible without upsetting the whole neighbourhood, even operating the throttle was difficult. A Fi-Glass of Edenbridge fairing was fitted to streamline the unit.

The main competitors to Bill Ivy and the Chis-Itom were other Chisholm team members Maurice Thomas and Sid Lovell on their own machines, Howard German on Frank Sheene's Special, Alan Dawson on the Pope brothers's machine, Mike and Dave Simmonds and Charlie Mates who were all striving to get more performance from their machines.

Bill Ivy's size and weight were considerable advantages, as was his very brave riding style.

As part of the development programme the next major job undertaken almost totally in-house was to build a six-speed gearbox to enable the narrow power band to be exploited. This was tackled by the brothers, Don and Bill, casting an alloy extension of the gearbox housing plus machining an extension gearshift and selector mechanism, together with a foot change. The blank gears were taken to a company in Rochester for the teeth to be cut and hardening to be carried out. Delivery and collection of these items was made by Roy Francis who had by now also joined the staff at Chisholm's of Maidstone, having been recommended by Bill Ivy.

All this improvement in performance and reliability of a basic motorcycle by these two enthusiasts, Don and Bill Chisholm, in out-of-hours time, independent of worldwide two-stroke development, was remarkable and unknowingly in tandem with the giants of the motorcycle industry: Suzuki, Yamaha and MZ, etc.

Things gathered pace very quickly in the early 1960s with production racers appearing from Japan in the form of the Honda CR110, Tohatsu and Suzuki TR50.

The Chis-Itom was retired and dismantled when Bill Ivy moved on to pastures new. In the years to come the engine was purchased by Brian Woolley and on the death of the Chisholm brothers the racing chassis went to Governors Bridge Motorcycles.

All three meetings so far had been held in relatively cold weather, but all this changed on Sunday 5 July with what can only be described as a scorcher of a day. As *Motor Cycle News* said: 'The temperature was in the "80s" and it was really sweltering around this shadeless circuit.' The meeting was organised by the Gravesend Eagles club, and the 10-race programme began with a five-lap affair for the 50cc machines.

C.V. Dawson (Itom) snatched an immediate lead from the start, winning easily, and pushed the race record speed up to 50.24mph (80.83km/h).

50cc Brands Hatch – 5 laps – 6.2 miles

1st	C.V. Dawson (Itom)
2nd	L. Howard (Itom)
3rd	W.D. Ivy (Chis Itom)
4th	S. Lovell (Itom)

Another German Victory

Howard German was back to winning form on Sunday 23 August, leading the field home comfortably and putting both the race and lap record speeds up to 52.10mph (83.82km/h) and 54.17mph (87.15km/h) respectively. As for Bill, he was to suffer his second retirement.

Then, precisely four weeks later on 20 September, in what were described as ideal conditions, Bill brought his machine home to another third position. And although every one of his finishes so far had been an identical one, this was his best performance to date as both men who beat him were seen as expert competitors with many class wins to their belts – Roy Nicholson and Howard German.

50cc Brands Hatch – 5 laps – 6.2 miles

1st	R.A. Nicholson (Itom)
2nd	H.D. German (Sheene Special)
3rd	W.D. Ivy (Chis Itom)
4th	E. Chiles (Itom)
5th	A.A. Stride (Itom)
6th	L. Howard (Itom)

A Press Mention

The 1959 Brands Hatch season ended on Sunday 10 October and with it came Bill's first mention in the national motorcycle press – other than a name in results – with the following extract from *Motor Cycle News* dated 14 October 1959: 'the 50cc class is now firmly established at Brands with Howard German (Sheene Special) at the top, and it came as some surprise when he was being led by W.D. Ivy (Chisholm Itom) in the opening lap of the first event.' In fact, Bill led for three laps until he was forced to retire with mechanical problems; but not before establishing a new class lap record of 55.11mph (88.67km/h). German then rode out on his own, winning easily with a new race record speed of 52.76mph (84.89km/h).

And so Bill had at last shown the first glimpse of his potential, and he had repaid some of the confidence the Chisholm brothers had placed in him with this exciting performance.

The following month, in November 1959, came the welcome news that Brands Hatch would remain open for practising on Wednesdays and Saturdays throughout the winter, weather permitting. Practice began at nine and ended at five, with an hour's break for lunch. Cost, which included insurance, was given as 'thirty-five shillings all day' (£1.75 equivalent). Cars and motorcycles took it in turn to use the track.

Maurice Thomas

Maurice Thomas during his early racing days, *c.*1957. The machine is a 250cc Velocette MOV.

Maurice Thomas – who was Bill Ivy's co-rider on the Chisholm Itom in the first two 50cc 250-mile Enduros – was born at Lenham, Kent, on 15 January 1936; Lenham is a small village halfway between Maidstone and Ashford in a rural location.

Maurice's first experience of motorcycle racing came in 1951, when together with his father, Robert, he cycled to Brands Hatch. He remembers saying: 'I would like to do this one day.'

Maurice winning the 50cc race at Brands Hatch aboard his privately-owned Chis Itom, 17 September 1961.

An *MCN* advertisement showing the results for 17 September 1961, a round of the 1961 Brands Hatch Championships.

After leaving school, Maurice went to work for a local car garage, but his real interest lay with motorcycles. And to this end he purchased his first machine, an old pre-war Triumph 250. The Triumph was followed by a 125 James. Then in 1955 he became the proud owner of a Rudge 250, which was subsequently converted into racing trim, having its first meeting (at Brands Hatch) later the same year. In 1957 the Rudge was replaced by an MOV Velocette. On the latter machine he raced against many of the sport's top names, including Mike Hailwood, Derek Minter and Dave Chadwick.

Towards the end of 1959 Maurice joined Maidstone dealers Chisholm's. And thus began his Itom racing career. Not only did he purchase a second-hand Itom racer from Sid Lovell, but Maurice shared the Chisholm machine with Bill Ivy in the Snetterton Enduro in both 1960 and 1961. As is fully documented in the main text, the pairing won the event in the first year but were controversially disqualified some months later. The following year Maurice and Bill came home in fourth place.

In 1962 Maurice quit his job at Chisholm's and moved to Snodland in the Medway area of northern Kent, working at an engineering works, producing, among other things, small air compressors.

This move and change of occupation also saw Maurice stop racing.

Nothing happened on that front until 1964, and then his return to the sport saw him passengering for John Sweet (who campaigned a Manx Norton 'sitter' outfit). This lasted a single year.

Then came a long gap in his competition activities before returning (again as a sidecar passenger) with Brian Reeves, the latter's original passenger having gone to live in the Isle of Man. The Reeves outfit was powered by a BSA A65 six-fifty twin-cylinder engine.

In 1984, with the birth of classic racing, Maurice made a return as a solo racer riding a five-hundred Gilera Saturno. Then in 1986 his son Nigel – Maurice having married his wife Jay back in 1960 – took up sidecar racing (again with an A65 outfit), recruiting dad as his passenger!

In 1992, Maurice Thomas finally called it a day and retired from racing once again – this time for good.

A New Season and a First Victory

As was traditional at that time, the Good Friday National was the first race of the 1960 Brands Hatch season; this taking place on 15 April. *Motor Cycle News* were enthusiastic: 'Bang Go Brands Records' and 'What a crowd and what magnificent racing.' Continuing: 'By the end of the afternoon all existing solo and lap records had been knocked for six.'

Of course the established stars, in the shape of Derek Minter and Mike Hailwood, grabbed all the column inches. However, it was also a great day for Bill, as not only did he raise his existing lap record but also scored his first-ever race victory into the bargain.

50cc Brands Hatch – 5 laps – 6.2 miles

1st	W.D. Ivy (Chis Itom)
2nd	H.D. German (Sheene Special)
3rd	R.A. Nicholson (Itom)
4th	M.E. Chiles (Itom)

The Snetterton Enduro

Then came Bill's first really long-distance race, the 250 mile (402km) Chilton Enduro. Organised by the Racing 50 Club and held in superb, sunny, dry weather, this was the first-ever long-distance event for the midgets of motorcycle racing. It was staged over 92 laps of the 2.71 mile (4.36km) Snetterton circuit in Norfolk, some 18 miles (29km) south of Norwich. Bill was partnered by his friend and fellow Chisholm's employee, Maurice Thomas (see boxed section within this chapter).

As the 18 May 1960 issue of *Motor Cycle News* reported: 'After a delay of half an hour the 50 starters for the first-ever long-distance 50cc race in England got away in a buzzing, weaving mass.' At the end of the first lap Dick Dedden (Itom) led from Bill Ivy on the Chisholm-entered machine; third was yet another Itom, piloted by Charlie Surridge. By the third lap Dedden (partnered by the journalist Mick Woollett) had dropped back to third spot with clutch slip and Surridge went into the lead ahead of Ivy. With 10 laps of the 92 completed Surridge and Bill had pulled half a mile clear of R.G. Harris (Fruin). After 30 laps – third race distance – the Charlie Surridge/Roy Nicholson Itom led by a 'wide margin' (*MCN*), because the Bill Ivy/Maurice Thomas machine had crashed (Bill the rider) and was off the leaderboard. Then the leading Itom slowed and with half the race distance covered it was the Johnson/Bone team in the lead, but the Ivy/Thomas machine was right back in the picture and gaining ground on the leaders all the time. A long stop dropped the Bone/Johnson Itom to sixth place and the Ivy/Thomas machine swept into the lead, which they held until the flag. The Bill Ivy/Maurice Thomas pairing also set the fastest lap (Bill) at 55.95mph (90.02km/h).

On 14 May 1960 Bill, together with co-rider Maurice Thomas (a fellow employee of Chisholm's), took part in the very first 50cc Enduro at Snetterton. Here Bill sets off after a refuelling stop, while Don Chisholm in his white coat looks on. The team won but were disqualified some months later.

50cc Chilton Enduro 250 mile – 92 laps – 250 miles

1st	W.D. Ivy/M. Thomas (Chis Itom)
2nd	V.J. Dedden/M. Woollet (Demm)
3rd	D. Frost/D. Weightmann (Itom)
4th	P. Lucas/J. Snow (Itom)
5th	K.I. Johnson/A.D. Bone (Itom)
6th	R. Kemp/P.E. Ranford (Itom)

Unfortunately, the pairing of Ivy/Thomas was to be disqualified some months later, but morally they were the victors of this very first 50cc Enduro (the last of which, held at Lydden Hill, Kent, took place in 1972 – the author and his co-rider coming home fifth). Bill and Maurice were never given an official answer as to why they had been disqualified. But Maurice told the author that he thinks it was because they refuelled while keeping their engine running (due to a sticking throttle).

The second 50cc Enduro took place on Sunday 7 May 1961. Here, Bill is seated on bike, while Maurice Thomas and Bill Chisholm are refuelling the Chis Itom. The pair came home fourth.

Back at Brands

Straight from his victory the previous day at Snetterton, Bill was back at Brands Hatch on Sunday 15 May 1960. Since the previous meeting at the Kent circuit a month earlier on Good Friday a great deal had been carried out to improve the course, especially at Clearways. The verdict of the 50cc race – as usual the opening event – was, as *Motor Cycle News* said in its 18 May issue: 'Expected to be between the respective race and lap record holders, Howard German (Sheene Special) and Bill Ivy (Itom).' But this was not the case. From the start Charlie Mates (Itom) made the running, and although German was hard on his tail and took the lead on the second lap, Bill was never in the picture and from seventh place on the first lap he dropped down the field to eventually finish 12th.

Perhaps more notable was his first-ever race on his recently acquired 175cc Gilera. This machine, a converted road model, was to be used in the then current 200cc class races at Brands Hatch that year, before being increased in size to 190cc the following season. Ranged against Bill at the May 1960 meeting in the 200cc race were Mike Hailwood (124cc Desmo Ducati), Bob Anderson and Ken Whorlow (both riding 175cc MV Agustas – entered by importer Ron Harris) and Dan Shorey (125cc Ducati GP). Against riders and machinery of this quality, the Gilera was outclassed and eventually retired.

Three weeks later, on Sunday 6 June, Bill was back in action at Brands Hatch, finishing third in the five-lap 50cc event behind the winner Howard German (Sheene Special) and Charlie Mates (Itom). And having his second ride on the 175cc Gilera, he was unplaced in the 200cc event, which was won by Ken Whorlow (MV Agusta).

Bill converted his road-going Gilera 175cc Rossa Extra into a racer, the first meeting coming on 15 June 1960 at Brands Hatch, but he was a non-finisher.

The Big Crash

Bill's next outing, again at Brands Hatch, was scheduled for 21 August. But he was to be a non-starter in both races he had entered (the 50cc and 200cc on the Itom and Gilera respectively). This was because of the massive injuries he sustained in a road crash, riding a 650cc Triumph Thunderbird, as described in Chapter 1. The accident resulted in him breaking both legs and his pelvis. The Chisholm brothers were to comment that they had 'never seen a bike so badly wrecked; virtually everything was a write off'. Even the engine and gearbox assemblies were destroyed, such was the force of the impact. The machine had slid into the base of a telegraph pole situated a mere 2ft from the edge of the road: even the top gearbox lug had pulled out of the casing.

But Bill was not one to remain idle. And as Alan Peck says in his 1972 book, *No Time To Lose*: 'When the brothers [Chisholms] visited Bill in hospital they found him encased in plaster of Paris, propped up with pillows, with bits of balsa wood strewn all over the bed – helping some of the younger patients to make model aeroplanes.'

Bill spent well over six months in plaster and it was not until early 1961 that he was making progress. During the time Bill was recovering many of his friends and family were convinced that his accident would put him off racing. But already Bill was planning a comeback and soon told everyone: 'I'll be back on the track for the first meeting next season.'

Back to a Winning Start

As anyone will know who has broken a leg or ankle, being unable to walk for a considerable amount of time means muscles are not used and fitness is decreased. And with Bill's even more serious injuries he was still far from fully recovered when he travelled to Brands Hatch for the circuit's season opener on Good Friday, 31 March 1961. This meeting was run on the long 2.65 mile (4.26km) circuit, in ideal conditions before a near record crowd. And he made an impressive return – winning from fellow Chisholm employee Maurice Thomas (both riding Itoms); Michael O'Rourke was third on Frank Sheene's machine.

50cc Brands Hatch – 3 laps – 7.95 miles

1st	W.D. Ivy (Chis Itom)
2nd	M. Thomas (Itom)
3rd	M.P. O'Rourke (Sheene Special)
4th	C.C. Mates (Itom)

A Larger Gilera

Bill had also found time to increase the Gilera's exact engine displacement from 172 to 190cc. This was achieved by fitting a Triumph Tiger Cub piston into a newly created cylinder barrel. The latter work was done by Bill's father, who hand-cast this by melting down a quantity of old pistons in a biscuit tin. The barrel then had to be machined and the cooling fins created. A larger carburettor was also fitted. These modifications increased the performance considerably. Unfortunately, for the 1961 season Brands Hatch had scrapped the 200cc class, so Bill had to ride the enlarged Gilera in 250cc events.

At the first meeting of the 1961 Brands Hatch season on 31 March, this race was won by Mike Hailwood (FB Mondial) from Dan Shorey (NSU Sportmax) and Fred Hardy on another NSU. Ken Whorlow was sixth on the Ron Harris MV Agusta; Bill came home a very respectable 12th.

The four-stroke Italian Motom engine. The Milan company entered a team of three machines in the 1961 50cc Enduro, managed by multi-World Champion Carlo Ubbiali's brother, Armando.

The Second Chilton Enduro

A feature of the second Chilton Enduro, organised by the Racing 50 Club on Sunday 7 May 1961, was the appearance of the Italian works Motom team. As *Motor Cycle News* commented in its 10 May issue: 'Glamour and prestige were added to the meeting by the appearance of three Italian works machines from the Italian Motom factory complete with works mechanic and team manager – none other than Armando Ubbiali, brother of World Champion Carlo Ubbiali!'

The Motoms were ridden by British riders and one of them – piloted by Jim Pearson and Peter Inchley – led the race for many laps and set the fastest circuit at 56.26mph (90.52km/h) before retiring with a suspected broken valve.

Conditions were described as 'breezy.' The early lead was disputed between Peter Inchley (Motom) and Ian Johnson (Itom). But the latter's race was soon over after the machine spluttered to a standstill – the rev counter drive sheered and pieces dropped into the engine which ruined the magneto.

This left the Pearson/Inchley Motom ahead of the field with 87 laps of the 2.71 mile (4.36km) circuit still to be covered. The Motom was slowed by pit signals so that after 15 laps the Italian works machine led by only six seconds from Bill Ivy on the Chisholm Itom.

That lead was just a shade too slim and thereafter the Motom speeded up, and after 30 laps it led by a full lap and a quarter with the Ivy/Thomas machine second, a lap ahead of the third place bike – another Itom shared by Phil Latham and Brian Brader.

When Chisholm's became Kent's first Honda dealership in 1961, Bill was given the use of a 125cc CB92 sports model (seen here). This was fitted with the optional race kit and he made his debut on the machine (see separate boxed section) on 20 August at Brands Hatch.

Next came the eventual winners Geoff Votier and Roy Nicholson who lay fourth – and the fastest bikes were, according to *MCN*: 'Proving remarkably reliable for the same four had shared the leading positions after 15 laps.'

Then the Motom team ran into trouble. After 30 laps they held first, fifth and sixth places, but then the latter machine went out when Ted Broom came off at the Esses, breaking a collarbone – fortunately the only real injury of the day – and the leading bike slowed with minor ignition problems.

By the time these had been cured the leaders had dropped back to fifth place, so that after 45 laps the Votier/Nicholson machine had come through to the front ahead of Brian Smith/Roy Righini (Motom), with a Levis-Itom shared by Brian Woolley (later a journalist for *Classic Bike* magazine and a long-time friend of the author) and hillclimb specialist Roger Cramp. The Latham and Brader pairing had dropped to fourth place, while Bill Ivy and Maurice Thomas were in trouble with misfiring.

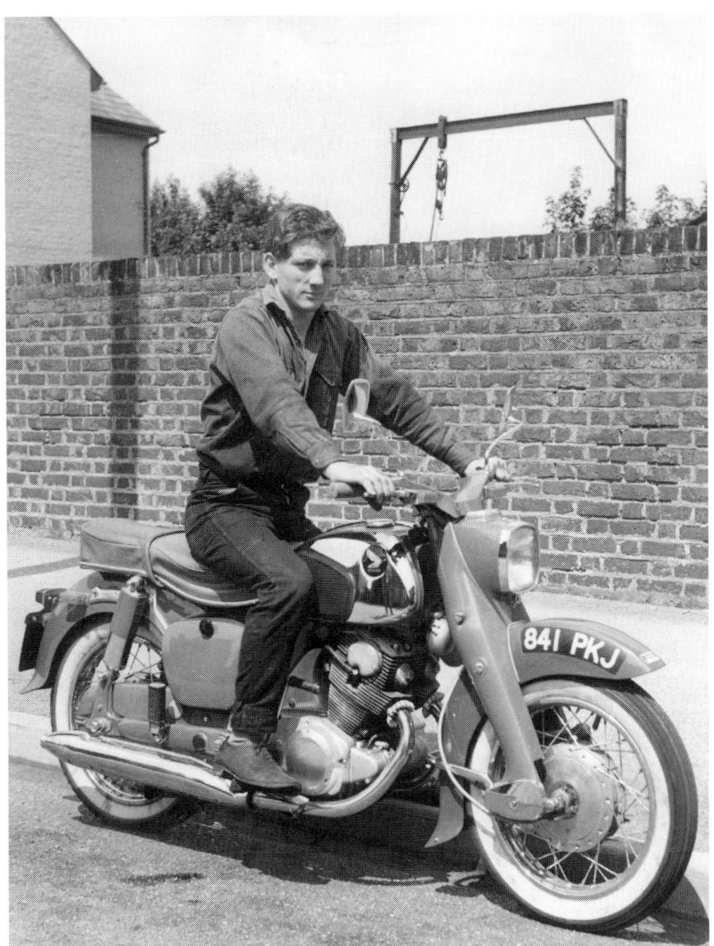

Bill pictured during 1961 with one of the first Hondas (a 250cc C72 tourer) delivered to his employers, the Chisholm brothers.

From then on Votier and Nicholson were never headed, although Woolley and Cramp put in a really determined challenge – the only other machine to complete the full distance.

The Smith/Righini Motom wavered up and down the results sheets before coming through with a strong burst to take third ahead of Bill and Maurice Thomas on the Chisholm-entered machine.

50cc Chilton Enduro 250 mile – 92 laps – 250 miles

1st	G.W. Votier/R.A. Nicholson (WMS Itom)
2nd	G.B. Woolley/F.R. Cramp (Levis-Itom)
3rd	B. Smith/R. Righini (Motom)
4th	W.D. Ivy/M. Thomas (Chis Itom)
5th	R.F. Smallcorn/A.E. Baxter (Itom)
6th	L.R. McLaren/M.C.T. Sampson (Maserati)

Maurice Thomas, Bills' co-rider on the Chis Itom during the 1961 50cc Enduro, at speed around Snetterton circuit.

Brands Hatch Trophy Day

The Brands Hatch Trophy Day took place on Sunday 25 June. And as *Motor Cycle News* reported, it: 'Was a great success – in spite of the lack of spectator support. The hottest day of the year undoubtedly made enthusiasts settle for the seaside rather than the race track.'

The 50cc race ended in a victory for Maurice Thomas on the Chisholm Itom, while Bill, riding the 190cc Gilera in the 176-250cc final, came home fourth after earlier finishing one place lower in his heat. The meeting was held over the shorter, 1.24 mile (1.99km) circuit.

176-250cc Brands Hatch – 6 laps – 7.44 miles

1st	B.T. Osborne (NSU)
2nd	E.J. Woodward (NSU)
3rd	E.R. Cooper (Ducati)
4th	W.D. Ivy (190cc Gilera)

Bill and Maurice were back in action at a star-packed entry over the 2.65 mile (4.26km) 'long' circuit at Brands Hatch on Sunday 9 July 1961. Maurice Thomas had a superb day, not only winning the 50cc race but also setting a new class lap record for the longer Brands course at 62.51mph (100.57km/h); the old record having been held by Howard German on the Sheene Special at 60.99mph (98.13km/h). But, with a star-studded field in the 250cc event including Mike Hailwood, Tommy Robb and Dan Shorey, Bill, on the 190cc Gilera, was unplaced.

Best Ever 50cc Event

'Best Ever 50cc Event.' So read the headline in *Motor Cycle News* dated 23 August 1961, in reference to the previous Sunday's meeting at the Kent course over the 2.65 mile 'long' circuit. It went on to say: 'the 50cc race was certainly the best ever seen at Brands. In a tremendous four-cornered struggle which ended in a blanket finish, with half a second covering the quartet, Maurice Thomas (Chis Itom) beat Charlie Mates (Sheene Special), Bill Ivy (Chis Itom) and Dave Simmonds, who was riding one of the works four-stroke Motoms.'

50cc Brands Hatch – 4 laps – 10.6 miles

1st	M. Thomas (Chis Itom)
2nd	C.C.W. Mates (Sheene Special)
3rd	W.D. Ivy (Chis Itom)
4th	D.A. Simmonds (Motom)
5th	P. Lucas (Lucas Itom)
6th	G.W. Votier (WMS Itom)

Brands Hatch, 20 August 1961. Bill (107) leads Maurice Thomas (Chis Itom) number 156.

Roy Francis

Roy Francis has the distinction of not only growing up with Bill Ivy and going to the same schools, but also working alongside Bill at Chisholm's – and acting as his race mechanic and co-rider in the Chis racing team. So Roy has a unique position in the Bill Ivy story.

He was born on 26 June 1943 at Brissenden Farm, East Sutton, near Sutton Valence in Kent. His father James Alan Francis (Jimmy to all his friends and colleagues) was a farmer and keen motorcyclist; having owned a variety of machines, including a 600 Ariel Square four, a 1930s Sunbeam and even a pair of BSA Slopers – one in solo guise, the other equipped with a sidecar. The latter machine was used to transport churns of milk from the farm's dairy herd. Interestingly, the two BSAs sported one set of number plates...well one was for pleasure and one for work, so saving on road fund tax!

As with Bill Ivy, Roy attended first Sutton Valence Primary School and later Oldborough Manor Secondary School.

Up to 18 years of age Roy lived with his parents at the farm. Then, in 1961, he got a job (via Bill Ivy) at the Chisholm motorcycle dealership in Maidstone; Chisholm's being Kent's first Honda dealer – appointed by the then importer, Hondis Ltd. Around the same time Roy purchased the second CB92 Honda in Kent – from Chisholm's, of course.

As is revealed in the main text, Roy and Bill worked together at Chisholm's; in fact later the pair often worked in the Chisholm's Boughton Monchelsea workshop. The premises of this operation were, as Roy describes, 'At the bottom of my garden where I live now with wife Sandra who lived next door.'

As for Roy's racing career, he freely acknowledges: 'I was always one step behind Bill.' And in the author's opinion akin to Alastair King in regard to Bob McIntyre. In both cases without their close friends, both Roy and Alastair would have garnered more fame for themselves. But, in truth, they were friends first, competitors second. And, of course, both quit racing immediately when their respective friends suffered fatal racing accidents.

Roy Francis winning the 1964 Brands Hatch Stars of Tomorrow 125cc race on Bill Ivy's Chisholm-sponsored Honda CR93

Roy's racing career began in 1962 when he raced his own CB92 road bike. By this time Bill was sponsored by Chisholm's on the Chis Honda CB92 (see separate boxed section in this chapter). When Bill moved on to ride the Chis CR93, Roy looked after it and also raced Bill's CB92.

Roy's first success and mention in the press came in July 1964, when he rode Bill's CR93 to victory in the 'Stars of Tomorrow' meeting at Brands Hatch.

After competing in the 1966 TT on the Honda (held in late August that year due to the seaman's strike), as Roy says: 'The CR93 needed a new crankshaft and the exhaust valve had turned into a tulip.' And with the motorcycle trade in the doldrums, the Chisholm brothers were not able to spend money on the bike. So Roy left the firm and drifted out of racing for a while, and he went to work for a local firm who had a contract to straighten Lotus racing car chassis for a Brands Hatch racing school.

While working at the above firm, Roy bought himself a car, a Ford Zodiac Mk III. As he described it: 'a real jack-the-lad's motor. It was the thing to have in those days, but I didn't have it long as some berk in another car rammed it sideways at high speed and wrote it off.' This made Roy think of taking up racing again 'as it would probably be safer!' So he bought a Cotton Telstar, with the help of a friend, Mick Vidler.

He raced the Cotton throughout 1967 and had several victories at Brands Hatch and Lydden Hill, selling it afterwards.

Becoming restless during the closed season of 1967–68 'I went to visit Geoff Monty at his dealership in Edenbridge.' As Roy says: 'I knew him from the days when he'd sponsored Bill. I found a DMW Hornet that I fancied, but Geoff said "you don't want to *buy* that do you? Why not take it with you and the Honda CR93 out back and let me sponsor you." It was marvellous and totally unexpected. I went to buy one bike and came away with two, for free.'

At the April 1968 Lydden meeting Roy finished runner-up on the DMW to Yamaha-mounted Brian Kemp – then one of the top riders in the class and Lord of Lydden at the time. He followed this performance up with a win on the CR93 at Lydden.

As Roy recalls: 'I was at Brands one Wednesday for practice when I met Geoff. He used to take his customers out there to try his bikes and he offered me a job as a mechanic – and also offered me the Aermacchi and the Monard which Ray Pickrell had raced for him.' He continues: 'My first race on the 'Macchi was the May meeting up at Mallory, just before I started work for Geoff. At the Esses I dived inside Don Padgett and that's the last I remember until I woke up in the First Aid room with Smartie [Paul Smart] bending over me.'

Roy turned up for work on Monday, limping, with the wreckage in the van – hardly a good start. But Geoff was not bothered about the damage, as Roy recalls: 'He said he thought that it might happen as the tyres were rather old and had probably gone hard. It crossed my mind to say he might have mentioned it before, but Geoff was such a fantastic sponsor. I had the CR93, the 250cc Aermacchi [ex-Alberto Pagani works bike], a 350 Greeves Oulton and a 500cc Monard.' This meant four different machines to prepare, practice with, set-up, qualify in heats and ride in finals – an experience few other riders ever experienced at the same time.

Roy also learned a lot from Geoff, as he says: 'He taught me an awful lot about machine preparation and motorcycle dealing.'

Then came that fateful day on Saturday 12 July 1969. Roy was working in Geoff's garage preparing the bikes when he heard on the car radio that Bill had crashed in East Germany and had been seriously injured. He was worried and upset but knowing just how resilient his old friend was he tried hard to convince himself that Bill would be alright.

However, 'Listening to the radio in hope of some good news the report came through that Bill had died. I threw the spanners down and gave up racing there and then.'

Roy continued working for Geoff Monty until early 1970 when he rejoined Chisholm's. He also worked odd days for Karl Pugh (one-time foreman/team manager of the Ashford-based Norman motorcycle company), who owned a dealership at Tenterden; plus occasional work for Rochester-based Roy Baldwin.

Then on 14 November 1970 Roy was offered Karl Pugh's workshop, which he rented for some two years. During 1974 Paul Smart brought his TR750 Suzuki racing machines for Roy to fettle. Later that year Paul also had one of the factory prototype RG500 (XR14) square fours to race; again Roy got involved with its maintenance.

Around the same time, in the summer of 1974, Roy walked into Chisholm's one day and was greeted by the question: 'Do you know anyone who wants to buy the business?'

As referred to elsewhere in this book, Roy and Paul Smart eventually became the owners of the Chisholm business the following year.

The Chisholm's dealership was by then 100 per cent Honda, but later, now called Paul Smart Ltd and with Roy and Paul equal partners, it was to also take on Norton and Triumph agencies.

Next, in late 1975, fellow racer Trevor Springett who had a garage in Paddock Wood joined forces with Roy and Paul to set up Paddock Wood Kawasaki. But following an accident Trevor relinquished his involvement in the firm, while Roy and Paul also bought out Karl Pugh's business in Tenterden.

In the early 1980s the Tenterden shop was closed, with Karl retiring and his son Alan coming to work on the spares side at the Maidstone branch. However, tragedy later struck when Alan was run down by a lorry in Tenterden High Street.

Later that decade after mounting problems due to parking problems and a change in customer type (from small to big bikes) it was decided to close the Maidstone branch and concentrate the business at Paddock Wood. This also saw the Honda agency moved to Paddock Wood and the dealership name changed from Kawasaki to Paul Smart Ltd.

This traded until July 1998 when it was sold out to the Motorcycle City Group (although Roy and Paul retained ownership of the property).

Since then Roy has been involved in running the Tenterden & District Motor Cycle Club, which specialises in trials, notably the 'Man of Kent' and 'Weald of Kent' events. He also became the owner of the 650cc Monard, purchased from Geoff Monty, to add to his CR93 Honda.

Sandra and Roy had two children, daughter Corinne and son Keith. The latter was born in 1975 – the same year as Scott Smart, Graham Hurry's son Paul and Don Godden's son Mitch, the quartet being close friends.

Roy often attends classic events both in the UK and abroad, including the 1998 Centennial TT at Assen, which both he and the author consider to have been the greatest of all such events ever staged.

An Equally Brilliant 125cc Race

Although the Australian works Honda rider Tom Phillis was a non-starter due to his crash in the Ulster Grand Prix the previous weekend, excitement was certainly not lacking. And Bill was having his first-ever outing on the Chisholm Honda CB92 (see separate boxed section for this machine's history). Dan Shorey (Bultaco) streaked off the grid leaving Phil Read (Sheene Bultaco) to get his machine going. At the end of the first lap Shorey had a comfortable lead over Fred Hardy (MV Agusta) and Read was through to third place – incredible riding after being last away!

By the third lap Read had passed Hardy and was striving to whittle down the 500 yard lead that Shorey had built up in the initial stages. By the halfway mark and consistently as quick as the lap record, Read had caught Shorey and from then on the two Bultacos were never more than inches apart. Going into the last lap, Read led by a machine's length. And from then until the finish line the lead swapped on several occasions. But judging his effort to perfection, Dan Shorey came out of Read's slipstream and won

Brands Hatch, 8 October 1961. Ron Freeman (133, Honda CB72), leads Bill (7, Gilera – now converted to 190cc) and Len Rodda (24, NSU). Just study Bill's determined riding style!

Opposite: A previously unpublished – and certainly unposed – photograph of the husband and wife team Mr and Mrs Swain. Beryl is on the left of the picture in helmet, her husband Eddie is holding the refuelling funnel. The picture was taken at the 50cc Enduro, Snetterton, 4 August 1962. Beryl had made history that year as the first-ever female rider in the TT.

the race by a tyre's width. But even more exciting was Bill's performance on the Honda CB92 – coming home a truly brilliant fourth, behind the highly experienced Fred Hardy (MV Agusta) and in front of many other expert riders on much faster machinery.

125cc Brands Hatch – 8 laps – 21.2 miles

1st	D.F. Shorey (Bultaco)
2nd	P.W. Read (Sheene Bultaco)
3rd	F.D. Hardy (MV Agusta)
4th	W.D. Ivy (Chis Honda CB92)
5th	G.H. Hughes (Bultaco)
6th	B. Lawton (Ducati 125 Desmo Twin)

Bill's 1961 season ended at Brands Hatch on Sunday 8 October. But it was not to be his day. Instead, after retiring on the Chis Itom in the 50cc he was unplaced on the 190cc Gilera in the 250cc event; his last ever race on the latter machine. Quite simply he felt, correctly, that against full-blown 250cc pukka race bikes he was not only giving away 60cc, but his converted roadster was never going to match the machines he was trying to compete against. So from then on, for the coming season he would only ride the 50cc Itom and 125cc Honda.

Nineteen-Sixty-Two

Bill's 1962 racing season did not, as usual, begin at Brands Hatch. Instead, on Saturday 14 April, he, together with all the other leading lights of British 50cc racing, was at the first race meeting held on a banked track since Brooklands closed after the outbreak of World War Two; this was staged at the Gosling Stadium (normally a cycling venue), Welwyn Garden City, Hertfordshire.

Mike Simmonds' 50cc Watercooled Special photographed at Gosling Stadium, Welwyn Garden City on 14 April 1962. Mike dominated the meeting on this machine.

Organised by the Racing 50 Motor Cycle Club, the cold weather and lack of prior publicity might have kept the number of spectators down, but there was certainly nothing below par about the standard of racing, which was deemed as first class.

There were no less than four heats – these being won by J. Whale (Itom), Charlie Mates (Itom), Mike Simmonds (WCS) and Bill on the Chisholm brothers's Itom.

The main race of the 13-event programme was the Gosling final. At the start Charlie Mates on his Itom stormed into the lead followed by Bill, Phil Horsham (Itom), R.J. Smith (Itom) and Brian Brader (Itom), with the pre-race favourite Mike Simmonds a long way behind on his WCS (Water

36

Cooled Special – essentially a liquid-cooled Itom). But even though his machine was clearly the quickest out on the circuit, Simmonds could not quite snatch victory from Mates who had led all the way. Bill finished fourth behind Smith.

Good Friday at Brands

Only six days later, on Good Friday 20 April 1962, Bill was in action again, this time at Brands Hatch. Derek Minter got all the headlines with wins on single, twin- and four-cylinder machines, in front of over 45,000 spectators. As for Bill, he finished fourth in the 50cc race on the Chis Itom and eighth in the 125cc event on the Chis Honda CB92.

50cc Brands Hatch – 3 laps – 7.95 miles

1st	M. Simmonds (WCS)
2nd	C. Mates (Itom)
3rd	P. Horsham (Itom)
4th	W.D. Ivy (Chis Itom)
5th	G. Votier (Itom)
6th	D. Simmonds (Tohatsu)

125cc Brands Hatch – 5 laps – 13.25 miles

1st	D. Shorey (Bultaco)
2nd	D.W. Minter (EMC)
3rd	S.M.B. Hailwood (EMC)
4th	N. Surtees (Bultaco)
5th	F.D. Hardy (Sheene Bultaco)
6th	B. Lawton (Ducati Desmo Twin)
7th	R. Avery (EMC)
8th	W.D. Ivy (Chis Honda CB92)

Bill was back at Brands just over three weeks later, when he brought the Chis Honda home fifth in the 125cc event – again up against top line opposition.

125cc Brands Hatch – 5 laps – 13.25 miles

1st	N. Surtees (Bultaco)
2nd	M. O'Rourke (Sheene Bultaco)
3rd	J. Russell (Honda)
4th	B. Lawton (Ducati Desmo Twin)
5th	W.D. Ivy (Chis Honda CB92)

1962 also saw Bill's Isle of Man debut, in the newly introduced 50cc event. This was staged over two laps of the 37.73 mile (60.70km) Mountain circuit, but Bill's Itom did not complete a lap and he retired early in the race. Then at Brands Hatch on Sunday 11 June he was unplaced in the 50cc event and could not get an entry in the 125cc class.

In fact, at this time Bill was obviously not yet an acknowledged star name. This was not helped by the fact that, largely, he had to fund his own racing costs, except for the loan of the Chisholm machines. Sometimes the Chisholm brothers transported Bill's machines but occasionally Roy and Bill shared Bill's car and trailer, or whatever was available.

Co-riders

This tie-up (read friendship!) between Bill and Roy saw the two enter as co-riders in the 1962 running of the annual 50cc Enduro, run by the Racing 50 MCC. Riding the water-cooled Chis Itom, the pair practiced for the long-distance race over the 2.71 mile (4.36km) Snetterton (Norfolk) circuit, without experiencing any problems. However, this was not to be the case in the actual event, when after the first hour with Bill still doing his first riding stint the engine seized. So Roy never got to actually race the bike! It was the Simmonds brothers, Dave and Mike, who riding a Japanese Tohatsu ran out

Bill during practice for the 1962 50cc TT in the Isle of Man on the Chis Itom. But he was out of luck in the race, retiring on the first lap.

Ken Whorlow

Ken Whorlow, born in 1935, was an early racing career inspiration to the young Bill Ivy by the way the local lad progressed to national and championship success. Bill had met Ken when he visited Chisholm's shop in Maidstone to collect spares for his (Ken's) employer Mick Gunyon who had a motorcycle business in Faversham. (Mick, a former tank commander in the army, was a great friend of the Chisholm brothers and like them raced Velocettes.) Ken's first racing machine was one Mick had raced, a 250cc Velocette MOV, Ken purchased this and set off road racing in the mid-1950s and was soon enjoying himself so much he decided to add another machine to give him more races. He ordered a new Triumph Sports Cub from the Chisholms, specifying that it should have 19in wheels and a down swept exhaust.

With the Cub and Velocette he was able to ride in 200cc and 250cc class races. The ageing Velo was parted with and a 175cc Gilera was purchased from Gunyon's used stock. On this at Brands Hatch on 26 May 1958 Ken finished a very creditable fourth in the 200cc race and ninth on the Sports Cub entered as being 204cc in the 250cc race. Such was the faith Mick Gunyon had in Ken's ability he personally recommended him to entrant Ron Harris who had a stable of 125/175/203 racing MV Agustas, the machine to have at the time.

Late in 1958 Ken joined the Ron Harris set up on initially the 125cc MV. Progressing through 1959 Ken's best season was 1960 when he tied on points with Mike Hailwood for the ACU Star British Championship, riders having gained points at several meetings during the season. Mike took the title by the fact that he had more winning rides. The 1960 Championship was first Mike Hailwood, second Ken Whorlow, third Dan Shorey, fourth Fred Hardy, very illustrious company for the Charing, Kent-based rider. Wins came at Brands Hatch, Aberdare Park and Crystal Palace with two class wins on the same day in April 1960. The *Evening Standard* carried an article on Ken Whorlow being the man to beat at the Crystal Palace on the lightweight machines.

Ken Whorlow was something of a lightweight 125–250cc star at Brands Hatch during the late 1950s, riding for the Ron Harris MV team. Ken is seen here riding the dohc conversion Ron Harris CSS Super Squalo 175cc model.

Ken racing the 203cc Ron Harris MV Agusta at Brands Hatch during the late 1950s.

A trip to the Isle of Man was a low point when the MV broke a big end on the first lap of the race at Union Mills. In retrospect Ken feels the bike had been used by Bob Anderson, another of Ron Harris's riders, prior to the TT and with no time to fully check the machine it was sent to the island.

Ken only crashed twice throughout his career, both times at Brands Hatch on the MVs and in the company of Mike Hailwood. Exiting Druids hairpin in very close company of one another Mike's machine lost adhesion and with Ken being so close he also went down. The press carried a photograph of his somersaulting machine. The other occasion was travelling in a formation of riders including Mike exiting Clearways onto the main straight fast catching lapped riders closely slipstreaming each other, when one of the formation suddenly moved over to avoid a lapped rider clipping Ken's front wheel sending him tumbling down. On the 9 October 1960 at Brands Hatch in the 200cc race Tom Phillis won, Ken Whorlow second, Mike Hailwood third and Dan Shorey fourth. In the 250cc race Ken finished fifth. Ken's last racing season was 1961 as Ron Harris decided to move over to motorsport and although he offered Ken the chance to follow on four wheels Ken felt it was not really for him. The need to provide for a young family became a priority and Ken moved away from the motorcycle trade and racing, taking a job as a fitter with Batchelors Foods factory at Ashford. The same determination shown in racing to get on eventually led to Ken Whorlow becoming the proprietor of Sunnybank Garage at Chilham near Canterbury which he eventually sold to retire in 1986.

Motorcycle racing came back into his life when son Simon went grasstrack racing becoming first British junior pairs champion with Tony Reynolds and then in adult grasstrack winning the Kent Kracker meeting. Now living in retirement in Mersham in Kent, Ken is an active member of the Norman Motorcycles Owners Club based at the Willesborough Windmill. Ken and the club are dedicated to keep the Ashford factories machines on the road and in exhibitions. His particular interests are the twin cylinder models and at present he has a very well presented B4 model on the road. During a visit to the classic show organised by the West Kent section of the VMCC in 2004 Ken was reunited with one of the MV machines, the 203 unrestored, that he rode for Ron Harris, now owned by Mole Benn.

Ken reunited with the ex-Harris 203cc MV at a classic motorcycle event in the summer of 2004.

In 2008 remembering his road racing career Ken recalled the one and only occasion he passengered a racing Norton sidecar outfit. Maurice Candy, one of the Chisholm/Gunyon group of friends, was without a passenger for a meeting and coerced Ken into the outfit. The horrendously noisy experience was something Ken never wished to repeat.

the victors at the end of the 250 miles (402km) race distance. Second home was Beryl Swain (known as the 'Walthamstow Flying Housewife') and her husband, Eddie, riding their CS Itom. Third was Brian Woolley and Roger Cramp (Itom). Besides Bill and Roy, there were two other Chis Itom teams in the event: Bill Stevenson/Maurice Thomas (who retired with big-end failure) and the sixth-placed finishers John Tompsett/C. Campbell.

All the remaining meetings which Bill undertook in 1962 were at Brands Hatch, on 19 August, 23 September and finally 14 October. Riding the Chis Itom and Chis Honda CB92 his best results – both coming on 23 September – were seventh in the 50cc and eighth in the 125cc. However, at the October meeting he crashed spectacularly, when on the first lap of the 125cc race Rex Avery (EMC) fell and his bike struck Bill's Honda. The two of them then brought down Derek Minter on the second works EMC (the author witnessing this crash as a spectator). And so Bill was unable to ride in the 50cc event later in the day; not a happy end to the 1962 season by any means.

At that time it would have been hard to imagine that not only would Bill be riding for Frank Sheene the following season but that before its end he would have been signed up by another big name race entrant, Geoff Monty.

The Maudes Trophy Attempt

On Wednesday 24 October 1962, there began an ambitious seven-day test, 24 hours a day, with a trio of Honda 50cc machines.

A team of 18 riders – including Bill – were to take turns riding the machines for two hours apiece. At each pit stop it was intended to keep the engines running. No less than nine ACU observers were on duty.

In charge of the models – a C114 sports motorcycle and two step-thru's – and riders was Geoff Monty. Said to have cost £5,000, the test involved more than 40 officials, riders and mechanics.

Apart from demonstrating reliability, Honda hoped to win the coveted Maudes Trophy, a special award for manufacturers for outstanding achievement in the motorcycling sphere. The trophy had been held since 1962 by the BSA factory.

Organised by the European arm of the Honda Motor Company, the test was among the most severe ever held in Great Britain: 168 hours circulating the Goodwood circuit in Sussex. The total mileage of the three machines was some 16,000 miles (25,744km). The weather conditions experienced over the seven days could not have been worse, with torrential rain, biting winds and night-time ice throughout the week.

It was this event that first brought Bill and Geoff Monty together – Bill having been nominated by Chisholm's who were, at the time, the main Honda dealer for Kent.

Why was Goodwood chosen? Well, it was handy for London, rather more hilly than Silverstone but less so than, say, Oulton Park or Cadwell Park. The machines circulated in the opposite direction to that normally used for car racing – mainly so that advantage could be taken of prevailing winds, but, as it happened, this proved of no advantage because the wind-sock at the adjacent Goodwood airstrip went full circle three times while the test was in progress!

Besides racing men such as Bill there were a couple of London policemen plus two well-known lady riders, Olga Kevolos and Beryl Swain.

No mechanical problems were experienced during the test, and, eventually, Honda were awarded the Maudes Trophy for their efforts; the first non-British manufacturer to do so.

Chisholm's the Second coming

As is fully detailed in Chapter 3 – Frank Sheene, Bill did not ride for the Chisholm brothers during 1963, considering the race-kitted CB92 outclassed.

There is no doubt that Bill believed in his own abilities – and decided to accept Frank Sheene's offer to join him. But, equally, Bill had loyalty to the Chisholms, so when they decided to purchase a brand new Honda CR93 a year later at the beginning of the 1964 season, Bill returned to the fold so to speak. And so came about this second period as a Chisholm

The Chisholm Brothers

Don and Bill Chisholm were two bachelor brothers, both over 6ft tall, who lived with their parents until the latter died in their late 90s. They were often mistaken for twins as they did everything together. They made their own bread and grew a comprehensive selection of vegetables in their garden. Motorcycling was initially a hobby and means of transport to work in south London.

Before purchasing one of his early machines from a south London motorcycle dealer, Don insisted on taking it for a test run, only returning some hours later to discover the dealer about to report the machine stolen.

The brothers were soon attracted to motorcycle sport and they took up grass track racing, often competing at Layham's Farm. Velocettes were the machines of choice and they soon became experts on their preparation and repair. On moving to Maidstone they joined the local club, Maidstone Aces, entering grass track events and gymkhanas. They formed a close friendship with another local enthusiast, Tom Hartridge, and the trio decided to set up in business as motorcycle dealers and rented premises at 109 Upper Stone Street, Maidstone. Chisholm and Hartridge motorcycle dealers were launched. A discontented Tom Hartridge left after a short while and the two brothers progressed, taking on new machine agencies.

The elder brother, Don (born 1908), was the innovator and engineer and Bill took care of the sales and administration. In later years they purchased an oasthouse at nearby Boughton Monchelsea and installed a full engineering facility with belt drive lathes and a milling machine etc. From this workshop they produced motorcycle accessories such as ace bars, clip-ons, headlamp brackets, carriers and fairings, together with special clips for the Fire Brigade to fasten hose reels.

The brothers had a reputation not only for their skills in repairing almost anything, but also for being extremely hard working and honest.

Another product they manufactured was strawberry carrier trays, lightweight and made from stiff wire enabling the fruit to be picked straight into the marketing unit. After selling their business and not manufacturing the carrier for some years, they decided to return to production in their

Left to right: Don Chisholm on his 1928 Cotton fitted with a Velocette KTT Mark IV engine; Bill Chisholm standing; Sam Simmonds on a Velocette Mark IV; two unidentified people; Tom Hartridge on a Velocette KTT Mark IV.

Bill Chisholm and his 1932 Velocette KTT Special in 1959. During the early 1950s Bill had a serious accident on this machine. It was subsequently rebuilt. This included conversion to swinging arm rear suspension, (using BSA telescopic forks) and the fitment of a Mark I KSS engine and three-speed gearbox.

garden shed. The by now elderly brothers spent an entire winter making hundreds of the strawberry carriers and went on the road in spring to sell the finished product to local farmers only to discover that a new size of tray was now being used and their efforts had been futile.

They both competed at club level in grass track and Don progressed via a Cotton-Blackburne on to riding 250 and 350 Velocette KTT models at road racing, mainly at Brands Hatch. In the last few years of his riding career he purchased ex-factory rider Frank Fry's Mark VIII Velocette, something he was extremely proud of.

A fellow competitor and local enthusiast Maurice Candy struck up a lasting friendship with them and for a period of time assisted them in their business before moving to a highly successful career with the Dupont Corporation in the USA. Maurice took up sidecar racing and built his own twin-cylinder engine, competing in the Isle of Man TT many times, once bringing a member of the Dupont family with him to ride an Aermacchi which Chisholm's supplied. Maurice would appear before the TT and completely take over Chisholm's workshop finishing his outfit, making many parts and welding etc.

There were two other well-established motorcycle dealers in Maidstone so most of the agencies, i.e. Triumph, Vincent, BSA, Francis Barnett etc, were catered for. So the brothers turned to DMW and the Italian MV, Gilera and Itom and eventually became Kent's first Honda agency, gaining a nationwide reputation with their support of Bill Ivy and their other assisted riders including Roy Francis, Maurice Thomas, Sid Lovell and John Tompsett.

With Honda at Goodwood for their October 1962 7 days and 7 nights Maudes Trophy attempt, the brothers were back-up crew for the running of the C110 for the Filtrate Oil sponsored event, with Bill Ivy as one of the riders.

Bill had joined the Chisholm's staff in Maidstone after a short period working for the AMC factory at Plumstead where he was not learning or working on motorcycles, but was instead only expected to make cups of tea and sweep up, only for the foreman to kick the dust back over the floor and order Bill to sweep up all over again. A very angry and despondent little man went into Chisholm's shop and asked if they had any vacancies. A uniquely talented character was on his way, the tiger of a man was unleashed to make his mark in Grand Prix history.

In 1975 the Chisholm business was purchased by Paul Smart and Roy Francis, who took over the running on a Saturday night not having paid a pound or completed the paperwork, such was the trust between them. In retirement the Chisholm brothers kitted out a VW van into a camper and every winter set off for Spain, exploring extensively.

The Chis-Itom engine was sold to Brian Woolley; the chassis to Governors Bridge Motorcycles.

The Chis-Honda CB92 was sold to Governors Bridge Motorcycles and is currently owned by John Pitt.

The Chis-Honda CR93 was sold to Roy Francis.

The Mark VIII Velocette was sold to Maurice Candy.

Often seen out walking together, a routine they kept up for many years, the brothers passed away within a very short time of each other in the mid-1990s.

rider. But unlike his previous spell, this time it ran in parallel with his other sponsors – at first Geoff Monty and later Tom Kirby.

In the 4 March 1964 issue of *Motor Cycle News* the pre-season Racing Plans section carried news of Bill's plans. Entitled: 'Second to Tommy Robb' it went on to say: 'Bill of Maidstone, Kent, has two contracts for 1964 – riding a 125 Honda for Chisholm's of Maidstone and four machines for Geoff Monty. These will be a 250 Yamaha, a 350 Norton, a Norton or Geoff's Triumph-engined Monard special in 500 races, and Geoff's 650 Triumph Monard for unlimited events. His most memorable race last year was at Brands Hatch when he was second to Tommy Robb in the 125 race. He was also runner-up to Robb in the 250 event.'

CR93 Debut

Bill's debut on the newly-acquired Chisholm Honda CR93 (see separate boxed section in Chapter 6 for development history and technical details) came at Mallory Park on Sunday 22 March, the first meeting of the 1964 British racing season. It was also Bill's first visit to the Leicestershire circuit. And even though he did not make it a winning debut for machine or circuit, he did the next best thing by finishing runner-up behind the quick starting Chris Vincent on Bill Hannah's CR93.

125cc Mallory Park – 10 laps – 13.5 miles

1st	C. Vincent (Hannah Honda)
2nd	W.D. Ivy (Chis Honda)
3rd	A. Dugdale (Ducati)
4th	J. Russell (Honda)
5th	G. Riches (Bultaco)
6th	G. Collis (Bultaco)

Following Mallory came meetings at Brands Hatch on Good Friday 27 March, when after a crash at Druid's Hill Hairpin, Bill remounted to finish eighth. Then at Snetterton two days later on Easter Sunday he finished fifth, then at Oulton Park on Easter Monday he finished second and at Brands Hatch on 19 April he again finished second.

The 1964 CR93 differed from the original model by having a singled-sided 2LS front brake, as seen here, rather than a dual SLS device.

First Victory

Then it was back to Mallory Park on 3 May, where Bill gained his first victory on the CR93 – and set the fastest lap into the bargain. Besides all this his speed of 76.10mph (122.44km/h) for the 10 laps broke the race record of 74.59mph (120.01km/h) which had been established by Chris Vincent back in March.

125cc Mallory Park – 10 laps – 13.5 miles

1st	W.D. Ivy (Chis Honda)
2nd	D.A. Simmonds (Tohatsu)
3rd	M. O'Rourke (Honda)
4th	J. Russell (Honda)
5th	M. Bancroft (Honda)
6th	R. Scivyer (Honda)

Just by studying this latest Mallory result, one can immediately see the dominant nature of Honda's CR93 machine in British short circuit racing during 1964.

Two other meetings on the Chis Honda that month illustrate that by now Bill was rapidly becoming the top rider in the 125cc class at British meetings. A week after Mallory came Snetterton on 10 May where in finishing runner-up to Dave Simmonds (Tohatsu) he set a new class record lap of 82.96mph (133.48km/h), followed on Whit Monday 18 May at Brands Hatch with victory and another record lap, this time at 79.36mph (127.69km/h).

125cc Brands Hatch – 20 laps – 24.8 miles

1st	W.D. Ivy (Chis Honda)
2nd	D.A. Simmonds (Tohatsu)
3rd	R. Bryans (works Honda twin)
4th	M. O'Rourke (Honda)
5th	C. Vincent (Hannah Honda)
6th	R. Pladdys (Honda)

Dave Simmonds

Dave Simmonds was both a rival and close friend of Bill Ivy, as both men came into racing via the 50cc class on Itoms: Bill in 1959, Dave the following year.

Born in London on 25 October 1940, Dave and his brothers Mike and Colin had an unusual childhood. Shortly after arriving in this world the family's home was bombed and thereafter they spent several years in Asmara, Ethiopia, where his father, John, worked for British Overseas Airways at one of the staging posts on the old route to eastern and southern Africa. John Simmonds was a great motorcycle enthusiast – and this was passed on to his sons Mike and Dave (the latter in particular).

During the 1950s a transfer back to Great Britain saw the Simmonds family move to Stanwell on the southern edge of London's new Heathrow Airport. Simmonds Snr was working for BOAC (British Overseas Airways Corporation – the forerunner of today's British Airways).

On leaving school, Dave's career was as an apprentice electrician, and with his first wages he purchased a 200cc Zündapp two-stroke motorcycle for everyday transport. Although money was now at a premium he managed to make his racing debut aboard a 50cc Itom in 1960. Elder brother Mike was campaigning a similar machine and together they made steady, if unexceptional progress. And during the remainder of 1960 and 1961 the brothers often competed against Bill on their Itoms.

But for the Simmonds the real breakthrough came in 1962, when, thanks to their father, a 50cc Tohatsu Runpet was tracked down in Tokyo. This was subsequently transported by air to Britain and, as the elder rider in the Simmonds team, Mike rode the machine in the 1962 Isle of Man TT, finishing 13th, the first owner home behind the hordes of works Suzukis, Kreidlers and Hondas. Interest in this event was considerable and not only was it the very first 50cc TT, but it was also the first year of the newly introduced 50cc World Championship series.

Following this, Tohatsu sent brand new 50 and 125cc twin-cylinder models, which the brothers, Dave in particular, raced with considerable success during the next couple of seasons – even though Tohatsu themselves ended up on the financial rocks. During 1963 Dave won the 125cc ACU Star (the British Championship) title.

After visiting Japan, where he finished 13th in the 50cc Japanese Grand Prix at the end of 1963, with Tohatsu's subsequent demise much of 1964 was a state of limbo for the Simmonds equipé. However, another break came with the purchase of 250 and 305cc Honda CR dohc twins. On the smaller model Dave gained a second ACU title, this time the 1965 250cc crown; while the larger Honda engine was fitted into a Norton frame.

Although the 1965 season ended with a crash at Mallory Park in which Dave suffered a broken ankle, a letter arrived shortly afterwards from Kawasaki offering a factory 125cc ride in selected Grand Prix races during 1966.

The original machine which Kawasaki engineers built was an air-cooled twin which proved unreliable during testing, resulting in a re-design and liquid-cooling. However, this was not deemed fully enough developed to send over to Dave, and instead Kawasaki dispatched its own test rider/racer Toshio Fujji. But even this plan did not work too well; Fujji crashing fatally during practice for the (postponed) Isle of Man TT in 1966.

The Simmonds brothers at the Snetterton Enduro, 4 August 1962. Dave is without a helmet with his brother Mike seated on the Itom-based machine.

That year ended with Dave's second visit to Japan and his debut race for Kawasaki. The factory invited him and Chris Vincent to race works 125cc twins in the Grand Prix at the Fisco circuit that October. The British pairing finishing 8th and 10th, being outpaced by the latest Yamaha and Suzuki machinery.

Then Kawasaki stated that they could not afford to contest European events. In fact, the company was not even prepared to finance a mechanic to look after the bike. But Dave Simmonds had the answer to this dilemma – he would look after the machine himself! At first Kawasaki were hesitant, but after Dave returned to Japan and completed a full course during which he proved just how competent he was, Kawasaki relented and agreed to loan him a bike and spares for 1967. Not only this, but a production AI-R air-cooled 250 twin into the bargain.

But 1967 was to prove a disaster, as both bikes suffered from poor reliability. The 125 was plagued by constant piston failure, while the 250 was also not quick enough at GP level. To cap all this Dave was to crash heavily during the Ulster round, which sidelined him for several months.

This injury, coupled to still unreliable bikes, put a damper on the 1968 season and it was not until the Italian Grand Prix at Monza in September that things at last turned around. There, he came home fourth in the 125cc event, beaten only by the four-cylinder Yamahas of Phil Read and Bill Ivy, plus the works Suzuki of Hans Georg Anscheidt.

Then, virtually overnight, the FIM changed the rules for Grand Prix racing. This saw the number of cylinders in the 125cc class cut to two. So, Dave and Kawasaki were at last on equal terms with the leading competitors, and Yamaha had quit.

Even though Dave missed the first round in Spain, he went on to win the 1969 125cc world title. From round two (West Germany), when he gave Kawasaki its first GP victory, he never looked back, winning no less than seven 125cc Championship races in succession: Isle of Man TT, Holland, Belgium, Czechoslovakia, East Germany, Finland and Italy.

He also found time to marry Julie Boddice – daughter of sidecar star Bill Boddice. Julie recalled to the author: 'Getting married and winning the World Championship – David said life was perfect.'

For the 1971 season Kawasaki supplied a six-speed gearbox, as from 1970 the FIM had banned the original eight-speed device.

However, Dave was unable to retain his title – quite simply the 125 was no longer fast enough against the latest opposition. But he did put in some excellent performances on the new HIR500 triple – especially once a new, lower, better-handling frame had been constructed by Ken Sprayston of Reynolds.

Dave's final GP victory came at Hockenheim in spring 1971 on the 125 twin, while his last GP came the following year at Montjuich Park, Barcelona, where he was fourth in the 125cc race and a close runner-up in the 500cc, fractionally beaten by Yamaha-mounted Chas Mortimer.

A few weeks later tragedy struck, when at a non-Championship meeting at Rungis on the outskirts of Paris, he and fellow racer Billie Nelson had rushed to help when they learned of a fire which had broken out in Jack Findlay's caravan. An explosion occurred and the caravan was engulfed in flames. Julie bravely dashed inside and dragged Dave out, but it was too late. Julie eventually recovered after being on the critical list with severe burns.

No TT But a String of Wins

Bill did not contest the Isle of Man TT in 1964. As explained in Chapter 4 – Geoff Monty, the Twickenham dealer/sponsor did not wish to enter the event, so with only the Chisholm Honda, Bill stayed away.

There followed a tremendous run of success on the CR93, with wins and records all over the country. This began with a victory at Snetterton on 26 July, followed by further wins at Brands Hatch (16 August), Aberdare Park (22 August), Mallory Park (30 August), Castle Combe (5 September), Snetterton (6 September), Cadwell Park (13 September), Brands Hatch (20 September), Oulton Park (4 October) and finally Brands Hatch (11 October). And at many of these he also set either fastest lap or record lap time.

This run of success culminated in Bill being crowned 125cc ACU Star Champion (in effect the British Champion).

As fully covered in Chapter 4, Bill also shared the winning Honda CR110 with Paul Latham in the Racing 50 Club's 250-mile Enduro at Snetterton on 17 October.

By now, Bill Ivy had become a national star rather than, as previously, a local hero at Brands Hatch. And the Chisholm Honda machine had been the one bike, more than any other, which had made this success possible. It is also worth recording that during the 1964 season the machine had never suffered a mechanical failure during a race. This, it must be said, was helped by the preparation which was lavished on it in the Chisholm workshop – and the fact that parts were replaced regardless of cost at the mileages recommended by Honda. This was a remarkable fact considering Bill often revved the motor way above the 13,000rpm limit.

After a season riding a Bultaco in the 125cc class for Frank Sheene in 1963, the following year Bill returned to the Chisholm fold courtesy of a brand new machine; the now legendary Chis Honda CR93. He finished the season as ACU Star (British) Champion.

More Successes

When the 1965 racing season began for Bill at Mallory Park on Sunday 7 March, he

Bill Ivy on 19 April 1964, with the then brand new Chisholm Honda CR93.

27
113
HONDA
113

immediately continued the form with which he had finished the 1964 season, with victory on the Chisholm Honda and a fastest lap.

The wins just kept coming: Brands Hatch (21 March), Snetterton (28 March), Snetterton (18 April), Mallory Park (20 April), Brands Hatch (9 May), Snetterton (16 May), Mallory Park (23 May), Mallory Park (20 June) and, finally, at Brands Hatch (27 June). That last outing was to be his swansong on the Chisholm Honda. As is explained elsewhere, the Chisholms withdrew their support because with an ongoing recession in the motorcycle trade at that time they were feeling the pinch, and therefore they could not afford to keep throwing replacement parts at the CR93's engine, which was vital to maintaining its continued health. In fact, as in the previous year, the machine had maintained a 100 per cent reliability record; an achievement in itself.

Thereafter, following Chisholm's withdrawal, Bill raced a similar (but not the same) machine for Liverpool dealer Bill Hannah (see Chapter 6).

But the lasting – and fitting – tribute to the Chisholm brothers is that their support over the years gave Bill the chance to show his talents to a wider audience, including, most importantly, Yamaha.

Bill (Chisholm Honda CR93, number 113) leads Dave Simmonds (Tohatsu, 127) at Mallory Park in August 1964.

Bill (number 4) getting the Chis Honda CR93 away at the start of a 125cc race at Snetterton, summer 1965.

The Chis Honda CB92

As Kent's first Honda dealership, Chisholm's of Maidstone, where Bill Ivy worked at the time, received an early delivery of the CB92 sports model in 1961 via the Japanese company's British importers, Hondis Ltd. And so the saga of the Chis Honda CB92 racer began. Don and Bill Chisholm employed among mechanics at the time, Bill plus his long time friend Roy Francis. The Chisholms decided to put one of the new CB92s on the road and once run in fitted it with one of Honda's race kits for the model plus a home-made thinner copper head gasket to enable the compression ratio to be raised. Bill Ivy knocked up a rather crude home-brewed seat, fitted 'Ace' handlebars and changed the brake and gear pedals to opposite sides (to match British taste at the time) – and set off to the local Brands Hatch circuit to test their handiwork.

It soon became apparent that however good the rest of the machine was the suspension, in the shape of the leading-link front fork and Japanese-made rear shock absorbers, were simply not up to the job. Looking around for an improvement, the Chisholm brothers had in stock a blown-up MV Agusta 175 (now it can be revealed that none other than Bill Ivy had been responsible for its mechanical demise!). So the MV's telescopic front forks, together with the rear shocks, were removed from the Italian machine and utilised on the race-kitted CB92. It was also necessary to cast a special top fork crown to enable the MV forks to fit the Honda, and this was carried out by the brothers themselves. A clamp half way down the nearside fork took care of the Honda's front brake torque arm.

Thus equipped, the handling was, as Roy Francis described it: 'transformed'. This enabled Bill Ivy to achieve a number of top 10 places at Brands Hatch, even at national level, during 1961 and 1962 – plus, as described in the main text, a notable 'get off' when running at the front of the field with the EMC works duo of Rex Avery and Derek Minter in

Bill Ivy's Honda CB92 – the tank is inscribed 'Chisholm's Benly'. Note the MV Agusta 175 front forks and home-made saddle.

Current owner John Pitt riding the Chisholm Honda CB92 racer in an Isle of Man TT parade lap.

October 1962 (witnessed at first hand by the author, who was spectating at the exact spot that day!).

But with Bill moving to ride for Frank Sheene (Barry's father) for the 1963 season, Don and Bill Chisholm then promoted Roy Francis to the Chis Honda CB92 ride, in place of Roy's existing standard-forked CB92 racer.

Roy well remembers 19 April 1964. This was the day when challenging for the lead at Cadwell Park's 'Boys' Day' on the second lap he fell off at the infamous Barn Corner with its adverse camber (which is still there today).

When Bill Ivy returned to the Chis Honda setup upon the arrival of a brand new CR93 production racer at the beginning of 1964, Roy Francis's routine was, in his own words: 'to warm up my own machine (the Chis CB92) early, park it in the assembly area and then get Bill's ready, as he [Bill] was riding in several classes. I had his trust to make sure the Chis Honda CR93 was ready for action.'

Roy ends by saying: 'Happy days, little did we realise what the future held for this Maidstone group of enthusiasts.' Bill Ivy went on to become 125cc World Champion, Don and Bill Chisholm in 1975 sold their business to Roy Francis and Paul Smart, Roy and Paul sold out to the Motorcycle City Group in 1998 and returned to motorcycling as a hobby, tending their respective race machines of yesteryear.

As for the Chis Honda CB92, it was sold to Governor's Bridge Motorcycles and is currently owned by John Pitt of St Leonards, Ringwood, Hampshire.

Chapter 3
Frank Sheene

To Frank Sheene must go the honour of being the first 'outside' sponsor to appreciate Bill Ivy's racing talents – if one moves away from the obvious help and assistance given to Bill by the Chisholm brothers, Bill and Don.

Howard German

For several years during the late 1950s and early 1960s, Howard German had been Frank Sheene's main rider; certainly in the 50cc class, where on the Sheene Special (essentially an Itom) the combination had won the Brands Championship in the tiddler class on more than one occasion. Frank had also been on hand from day one of Bill's racing career which had begun back in the spring of 1959 – aboard, of course, an Itom in the 50cc class. In fact, quite often Bill had managed to give Howard a run for his money.

But with the entry of Bultaco into the 125cc class in Britain during 1961, Frank had begun to be involved in the class, as well as the 50cc division.

During 1962 it could be said that Frank put much of his efforts into the bigger class, with both Fred Hardy and Michael O'Rourke riding Sheene Bultacos. And so Frank had not had much opportunity to contest the 50cc category.

All Change

Over the winter of 1962–63 Frank had commenced work on a new Sheene Special 'fifty'.

By the end of 1962 he had finished constructing a new frame – which really did give the impression of being a pukka racing job in miniature.

For the early part of the 1963 season at least this would be fitted with a Spanish four-speed Ducson single-cylinder, two-stroke power unit. This was reputed to churn out around 11bhp at 11,000rpm. Frank said that this engine might possibly be replaced at a later date with a similar five or six-speeder.

As for a rider for the new machine, this had not been finalised by the beginning of 1963. At that time it was thought that Frank still favoured his old friend, Howard German; certainly there was no mention of Bill Ivy.

Meanwhile, it was widely held that O'Rourke and Hardy, who on Sheene Bultacos had finished first and second in the Brands Hatch 125cc Championship the previous season, would continue as Frank's runners in this class. And Fred Hardy proved his worth by finishing runner-up behind race winner Ralph Bryans (Honda CR93) at the Mallory Park season opener on Sunday 31 March.

Bill joins Frank

That very same week it was announced that Bill Ivy would be riding Frank's latest 50cc, which was claimed to be the only machine fitted with a Ducson engine on British circuits.

The motor, said to be an 'ex-works unit' (*Motor Cycle News*, 3 April 1963), was fitted in the previously described frame – built by Fred Hardy using Reynolds 531 tubing and fitted with Italian Demm front forks. The 19in wheels were fitted with Ducson hubs and Dunlop alloy rims, tyres and tubes. The weight of the new Sheene Special was quoted as 85lb (38.5kg).

Michael O'Rourke (Sheene Bultaco) finishing runner-up to race winner Peter Preston (Bultaco, in the 125cc event; Brands Hatch 14 October 1962.

Dennis Ainsworth

So who were the men who inspired Bill Ivy? Well, of course, there were Mike Hailwood and Ken Whorlow, but there was also Dennis Ainsworth.

Although a Londoner as far as the racing world was concerned, he had actually been born at Altringham, Cheshire, on 17 August 1942.

And for as long as he could remember Dennis had been interested in motorcycles. Even when he was a mere three years old he rode between his father's knees on the parental Triumph Tiger 80 three-fifty. And, like many a teenager at the time, he could hardly wait for his 16th birthday to arrive.

He passed his test on a second-hand AJS but touring was hardly up his street. Instead, right from the off, Dennis wanted to be a racer. He was only 17 when he purchased his first racing bike, a 1950 AJS 7R. And he soon showed that he was competitive, finishing in the money at Cadwell Park in only his third race.

Until the end of the 1962 season he had remained faithful to AMC machinery – a more modern 7R being joined by a Matchless G50. And with these he had considerable success, notching up victories at Thruxton, Castle Combe, Silverstone, Brands Hatch and Cadwell Park.

By trade he was an engineer – having been with the same engineering firm since leaving school at 15. And it was no doubt that this background was why so many people admired the finish of his privately owned bikes – including Bill Ivy!

There was never an oil leak or even a scratch to mar the perfect finish. Equally polished on the track, Dennis Ainsworth was truly a perfectionist in both his preparation and riding.

If he had a fault, it was that on occasions he would try just that wee bit too hard and fall off.

Dennis Ainsworth's superbly maintained AJS 7R with Peel Mountain Mile fairing; Cadwell Park international road races, September 1962.

One of the riders Bill Ivy most admired during the early stages of his career was Dennis Ainsworth.

No doubt about it, Oulton Park in Cheshire was his favourite circuit. For example, in 1962 he won the 500cc Clubmans, was third in the 350cc Clubmans and in addition won the coveted Dave Chadwick Memorial race.

But it was August Bank Holiday Monday 1963 that Dennis really shot to fame, when in the 350cc British Championship race he won a thrilling duel for fourth place with the highly experienced Fred Stevens.

At that meeting Ainsworth piloted a Norton for his new sponsor/tuner Ray Petty, the man who had prepared Derek Minter's bikes. Dennis commenting: 'It's my big break.' Already that year he had taken runner-up spot on the 350 Petty Norton at the international Brands Hatch meeting on Whit Monday. His first foreign foray had seen him gain a ninth place in the 350cc Dutch TT at Assen, sandwiched between Fred Stevens and Dan Shorey.

Dennis Ainsworth, at Oulton Park on 5 August 1963, riding a 350cc Norton in the British Championships.

However, it was to be at Assen a year later, at the end of June 1964, which was to signal a change in the fortunes of this young rider, when he crashed heavily during practice. He was severely concussed, not regaining full consciousness for some considerable time. And although he returned home from Holland in early August he was confined to bed due to the crash. Although he made a reasonable recovery, and continued to race, his drive to the very top was over.

The engine (four-speed) used conventional piston-port induction and was equipped with a 17mm Dell'Orto carburettor. Power output was given as being in the region of 9bhp at 11,000rpm (compare these figures with those which had been given earlier).

Frank also revealed that he hoped to replace this unit with a five-speeder incorporating two overdrives, thus providing 10 gears.

Brands Hatch

On Good Friday 1 April 1963, Bill made his Sheene debut aboard the Ducson-engined special and finished runner-up to Tohatsu-mounted Dave Simmonds.

He also had his ride on the Chis Honda CB92, coming home 10th. It was at this stage that Bill realised that although the Honda had served him well, quite frankly it was no longer competitive at the highest level.

So by the time the next Brands meeting came along a month later on Sunday 12 May, Bill was Sheene-mounted in both the 50 and 125cc events. It was that man Simmonds who again proved the stumbling block to an Ivy victory – with Bill coming home runner-up to the Tohatsu rider in both their races. In truth it was obvious that Bill still had a lot of learning to do. This is because in the 50cc event (over three laps of the long GP circuit at the Kentish track) he was almost a mile (1.61km) behind the winner, and in the 125cc class Dave Simmonds charged through the field to gain his victory while, as the *Motor Cycle News* race report says: 'Bill Ivy (Sheene Bultaco) nearly bought it at Druids Hill.'

Preparing for the TT

Next in Bill's racing schedule came the Isle of Man TT, and this was to see him not only have a 50cc entry but a 125cc one too. Bill's machine in the latter was Frank Sheene's Bultaco Special – the frame of which had been built by Reynolds. In the tiddler category Bill was down to race another Spanish bike, a Derbi.

The 125cc (Ultra Lightweight) TT came first, on Wednesday 12 May. The start was delayed by nearly two hours due to fog. With 26 non-starters, the grid was reduced to 53 competitors for the three-lap, 113.19 mile (182.12km) event. But it was not to be a happy race for Bill, his machine being forced to retire with, of all things, a broken carburettor needle.

History was made in the Isle of Man on Friday 14 June 1963, when Mitsuo Itoh (Suzuki) became the first Japanese rider to win a TT race – the two-lap 50cc event. But it was a poorly supported race, with only 18 riders completing the 75.46 mile (121.41km) distance.

As was to be expected, the works Suzukis and Kreidlers dominated, while Bill, suffering from cramp, brought his Sheene Special home in seventh; the expected Derbi had not arrived in the Island. Bill averaged 61.12mph (90.34km/h) for the two laps compared to the winner Itoh's speed of 78.81mph (126.80km/h).

Certainly at this time there was little to show that within a couple of years Bill would be among the very top stars in world motorcycle circles.

Things did not improve much when Bill returned to the mainland and Brands Hatch on 14 July. First he was unplaced in the 125cc event and then came home fifth in the 50cc behind Hugh Anderson (Suzuki), Dave Simmonds (Tohatsu), Ian Plumridge (Honda) and Mike Simmonds (Tohatsu).

Bultaco

There can be few of the world's motorcycle marques which owe their origin to the events of another company's board meeting. None, perhaps, save Bultaco.

In May 1958 a meeting of directors was called at Montesa, then the largest of Spain's motorcycle factories. There had been heated disputes for some time over a single, central issue – to race or not to race – and this meeting was to prove the final straw.

The two key figures at the centre of the disagreement were the factory's founders, both of whom were not only directors but also major shareholders. Francisco Xavier Bulto and Pedro Permanyer were men whose partnership had seemed ideal when they had founded Montesa in 1945. Now they found themselves on opposite sides of completely irreconcilable views. Permanyer, the majority shareholder, was backed by the other Montesa directors in his opinion that the factory should withdraw completely from racing for the same economic reasons that had influenced other factories. To Bulto, the firm's racing involvement and reputation was all-important and without it he saw no future for Montesa.

That May meeting proved to be a watershed. Bulto, then aged 46, left Montesa, intending to devote his time and energy to other business interests; a textile plant and a piston manufacturing concern. It was not to be. Learning of Bulto's departure, most of Montesa's racing department followed suit and within a few days the 'old man' received an invitation to dinner with several of his former technical staff, mechanics and riders. There, Bulto's ex-employees pleaded with him to start a brand new motorcycle concern – one which could follow through their shared love for the sport.

Impressed as much by their enthusiasm as by their logic, Bulto agreed to set about the huge task of creating a completely new name within the Spanish industry at a time when so many others were floundering and when even mighty Montesa was feeling the squeeze. Despite their love of racing, all those at the meeting were only too aware that they would only survive if their machines were commercially viable – and that meant that they had to build roadsters. On 3 June 1958, a group of 12 former Montesa

A catalogue illustration of the 1962 air-cooled four-speed 125cc Bultaco TSS production racer.

An early, modified, 125 Bultaco pictured in the Snetterton paddock during the early 1960s.

engineers met Bulto at his home. The purpose of this meeting was to discuss the design of a brand new 125cc road bike, which could not only be sold in satisfactory numbers as a means of transport but would also form the basis of a simple, effective racing machine.

Later that month, the embryonic company moved to a farm owned by Bulto at San Adrian de Besos on the northern outskirts of Barcelona. Conditions there were spartan in the extreme, especially for an engineering-based company. The offices were in the farm outbuildings, many of which were crumbling with age and disrepair. Engineering facilities were even more primitive; for example, the lathe and other machine tools were set up with only a roof to cover them so far as was essential for production purposes.

It took four months for the design team, headed by Bulto himself, to conclude its work and so turn the initial design sketches into metal. Of course this was all done by hand – no computer-aided methods here! As Francisco Bulto himself was a keen and active motorcyclist, he often took a hands-on approach, riding prototypes to assist the road test programme.

By February 1959 development work on the first design had been completed and a press day was planned to launch the new marque's first product. Only one detail was lacking – a suitable name for the farmyard company.

Johnny Grace, works rider and engineer, was the man who supplied the answer by using a combination of Bulto and Paco (the latter a Spanish nickname for Francisco) – hence Bultaco. The origins of the famous

Dan Shorey with his works Bultaco TSS 196 at Oulton Park British Championships meeting, August 1962.

'thumbs up' symbol adopted as the company's logo were equally fortuitous. Bulto himself came up with the idea – remembering how he had seen British rider David Whitworth giving a thumbs up to his pit crew. Asking what this meant, he had been told that it signified that all was well. And so, right from the earliest days, it appeared on all Bultaco machines.

The bike which was launched to the press was the Tralla 101 (in English the name translates literally to 'whiplash'). It was to prove an excellent little machine, with good performance and reliability in service, helping to establish the company both financially and in the eyes of those of the public who had invested their money. The engine was a two-stroke single with piston-port induction. From a capacity of 124cc it put out 12bhp at 6,000rpm, using a 22mm Dell'Orto carburettor, 10.5:1 compression ratio, and bore and stroke dimensions of 51.5 x 60mm. This provided a maximum speed of 71mph (114km/h). And, of course, given Bultaco's sporting instincts, certain performance goodies were also offered, such as close ratio gears, alternative sprockets and an expansion chamber exhaust.

Just two months after the company's official launch, Bultaco made its racing debut. This was in the production class (based on the successful Italian formula series) at the 1959 Spanish Grand Prix. And it was a successful debut too with a pack of Bultacos finishing second, third, fourth, fifth, seventh, eighth and ninth! Appropriately, the highest placed Bultaco rider was none other than Johnny Grace, who finished a hair's breadth behind the winning Montesa.

Spurred on by this encouraging start, the factory then decided to modify a stock Tralla 101 by replacing the standard 22mm carburettor with a larger 29mm instrument, tuning the engine and fitting a pukka racing expansion chamber. No one could have known at the time, but this set of relatively simple changes was to lead directly to the birth of the famous TSS series of racing motorcycles.

Prototypes of these were campaigned in Spain throughout 1960 before going on sale the following year.

Another significant milestone for Bultaco came in October 1960 when a machine with a specially prepared engine was taken to Montlhéry near Paris, with the objective of breaking a number of long-distance speed records. Although based on the existing 125cc engine the record breaker displaced 174.77cc and was specially prepared in the factory's race shop. With dimensions of 60.9 x 60mm, it ran on a 9:1 compression ratio and produced 18bhp at 8,000rpm. The engine retained the four-speed gearbox and was later to form the basis of the 196 and 244cc engines used to power a variety of roadsters, as well as racers, scramblers and even go-karts.

Bultaco TSS machines were first seen in Britain during 1961, when Dan Shorey and Tommy Robb rode factory-supplied TSS models in the 125cc ACU Star series (in effect the British Championships; Shorey winning the title that year). By now there was also a British importer – Bultaco Concessionaires, based in King Street, Blackburn, run by John Aneley and sales manager Ken Martin.

Frank Sheene (father of Barry) was to become a major entrant and tuner of Bultaco machines and in the process became a close friend of Francisco Bulto. And, as the main text reveals, Bill Ivy was to ride Bultaco machines for Frank during 1963.

Oulton Park

It might have been Bank Holiday Monday, but the international British Championship meeting at Oulton Park on 5 August 1963 was a particularly 'gray and gusty' (*Motor Cycle News*) event.

Although Bill was entered in both the 50 and 125cc Championship races he only completed the smaller-engined event, with the 125cc Sheene Bultaco posting yet another retirement.

The 50cc event was over six laps of the 2.71 mile (4.63km) Cheshire circuit. At the front the Suzuki works riders Hugh Anderson and Ernst Degner immediately broke clear of the pack, while the brothers Dave and Mike Simmonds (Tohatsus) headed the rest. However, at the end it was Anderson who won from Degner in second, followed by Honda-mounted Ian Plumridge.

50cc British Championship, Oulton Park – 6 laps – 16.5 miles

1st	H. Anderson (Suzuki)
2nd	E. Degner (Suzuki)
3rd	I. Plumridge (Honda)
4th	D. Simmonds (Tohatsu)
5th	C. Mates (Honda)
6th	G. Votier (Honda)
7th	W.D. Ivy (Sheene Special)
8th	M. Simmonds (Tohatsu)

Bill tucks himself away on the Ducson-engined Sheene Special at Oulton Park, 5 August 1963; he finished seventh.

A Wet Brands Hatch

Rain persisted throughout the programme at Brands Hatch on Sunday 25 August 1963.

Water got in the works to slow the Ducson-engined Sheene Special during the 50cc race, in which Bill could only finish sixth.

However, in the 250cc event, having his first outing on Geoff Monty's Yamaha TD1 (see next chapter), this played into Bill's hands as Joe Dunphy (Beart Greeves), who had been dicing for second spot, was forced to retire with waterlogged electrics. The race winner was works Honda rider Tommy Robb, with Bill in the runner-up berth.

Tommy continued his winning ways in the 125cc event but this time was made to work much harder for his victory, with Bill, on the Sheene Bultaco, pushing him hard for the entire race distance. Both of them finished well ahead of third man Dave Simmonds (Tohatsu).

125cc Brands Hatch – 8 laps – 21.12 miles

1st	T. Robb (Honda)
2nd	W.D. Ivy (Sheene Bultaco)
3rd	D.A. Simmonds (Tohatsu)
4th	P.R. Preston (Honda)
5th	G.H. Hughes (Bultaco)
6th	D.F. Shorey (Bultaco)

Tommy Robb

Like Bill Ivy, Tommy Robb was small in height and someone who made it to the very top in motorcycle racing. Tommy is also unique as he was the only rider during the 1960s who rode for both Honda and Yamaha.

Born in Belfast, Northern Ireland, on 14 October 1934, his father, Tommy Snr, was a well-known figure in motorcycle circles in Ulster as both an official and at one stage MCUI (Ulster Centre) President.

The Robb family lived in the south side of Belfast and together with life-long friend Sammy Miller (who hailed from the opposite side of the Ulster capital), Tommy Junior and Sammy trialled pedal cycles prior to their motorcycle days.

Tommy's competition debut came at Short brothers and Harland time trial in 1951, which he won on a 197cc Villiers-powered James Captain. The same machine was used in other trials and subsequently converted for grass-track racing when the youngster won the handicap award in April 1952.

Then, in 1955, Tommy entered his first road race, at Kirkistown Airfield on a 197cc Sun. Soon he was spotted by the well-known Belfast entrant Terry Hill, which led to Tommy riding one of Terry's rapid NSU Sportmax machines; two highlights being a third in the 1957 Ulster Grand Prix and runner-up in the same event the following year.

Next, in 1959, came involvement with English dealer/entrant Geoff Monty, who provided him with not only the famous GMS (Geoff Monty Special) but also a brace of Manx Nortons and later a twin-cam Ducati for the 125cc class.

Tommy did not move to England though, instead travelling to all the British mainland and Continental European races from his Belfast home. The Monty connection spanned 1959–61, though the 1960 season had a section missing in the middle due to Tommy breaking his neck in the fog at Windy Corner on Geoff's Matchless G50 on the first morning of TT practice.

In 1961 came a works Bultaco ride (together with Dan Shorey).

Then came the really big one – the offer of a Honda works contract

Tommy Robb (works Honda) during the 125cc event at the 1963 French GP at Clermont-Ferrand; he finished fifth.

during the closed season of 1961–62. The first race for Honda came at the 1962 Spanish Grand Prix. Although he rode in the 50cc World Championship that year, success came mainly in the 125cc class, where Tommy finished the season in third place in the table. But the undoubted highlight was victory on the four-cylinder model in the 250cc Ulster GP in August 1962. He also finished runner-up in the 350cc race. In fact Tommy created something of a record that year by finishing the season in the top six in the 50, 125, 250 and 350cc Championship tables.

Tommy, however, feels his best race that year was when he won the 350cc Finnish GP on the 285cc four, beating teammate Jim Redman and Alan Shepherd, the latter riding a works MZ.

In spring 1964, both Tommy and his teammate Kunimitsu Takahashi had their contracts terminated, Tommy telling me: 'I never found out the real reason, but I enjoyed my period with Honda and I feel that my World Championship placings do not belittle either the Honda name or my own. I am also pleased that today Honda still recognise these results by inviting me to the various celebrations connected with their history.'

Next came what Tommy says was: 'A wonderful experience riding the works Yamaha RD56 in 1964.' But due to plug oiling problems 'the results I achieved were not as good as I would have hoped in the short period I was with the team.'

Then it was back to the ranks of the privateers with a pair of new Bultacos, a marque he was to campaign for several seasons before switching to a Seeley G50. The high point of his time with this latter machine was a fourth place in the 1970 500cc World Championships.

The final couple of seasons were spent with private Yamahas (250 and 350) in 1972–73. His last race came at Kirkistown on Billy Guthrie's 500 Yamaha, which Tommy won, being crowned 'King of Kirkistown' in the process; thus beginning and ending his career at the same venue.

Tommy then began a career in Warrington, Cheshire, as a motorcycle dealer, finally retiring on 1 March 1999 after selling the business to Fowlers of Bristol.

The following is how Tommy recalls Bill Ivy: 'Bill was a cheeky impish young rider coming onto the scene, wanting to get to the top rapidly and equally determined that he would do so.' He continues: 'I first met him properly at Brands Hatch when I was riding for the Honda works team. Bill came and asked me to try and get him a ride with the factory. At that time Bill was riding the Chisholm Honda and on the lower rung of the success ladder.'

And as for his character: 'I saw a zest for life. Fun and determination in his own ability were a driving force in his career. He had an outstanding personality and enjoyed a joke. Like me, he was small in stature and took offence at anyone who thought this would reduce his ability to be a great rider.'

'I remember well the news of Bill's death reaching me when I was on holiday with my family in Spain. I was stunned, and saddened to the extent that I had a quiet cry to myself as I had lost a dynamic little friend and motorcycle racing had lost one of its most courageous riders.'

Finally, how far could Bill have gone in his career? 'An impossible question to answer, for with "Little Bill's" determination, anything was possible.'

Probably Bill's best ride on the Sheene Bultaco came at Brands Hatch on 25 August 1963, when he finished second to Honda-mounted Tommy Robb (the latter then a member of the Japanese factory's works team).

That same day at Brands, bedsides the Yamaha debut, Bill also rode Geoff Monty's G50 Matchless in two races; again, the full story is catalogued in the following chapter.

An Even Wetter Snetterton

Driving rain, a saturated track and appalling light combined to produce what *Motor Cycle News* was to describe as 'nightmare conditions' for riders at the national-status Snetterton meeting staged on Sunday 8 September 1963.

At one stage visibility was so bad that they were unable to see the full length of the Norwich Straight, while officials attacked vast puddles on Riches Corner with brooms in a desperate attempt to keep the track open.

But one man who refused to give in to the weather was Bill, who riding the Sheene Bultaco in the 125cc event overhauled Dave Simmonds (Tohatsu) to win the race at an average speed of 73.87mph (118.85km/h). Bill also set the fastest lap at around 75mph (121km/h). This result is notable as it was to be Bill's only win on the Bultaco.

125cc Snetterton – 5 laps – 13.90 miles

1st	W.D. Ivy (Sheene Bultaco)
2nd	D. Simmonds (Tohatsu)
3rd	J. Richards (Bultaco)
4th	G. Ashton (Bultaco)
5th	D. Shorey (Bultaco)
6th	R. Turner (Bultaco)

Frank Sheene

Frank (later known as Franco) Sheene was born at Newgate Street, a small village near Cuffley, Hertfordshire, on 21 November 1911. He attended the local Newgate School, and his father, Alec, ran a farm for the Royal College of Surgeons.

Later, Frank moved to London as resident engineer for the Royal College of Surgeons. During the war he was a fire service officer on the Euston Road in Central London. In the early stages of World War Two he met his future wife Iris when they both worked at the scientific research factory on Great Western Road, London. Later Frank and Iris married in Bromley, Kent (Iris' home town), during August 1942. When first married they lived in Kew Road opposite Kew Gardens.

Before their daughter (Maggie) was born on 5 February 1945, Frank packed Iris off to Brighton to avoid the bombing while he remained in London. As Maggie told the author: 'We lived with my grandparents.'

By now Frank was working in Queen Square, Holborn, London WC1, at the Examinations Hall of the Royal College of Surgeons.

Frank Sheene (centre) with son Barry (seated on a works Bultaco) and factory boss Francisco Xavier Bulto in October 1969.

A relatively little-known fact is that Frank took part as a competitor in many motorcycle races himself, notably in the Isle of Man.

He first competed in the Clubmans TT on a Douglas 348cc flat-twin in the 1950 Junior event, finishing 55th. The following year, 1951, Frank had switched to a Royal Enfield Bullet (still a three-fifty) for another crack at the Junior race. However, this was to be to no avail as Frank failed to complete a lap of the race. However, he was back the following year on the same machine, finishing 60th. He then made the decision to switch to a more competitive bike, the BSA Gold Star, and was rewarded with first a 40th in the 1953 Junior, followed by his best result in the Clubmans series in 1954 when he came home 25th at an average speed of 73.95mph (118.98km/h).

Interestingly, in 1954 Frank teamed up with fellow rider Howard German and the two men travelled together to the Island. They had met through racing at Brands Hatch and were both keen supporters of the Clubmans TT – when it ceased in 1956 the pair campaigned hard for its retention but without success. Howard was later to become Frank's first rider when he became an entrant/tuner later that decade.

Then, in 1955, Frank switched to the Manx Grand Prix, having changed his BSA for a pukka racing machine, an AJS 7R. On this bike he rode in four races in the Manx over two seasons, in 1955 and 1956; the first year finishing 44th in both the Junior and Senior races on the same bike. Then the following year, in 1956, he brought the 7R home 51st in the Junior and later went one better in the Senior with 50th.

His first race had been at the final Brooklands meeting ever held, on the eve of World War Two in 1939. As Frank would have been the first to admit, although he greatly enjoyed the racing and preparation of the machine, he was never going to become a star rider. So he stopped competing and instead decided to use his considerable engineering skills in helping others to greater glory. Even so, he did manage to race an Itom Astor to victory in the 50cc event at BEMSEE's Silverstone Trophy Day on Saturday 5 July 1958.

The first to benefit from Frank's expertise was his old racing friend Howard German. The machine selected was the 50cc Italian Itom referred to above. This in itself was quite a step, because up to that time all Frank's racing had been concentrated on British bikes – and four-stroke ones at that.

However, as *Motor Cycle News* said in its 5 August 1959 issue: 'H.D. German of Harrow thwarted any attempt to make it Itom 1–2–3 when he took his Sheene Special through the field to win in 6m 35s, setting up a new lap record of 55.11mph [88.67km/h] in the process.' And just three weeks later *MCN* were to report that Howard German had broken the lap and race records on the Sheene Special at Brands Hatch.

Thereafter Frank became ever more involved in tuning and sponsoring riders – not just Howard German and Bill Ivy, but Fred Hardy, Michael O'Rourke and Phil Read.

Frank and Iris had their son, Barry, born on 11 September 1950. From an early age Barry had motorcycles all around him, so it was probably no surprise when, in March 1968, Barry rode his race debut (on a Bultaco of course!) at Brands Hatch. Barry went on to become a household name in a career which included winning many Grand Prix races and being two-times 500cc World Champion (on Suzukis) in 1976 and 1977. And it would

Frank's daughter Maggie, with her husband Paul Smart, a few hours after the couple got married at the end of 1971.

be true to say wherever Barry went you were sure to find Frank. This included moving to Wisbech, Cambridgeshire, thanks in no small part to Barry's friendship with John Blunt, stores manager of the author's former motorcycle dealership in the town. The family then relocated to Charlwood, Surrey, before Frank, Iris, Barry and Barry's wife Stefanie finally emigrated to Australia in 1987. Sadly Iris died in 1991. Barry succumbed to cancer in March 2003. Finally Frank passed away on 2 August 2008, (but because of the 12-hour time difference Maggie got the news on the 1st!) at the ripe old age of 96. Maggie lives with husband Paul Smart – no mean racer himself – in Kent.

Certainly the Sheene name will be forever remembered in the annals of motorcycle racing for all the right reasons.

Back to Brands

Two weeks later Bill was back at Brands Hatch, on Sunday 22 September. Although his best placing was a sixth in the 125cc event on the Sheene Bultaco, he actually rode in four events – 50, 125, 250 and 500cc. He was either unplaced or, as in the case of his 250cc ride (on Geoff Monty's TD1 Yamaha), recorded a retirement.

It was also destined to be his last race on one of Frank Sheene's bikes in Great Britain, although as detailed in the next chapter Frank did accompany Bill to Spain the following month when he rode Geoff Monty's Yamaha.

Chapter 4

Geoff Monty

In retrospect, it was probably Geoff Monty who actually flicked the switch on Bill's transformation from a relatively unknown name to that of a world famous superstar. Certainly, it was 1964 when the beginnings of this transformation took place. And during that season, except for the Chisholm Honda CR93, our hero was mounted on motorcycles supplied by Geoff Monty.

Geoff Monty talking to Bill, with the 500 Monard on the Mallory Park grid, 1964.

A Former Racer

Besides his well-known motorcycle dealership – Monty and Ward (then based in Twickenham, south-east London) – and his engineering skills, Geoff had also been a successful racer in his own right. All this and more is related in a separate boxed section within this chapter.

Geoff had first met Bill at the week-long Honda Maudes Trophy marathon which took place at Goodwood in October 1962, described in Chapter 2. And, as Alan Peck was later to recall: 'It had not escaped his eye that Ivy had pushed the little Hondas round quicker than the other riders.' During the Goodwood event, Bill had asked Geoff if he would give him a test-ride on a bigger bike, and the latter had said he would consider it. Geoff later told Alan: 'I was impressed by his enthusiasm as well as his obvious riding ability – and he was very persistent.'

Bill's Debut Day

Bill Ivy's debut day as a Geoff Monty rider came at Brands Hatch on Sunday 25 August 1963. Although it was not a winning debut, with a couple of second places it was the next best thing. Besides an absolutely brilliant runner-up spot to Tommy Robb in the 125cc on the Sheene Bultaco (remember Tommy was mounted on a much superior works supported Honda), Bill, riding the Monty Yamaha TD1 production racer, followed Robb home in the 250cc event. Then to round off an impressive day's performance, Bill, unfamiliarly mounted on Geoff's G50 Matchless, finished eighth in the 500cc 'Redex Trophy' race, before moving up to fifth in his second outing on the machine in the 1000cc event.

250cc Brands Hatch – 10 laps – 26.4 miles

1st	T. Robb (Honda CR72)
2nd	W.D. Ivy (Monty Yamaha TD1)
3rd	T. Phillips (Greeves)
4th	W.S. Mizen (Parvel)
5th	P. Ownsworth (Aermacchi)
6th	C. Doble (Greeves)

1000cc Brands Hatch – 10 laps – 26.4 miles

1st	P.J. Dunphy (Norton)
2nd	W.S. Mizen (650 Dunstall Domiracer)
3rd	P. Preston Norton)
4th	T. Phillips (Norton)
5th	W.D. Ivy (Monty Matchless)
6th	G. Young (Norton)

A Second Monty Outing

Although history records that Snetterton on Sunday 8 September 1963 was the day when Bill scored his one and only victory on Frank Sheene's Bultaco in the 125cc race (beating Dave Simmonds with his twin-cylinder Tohatsu), perhaps more interesting is that Bill also rode a couple of machines for Geoff Monty that day – a 350 Norton (the special Monty model with the bottom frame rails removed) and Bill's one and only ride on the GMS two-fifty. On the latter he finished 14th in the 250cc race. Its lack of speed convinced Geoff that the machine's day was done, and this directly led to the birth of the Monards a couple of months later. These bikes were transported by Bill and his friend Roy Francis in a trailer to the Norfolk circuit.

As Alan Peck revealed in his 1972 book *No Time To Lose*, a 'rather amusing incident occurred.' As 'the Norton had been loaned on the basis that Bill transported it to the meeting himself and returned it a few days afterwards. But when he turned up with the bike still covered in track grime, Geoff promptly told him to take it back home and clean it. This was done, and Bill returned with the Norton really gleaming; it was some years later when Geoff discovered that Roy Francis had been responsible for cleaning it!'

Monty and Ward were Yamaha's British racing agent for the sales and service of the TDI two-fifty parallel twin two-stroke customer racer. Bill raced one of these from September 1963 until June 1964.

Brands Hatch

Brands Hatch was Bill Ivy's local circuit and certainly where it would be true to say he served his racing apprenticeship.

As for the circuit itself, its history is a long and interesting one. Situated on the Kentish downs to the south east of London, its origins date back to 1926, when a group of passing cyclists noticed what they saw as a natural bowl – at that time a mushroom field beside the road. This belonged to Brands Hatch farm. After discussions with the farmer, an agreement was reached to allow the cyclists to compete there. Motorcycles arrived in 1928, but the first real signs of organisation came in 1932 when the Bermondsey, Owls, Sidcup and West Kent clubs joined forces to become the original Brands Hatch combine; their first meeting – on the grass as were all pre-war events – took place on 28 March that year.

The first of a succession of events that had begun and Brands Hatch was on its way. The natural amphitheatre was ideal for spectators. The speeds grew and the oval grass track was extended to 1 mile (1.61km). After army occupation during World War Two, grass-track racing returned to Brands Hatch with some epic team battles between Brands and Wingfield (a grass circuit near Derby). In 1947, Brands Hatch Stadium Limited was created and during the closed season of 1949–50 the track was tarmaced; the first race meeting over the new surface was held on Easter Sunday, 4 April 1950.

A new Brands Racing Committee had been formed between the Gravesend Eagles, Rochester and Greenwich clubs. That first meeting in April 1950 saw several interesting names in the programme, including John Surtees (having his first-ever road race), his father Jack with passenger Charlie Rous (later to become a well-known journalist with *Motor Cycle News*), Alf Hagon, Bill Cheeson (later owner and founder of then Lydden Hill circuit), Vincent Davey (later boss of London motorcycle dealership Gus Kuhn) and perhaps most surprising of all, a certain Bernie Ecclestone (now Formula 1 car supremo). By the end of that season, Jack Keel (riding Jock Hitchcock's Triumph 500 twin) held the lap record at 68.96mph (111km/h).

During the winter of 1951–52 the track was completely resurfaced. Soon afterwards, to overcome too many crashes going up Paddock Bend, an experiment was tried and one race staged the opposite way (clockwise, as now), and although speeds were slightly slower it was agreed that after 29 June 1952 all races would be run in a clockwise direction.

From the 1954 season an extension loop was added between the end of Paddock Bend and the Bottom Straight, taking competitors up the 1 in 9 climb to Druids hairpin and down again to rejoin the old circuit at the Bottom Straight, bringing the lap distance up to 1.24 miles (2km). A crowd of over 45,000 watched the opening meeting on the longer course. Newly created grandstands were in place for spectators to witness the arrival of Geoff Duke and the four-cylinder Gilera (his only Brands two-wheel appearance) in October 1955, but the multi-World Champion had to settle for third behind local heroes John Surtees and Alan Trow (both Norton-mounted). Then in 1957 Trow and Derek Minter separately beat Surtees who by now was riding the works four-cylinder MV Agusta.

Minter continued his domination to earn the unofficial crown of 'King of Brands', with Bill Boddice doing the same in the sidecar classes.

On 9 July 1960 came the first meeting over the new 2.65 mile (4.26km) Grand Prix course; this extension utilised the old circuit and then left at South Bank Bend, going out into the winding and undulating countryside to rejoin the old circuit at Clearways. This initial meeting attracted over 40,000 fans and was the first full international permit meeting at Brands. This saw Mike Hailwood win all four solo races after Minter had crashed earlier in the meeting.

Less than a year later Grovewood Securities acquired Brands Hatch. Then in 1966 Grovewood formed a subsidiary company, Motor Circuit Developments Ltd, to administer not only Brands but also Mallory Park (acquired in 1962), Snetterton (1963) and Oulton Park (1964); John Webb became managing director.

As for Bill Ivy, he first raced at Brands on a 50cc Itom on Good Friday 1959 (also his first-ever race) and won many races over the years at the Kentish circuit on a variety of machines. He also had the satisfaction of taking the 'King of Brands' title off Derek Minter in 1966 (on the Kirby G50 Metisse). There is no doubt that Bill's journey to World Champion was in no small part due to his experiences at Brands over the years. It had been almost a second home to him.

Since Bill's untimely passing, Brands Hatch has continued to grow in stature and its facilities have progressed. For example, the paddock clubhouse restaurant, startline control tower and other additions were made. Then, after the 1974 season, the entire circuit was resurfaced, the first time it had been completely re-done since 1950.

To comply with Formula 1 car regulations, further extensive work, including a new paddock, were completed in 1976. New infield pits forced a slightly different line at Bottom Straight, Paddock Bend was eased and the lap distance was reduced to 2.61 miles (4.19km) and 1.20 miles (1.93km) for the shorter Indy circuit.

Further improvements have continued to be made, including the 'Kentagon' bar/restaurant at the rear of Paddock Bend and later still, in the 1990s, the Foulston Centre was completed, after the Brands Hatch empire had been acquired by John Foulston. After John died in a car accident, his daughter Nicola was in charge for several years before, finally, at the beginning of the 21st century, Brands Hatch portfolio of circuits (now comprising Snetterton, Oulton Park and Cadwell Park, plus Brands) passed to Motor Sport Vision Ltd (headed by former Formula 1 car racer Jonathan Palmer).

Back to Brands

His next outing on Monty machinery came at Brands Hatch on 22 September.

After finishing sixth in the 125cc event on the Sheene Bultaco, Bill did not have any luck with his Geoff Monty entries. In the 250cc race the Yamaha was never in the hunt and soon retired, while on a Monty Norton in bigger classes he was a non-starter.

Even so, Geoff had already seen enough of what Bill could do – even at this early stage appreciating his potential, which at that time was largely untapped. So when Bill mentioned that Frank Sheene wanted to take him to Spain the following month to take in a couple of meetings, Geoff was in full agreement.

Pain in Spain

After the Brands meeting, Bill travelled with Frank Sheene by van to Spain; taking with them Geoff Monty's Yamaha TD1 and a 500 Norton. The original idea was to compete at Madrid (7 October) followed by Zaragosa (14 October). But after crashing in practice and being taken to hospital, it was found that Bill had aggravated his old leg injury and could hardly walk. However, in typical fashion, Bill was absolutely determined to take part in the race, riding the Yamaha TD1. Getting permission to have Frank Sheene as a pusher and start from the back of the grid, Bill formed up on the start line with Frank. However, after policemen removed Frank, Bill was left to attempt to push-start the bike himself. After almost exhausting himself Bill eventually got the machine started, but by this time he was almost a lap behind. Riding supremely well he managed to catch everyone except the leader. Then came disaster as the gear linkage broke (weakened in the practice crash) and he was forced into retirement. But not before he had impressed everyone there, including Bultaco chief Francesco Bulto. He did not use the Norton because he could not agree any start money. Not only that, but his injuries meant he was ruled out of the following weekend's racing at Zaragosa.

Enter the Monard

In November 1963 came news of the Monard Specials to be built in 500 and 650 guises, and these machines would be raced successfully by Bill in 1964. The full story of their development is charted in a separate boxed section within this chapter. The original idea was that the Monards – the name derived from the first three letters from Monty and the last three from Geoff's business partner Allen Dudley-Ward's surname – were to build replicas. But this never came about. The concept was that with cost foremost in their minds, Monty and Ward also planned to market the Monard in kit form or similarly, to offer basic components such as complete frame assemblies. Geoff Monty was quoted as saying: 'We want to show that a machine can be built for the boys at a reasonable price, but is simple and non-expensive to maintain with spare parts that are easily and readily obtainable in this country.'

Essentially, the concept of the Monard was a tuned Triumph (pre-unit) twin-cylinder engine, with cycle parts from the successful GMS (Geoff Monty Special) 250 Gold Star-engined machine which had been ridden to many victories by Tommy Robb during the late 1950s and early 1960s.

Conversely, it was probably the very cost of their construction which meant that the Monards never entered production. Instead, they were used as racing testbeds for a range of tuning parts marketed by Monty and Ward.

Interestingly, in the very week that the news broke of the Monard project, Monty and Ward ran the following in their advertisement in *Motor Cycle News* dated 13 November 1963, headed 'Special Builders': 'I am offering my GMS 250cc engines and five-speed gearboxes for disposal. Both engines deliver 32bhp with complete reliability. Enough spares for years.'

Plans for 1964

As *Motor Cycle News* revealed in its 1 January 1964 issue: 'Geoff Monty's number-one rider for the coming season will be Bill Ivy on a 350 Norton, plus Geoff's "development" 500 and 650 Triumph-engined Monard Specials.'

As the 'Racing Plans' issue of *MCN* told readers in the 4 March 1964 edition, Bill: 'Has two contracts for 1964 – riding a 125 Honda for Chisholm's of Maidstone and four machines for Geoff Monty: a 350 Norton, the Yamaha 250, a Norton or Geoff's Triumph-engined Monard special in 500 races and Geoff's 650 Triumph Monard for unlimited events.' In the same issue, Charlie Rous told readers: 'Bill Ivy was out for the first time on Geoff Monty's Triumph-engined Monard at Brands Hatch last week and both Geoff and Bill were very pleased. Everything went perfectly. The bike handles, it steers, it stops and most of all it is very fast.' Bill commented: 'I've got to learn how to ride a bike on one wheel: I don't think the front wheel was on the ground at all as it came up the straight.'

The Mallory Park season opener on 22 March saw Bill take runner-up spot in the 125cc event (on the newly purchased Chisholm Honda CR93), but except for

Brands Hatch, 11 October 1964. Bill looks quite tall in this picture – that is because the photographer, Gary James, was only seven years old!

Another 1964 shot of Bill in action on the Monard, this time leading a group of riders at Silverstone.

this, Bill did not feature in the results at the Leicestershire circuit that day.

In the 1 April 1964 issue of *Motor Cycle News* it was reported that Geoff Monty now felt it 'not likely' that he would produce any of his 500 or 650cc Triumph-engined Monards for general sale that year. As mentioned earlier, it had been Geoff's original intention to construct a batch of them for resale in 1964, but he told *MCN* that he had now decided that it 'will be a better policy to take the development further' with his own test-bed machines before finalising a production specification.

The Easter Weekend

Over the previous week, which included the Easter period, Bill had taken part in meetings at Brands Hatch (27 March), Snetterton (29 March) and finally Oulton Park (30 March). His 125cc rides on the Chisholm Honda 125 are charted in Chapter 2, but on the Monty machinery his best placings on the Yamaha TD1 were a third at Snetterton and fourth at Brands Hatch.

A week later, on Saturday 4 April, Bill was entered for the BMCRC (British Motor Cycle Racing Club) international Hutchinson 100 meeting at Silverstone. As was often the case at early season meetings at the exposed Northamptonshire former-airfield, it was wet and windy.

Again it is worth quoting from the *Motor Cycle News* race report by Charlie Rous concerning Bill: 'An interesting dice in the 250cc race was between Dave Chester and Bill Ivy on production racer Yamahas and Mike Duff on the Royal Enfield racer. These machines seemed fairly evenly matched on performance.' Bill eventually finished in seventh position – all the top six being mounted on works machinery.

Causing Quite a Stir

Next came the King of Brands meeting at Brands Hatch on Sunday 19 April. And even though Bill did not win the title (this honour going to Tom Phillips), he still managed to cause quite a stir. Why? Well, in the 500cc race Bill caught and passed none other than Derek Minter (Petty Norton). But, sadly, just three laps from the end Bill (riding a Monard with Reynolds leading link front forks) ran out of petrol.

But even so, on the same bike Bill turned out for the 1000cc event and managed to complete the full distance this time, finishing fifth. He also came home third in the 250cc race on Geoff Monty's production racer Yamaha and runner-up to Chris Vincent in the 125cc event – both riding CR93 Hondas.

Then came Snetterton on 26 April. Here Bill brought the Monty Yamaha home fourth in the 250cc race. He followed this up with an excellent third in the 351-1,000 Senior Service Trophy race on the Monard – the larger 649cc version this time. As *Motor Cycle News* reported: 'The most surprised man after the big race was Bill Ivy, riding Geoff Monty's 650cc Triumph based "Monard". He finished third. But at the end of the penultimate lap he lay fifth. Without realising who they were at the time, he blasted past Chris Conn and Peter Darvill (Nortons) on the approach to the finishing line and literally snatched third place from under their noses.'

1000cc Senior Service Trophy Snetterton – 10 laps – 27.1 miles

1st	D.W. Minter (Norton)
2nd	T.F. Phillips (650 Norton Domiracer)
3rd	W.D. Ivy (650 Monard)
4th	P.J. Darvill (Norton)
5th	C.R. Conn (Norton)
6th	R. Pickrell (Norton)

Bill (partnered by Paul Latham) rode in the 50cc Enduro at Snetterton on 17 October 1964. Like the team of Rod Scivyer (shown here) and Paul Hutchins, they raced a Honda CR110. Bill and Paul won and Rod Scivyer and Paul Hutchins were runners-up.

The best Bill could do at Mallory Park with the Yamaha on 3 May was a fifth in the 250cc final. However, as is recorded in Chapter 2, on the Chisholm Honda CR93 he not only set the fastest lap of the race but also set a new race record time. He did not feature in the larger classes.

Moving up on the Yamaha

At Snetterton on 10 May Bill had probably his best performance on the Yamaha TD1. Although Tom Phillips, riding Syd Lawton's very fast Aermacchi, won by leading from start to finish, it was Derek Minter (works Cotton) and Bill who disputed second place. *Motor Cycle News* takes up the story: 'On laps two and three Derek was in command, then Bill took over. But on the final lap, as they approached the line, it was Minter ahead once more. Bill's superb timing, however, which had shown itself on numerous occasions this season, stood him in good stead, and a matter of yards from the finish he pulled out and got the verdict.'

250cc Snetterton – 7 laps – 18.92 miles

1st	T. Phillips (Lawton Aermacchi)
2nd	W.D. Ivy (Monty Yamaha)
3rd	D.W. Minter (Cotton)
4th	A. Harris (Orpin Greeves)
5th	K. Martin (Bultaco)
6th	R. Keys (Yamaha)

Brilliant Sunshine

Brilliant sunshine greeted race-goers and competitors for the Brands Hatch international meeting on Whit Monday, 18 May 1964. Bill celebrated with yet another victory on the Chisholm CR93 Honda. In the larger classes it was an entirely different matter, with his rides on Geoff Monty bikes either ending in retirement or being unplaced. But interestingly, in the 250cc event he did – for a very short period – rub shoulders with Phil Read, the latter riding an RD56 'works' Yamaha. And it was Bill's, albeit brief, competitive ride on the Monty TD1 production racer which was to lead to Yamaha's first direct interest.

Bill had not taken part in the Isle of Man TT fortnight in 1964 after Geoff Monty said he could not afford the cost. And with only the Chisholm Honda, Bill did not think it worthwhile with just a single bike.

Bill Ivy (Monty Cotton 9) leads Dave Degens (Aermacchi 16) in the Brands Hatch 250cc Race, 11 October 1964.

Geoff Monty

Geoff Monty was born in Colombo, Ceylon (now Sri Lanka), in March 1917. His father was a tea planter who had built up an estate of considerable size.

Geoff came to England when he was 10 and went to work at a garage four years later. Without an apprenticeship this meant doing any odd job that came along at first. Even so, within six months he was able to do the work of a skilled mechanic, which included complete stripdowns and rebuilds of car engines, gearboxes and rear axles.

The garage work – always on cars – kept him in full-time employment until 1939. During that period though, a number of motorcycles passed through his hands as well. By this time he had entered the garage business in his own right.

With the outbreak of war, Monty volunteered for service in the RAF but just prior to his entry he was invited to join Thorneycroft as an installation engineer on motor torpedo boats. He soon found the job to his liking as every conceivable type of engineering work was involved. Monty had also become interested in motorcycles, first with an HRD 500 single and later an Excelsior Manxman.

During the final stages of the war he met his future business partner, Allen Dudley-Ward. The first of the Monty specials appeared soon after the end of hostilities. This was a souped up Triumph Tiger 100 of 1939 vintage to which Geoff fitted a pair of telescopic front forks, while the engine was tuned and equipped with a supercharger using a cabin compressor from a Messerschmitt Bf 109 fighter.

Ridden by Geoff at Blandford, it proved faster than the recently introduced Triumph Grand Prix racers. But shortly afterwards supercharging

Tommy Robb and Geoff Monty with the 250cc BSA Gold Star-engined GMS in 1959. The cycle parts, including the frame, were later utilised for the Monard project.

Geoff Monty pictured with the Monard during 1964.

was banned and that was the end of that particular Monty effort. But if nothing else, it did whet the appetite for more track combat and acted as a prototype for the Monty and Ward pivoted rear fork and their own suspension units. During the late 1940s, together with the similar McCandless system, the swinging arm conversion became all the rage, both for road and track.

By now Monty and Ward had formed a business partnership, but this did not prevent the duo from becoming involved in the SPORT (Surrey Private Owners' Racing Team) equipe. Besides the partners, this set-up comprised Harry Bostock and Phil Webb.

At the time, in 1952, Geoff Monty's racing machine was a heavily modified AJS 7R, with a lightweight frame of his own design.

By 1954 the Monty-Ward partnership was in full swing (which did not stop either partner racing abroad, notably in Finland and Sweden). It was also in 1954 that the GMV (Geoff Monty Velocette) first appeared. This was quick enough to challenge the very fast Moto Guzzis of Cecil Sandford and Arthur Wheeler at the Silverstone Hutchinson 100 meeting that year. The machine was destined to become the fastest British 250 over the next couple of seasons.

The engine of the GMV was essentially a cutdown 348cc Velocette Mark VIII. The bore was left unaltered at 74mm but the stroke was reduced to 55mm. The magneto was replaced by battery/coil ignition. Other Monty modifications included a Manx Norton-type duplex frame and a major weight pruning exercise.

But if the GMV was an excellent piece of special builder's craft, the machine which followed it was even better. This was the GMS (Geoff Monty Special) which was built during the winter of 1955–56. The new machine's heart originated from a 348cc BSA Gold Star engine. At 71mm the bore was considerably up on the stroke and was dictated by the use of

Geoff's friend and business partner, Allen Dudley-Ward, working on a Manx Norton engine in his Kingston-upon-Thames workshop.

Geoff Monty pictured at Cadwell Park during 1957 with his AJS 7R-based GMS.

a barrel, head and piston from the 350, appropriately modified. To keep things within the 250cc limit the special one-piece crankshaft had a stroke of 63mm. Thus the displacement computed out to be 249cc; later, a shorter stroke 72 x 61mm, 247cc was constructed.

To reduce oil drag no internal flywheel was employed. Instead, an 8in (204mm) diameter outside flywheel was splined to the drive-side mainshaft inboard of the engine sprocket. The valve gear was virtually standard, but Geoff's expertise in welding and grinding was shown in the layout of the inlet port with an unusually steep downdraught and larger throat. Initial power output was a healthy 32bhp at 8,300rpm. In this area Geoff Monty readily acknowledged the valuable assistance of Roland Pike, the man then in charge of Gold Star development at BSA's Small Heath factory.

Mounted in a lightweight chassis with Manx Norton forks and brakes, the combination of Geoff Monty and the GMS proved hard to beat in the cut and thrust of British short circuits during the period 1956–58.

For 1959, Geoff decided to hang up his leathers and obtain the services of a rider for his bike – so Ulsterman Tommy Robb was signed. However, Tommy was not the first person to ride the BSA-engined GMS. As besides Geoff's own successes, Michael O'Rourke had ridden the bike to 11th spot in the 1958 Lightweight TT. However, it was from 1959 that results really began to flow, with Robb winning at several short circuits plus the 250cc class of the North West 200 and a brace of highly impressive fourth places in the TT and Ulster GP that year.

However, from the early 1960s, foreign manufacturers, notably Aermacchi and Bultaco plus British machines such as Greeves and Cotton, began to offer affordable 'customer' racers. And so the fortunes of the GMS as a competitive racer soon dwindled away.

Geoff Monty moved on to first the new Japanese Yamaha TDI in the 250cc class and then a Norton single for the 350cc, followed by 500 and 650cc Monard twins for larger classes.

The stories of these latter machines are to be found elsewhere in this book.

As for Geoff Monty, as the 1960s became the 1970s he moved from the Monty and Ward Twickenham showrooms to a newly created dealership by himself in Edenbridge, Kent. Retired, he now lives in Cornwall.

Besides Bill Ivy, Tommy Robb and Geoff himself, other riders to straddle Monty machinery included Bob Anderson, Ron Langston, Alan Shepherd, Tony Godfrey, Ellis Boyce, Michael O'Rourke, Bob McGregor, Gordon Bell and Roy Francis.

For most of Bill Ivy's time with Geoff Monty his mechanic was David Adby.

However, he did take part in the Post TT meeting at Mallory Park on Sunday 14 June. With the Monty TD1 Bill came home fourth in the 250cc event, which was won by Phil Read on a works Yamaha with Alan Shepherd on a factory MZ twin runner-up.

Little did Bill realise at the time, but his big break was only seven days away – an event which would ultimately catapult him from being a national to an international star.

A Slice of Luck

As is fully explained in Chapter 7 – Signing for Yamaha, a huge slice of luck came Bill's way at Brands Hatch on Sunday 21 June, when he got to ride one of the 1963 works rotary-valve RD56 Yamaha twins. The machine was one of the two lent by the Japanese factory for home events by Phil Read and Tony Godfrey. As a Yamaha agent, Geoff Monty had been loaned one of the bikes. Tony had been hoping to take over Phil's cancelled entry (he being on the Continent) at Brands. But this could not be arranged, so Bill, entered on Geoff's TD1, came in for this race. And what a slice of luck it turned out to be...as *Motor Cycle News* reported: 'It took just one lap of the 2.65 mile [4.26km] circuit for Bill Ivy to come to grips with the 1963 works 250 Yamaha which Geoff Monty, his Yamaha-agent-entrant, has been lent. After that he simply waltzed away to win.'

250cc Brands Hatch – 8 laps – 21.2 miles

1st	W.D. Ivy (Yamaha RD56)
2nd	D.W. Minter (Cotton)
3rd	D.A. Simmonds (Greeves)
4th	C. Doble (Greeves)
5th	D. Chester (Yamaha)
6th	T. Robb (Bultaco)

Bill later commented: 'It [the RD56] was a quick as anything I'd ever ridden. Power was about equal to the 650 Monard and both had handling problems.'

Almost forgotten in the excitement of the works Yamaha ride was that Bill also came home fifth in the 350cc race aboard an AJS 7R and fourth in the 125cc event on the Chisholm Honda. But in truth Bill's main priority had been making best use of his one-off ride on the Yamaha, which of course he most certainly did.

In *Motor Cycle News* dated 1 June 1964, there appeared the following in the Monty & Ward advertisement that week: '1962 AJS 7R, ex-property of well-known Irish rider. Low racing mileage. We can definitely say this is an exceptionally fast AJS, having used it ourselves, ridden by Bill Ivy, complete with fairing, sprockets £425.'

The national meeting at Mallory Park on Sunday 12 May was boycotted by several star riders – including Bill – the start money having been cut by 90 per cent! This was, said Grovewood Securities, because of an international car race meeting held at Brands Hatch the same day. It was a mistake by the organisers which was not to be repeated!

First Ride on a Cotton

The next piece in the Geoff Monty/Bill Ivy jigsaw was Bill's first outing on a Cotton. Already Derek Minter had been successfully campaigning one of the Gloucester-built, Villiers-powered single-cylinder two-stroke 250s. Bill's Cotton debut came at Snetterton on 26 July 1964 with him finishing fourth.

250cc Snetterton – 6 laps – 16.26 miles

1st	R. Everett (Broad Yamaha)
2nd	R. Watmore (Adler)
3rd	B. Lawton (Aermacchi)
4th	W.D. Ivy (Monty Cotton)
5th	O. Drixl (Aermacchi)
6th	P. Darvill (Cotton)

Bill also came home sixth in the 350cc final on Geoff's Norton. And, as was now becoming the norm, he won the 125cc event on the Chis Honda CR93. Meanwhile, he had failed to reach the start line in the 500cc class – the Monard having dropped a valve during practice.

The story behind the Cotton was as follows: Geoff Monty had collected the machine from the factory on the previous Tuesday, and it was 'run in' by Bill at Brands Hatch on Wednesday.

As for the production Yamaha TD1 which Bill had been racing, this had been sold to one of Geoff's customers when the Twickenham dealer/entrant thought he had the permanent loan of the 1963 works 250; but of course this proved not to be the case. Or maybe Geoff simply got the right offer for the TD1...

British Championship Meeting

The annual British Championship meeting took place at Oulton Park, Cheshire, on Bank Holiday Monday, 3 August 1964. Here Bill experienced mixed fortunes. With a host of full works entries in the 125 and 250cc races, the best he could do in the smaller classes was a fourth (albeit a lap behind) in the 125cc on the Chis Honda. But he did bring Geoff Monty's Norton home sixth in the 350cc race, which was held over 25 laps (69 miles – 111km). Although not in the first six in the 500cc Championship event, Bill did put in an excellent performance on the Monard in the Les Graham Memorial race later in the day.

Les Graham Memorial (500cc) Oulton Park – 8 laps – 22 miles

1st	J. Cooper (Norton)
2nd	P.W. Read (Kirby Matchless)
3rd	W.D. Ivy (Monard)
4th	B.J. Warburton (Norton)
5th	D.W. Minter (Norton)
6th	D. Woodman (Matchless)

Cotton Troubles

At Brands Hatch on 16 August, Bill was out again on the Cotton. This time he put in a brilliant performance, even though machine trouble ruled him out of the results. Everyone had expected the battle for honours in the 250cc race to be between Derek Minter (works Cotton) and Tony Godfrey (riding the works Yamaha RD56 Bill had been victorious on at Brands a few weeks earlier).

In the race it was Minter who got the early lead, in company with the Swiss rider Othmar Drixl (Aermacchi) and Reg Everett (Broad Yamaha). As for Tony Godfrey, he struggled to get the bike going and eventually came home seventh.

But behind the flying Minter, the big battle was for second spot. By half distance Bill had fought his way through the field to claim that position. *Motor Cycle News* said he had: 'Rushed through the field', but then he went out with a holed piston.

When Bill visited Aberdare Park in South Wales for the first time (23 August) he only rode in the 125cc race. This was essentially in pursuit of ACU Star Championship points. Also, the meeting, organised with traditional informality, was unfortunately notable for the largest number of spills in 15 years, with no less than nine riders being injured. So, perhaps Bill was wise not to ride any of his Monty machines.

Winning Heats and Finals at Mallory

As *Motor Cycle News* said in their 2 September 1964 issue: 'Pint-sized Bill Ivy was in dazzling form again at Mallory Park on Sunday.' This was in response to his impressive double heats and finals victories in the 125 and 250cc classes; the latter aboard the recently acquired Monty Cotton Telstar machine. He also won a 350cc heat on the Monty Norton and came sixth in the final. In the 500cc final he was fifth on the Monard.

To cap a very busy day he also took part in the Cadwell v Mallory Match races, as part of the latter team.

250cc Mallory Park – 10 laps – 13.2 miles

1st	W.D. Ivy (Monty Cotton)
2nd	R. Watmore (Adler)
3rd	W. Crossier (Greeves)
4th	M.W. Manley (Greeves)
5th	J. Jackson (Aermacchi)
6th	D. Jones (Aermacchi)

Then came two meetings in two days – first at Castle Combe on Saturday 5 September followed by Snetterton the following day. Although he won the 125cc event on both occasions, his best result on the Monty bikes was a victory in the 350cc heat at Snetterton and fourth in the final.

Bill (Monty Cotton) follows Ron Pladdys (182cc Honda) at the Cadwell Park International meeting, 13 September 1964. He finished second to Bill Rae (Yamaha) but set a record lap after making a bad start.

International Cadwell

New records in every solo and sidecar class, sunny and warm conditions and superb racing were the ingredients which greeted thousands of enthusiasts at Cadwell Park's international road race meeting on Sunday 13 September 1964. And certainly the conditions and the venue suited Bill, who produced some outstanding performances. As *Motor Cycle News* said: 'Bill Ivy set the record ball rolling when he led the ultra-lightweight [125cc] race from start to finish on his Chisholm Honda.' *MCN* continued: 'It was Ivy who attracted the attention in the lightweight [250cc] race too. At the end of the first lap he was way down in 11th spot on his Cotton, with John Ashworth leading Bill Rae, both on Yamahas. A lap later Ashworth had disappeared to give Rae a terrific lead over two Greeves ridden by Dave Simmonds and John Swannack. But Ivy was relentlessly cutting through the opposition until, with one lap to go, he was second and had almost wiped out Rae's advantage. As the pair rounded the hairpin to enter the finishing straight Rae was still in front, and, despite a great spurt from the Cotton, Ivy lost the race by three fifths of a second but he did set up his second-fastest lap (72.32mph – 116.36km/h).'

250cc Cadwell Park – 8 laps – 18 miles

1st	B. Rae (Yamaha)
2nd	W.D. Ivy (Monty Cotton)
3rd	D.A. Simmonds (Greeves)
4h	T. Phillips (Aermacchi)
5th	A.C. Wilmott (Norton)
6th	J. Swannack (Greeves)

Then in the 500cc race Bill put in another great performance. As *MCN* reporter Norman Bainbridge told readers: 'Ivy again shone to bring the Dudley-Ward/Geoff Monty Monard from eighth to second place.'

500cc Cadwell Park – 12 laps – 27 miles

1st	C.R. Conn (Norton)
2nd	W.D. Ivy (Monard)
3rd	D.F. Shorey (Norton)
4th	P.J. Dunphy (Norton)
5th	S. Griffiths (Matchless)
6th	A.C. Wilmott (Norton)

There was another fine day a week later at Brands Hatch on Sunday 20 September. However, the results were not a repeat of Cadwell – except Bill's by now familiar 125cc victory on the Chis Honda. In the 250cc race he had looked set for a win on the Cotton. However, this was to end in retirement. While on the larger machinery, the best he could manage was a fifth in round six of the 500cc 'Redex Trophy' – behind Minter, Dunphy, Driver and Cooper.

Race of the Year

The famous Race of the Year Mallory Park meeting took place on 27 September. And with a host of stars trying to win what was the richest prize in the sport, Bill got places rather than wins – even in the 125cc event. Riding Derek Minter's works Cotton model (with six-speed gearbox and Norton forks) he finished sixth. In the 25-lap, 33.75 mile (54.30km) 500cc race Bill came home fifth on the Monard.

Then came the main course, the 175-500cc 'Race of the Year' of over 40 laps. With men such as Mike Hailwood, Phil Read and Jim Redman in the entry – plus all the established short circuit stars – Bill and the Monard had their work cut out to get in the prize money. But give it a go he most certainly did, and he was finally rewarded with sixth position.

Race of the Year, Mallory Park – 40 laps – 54 miles

1st	S.M.B. Hailwood (MV Agusta)
2nd	J.H. Cooper (Norton)
3rd	D.W. Minter (Norton)
4th	J. Redman (305 Honda)
5th	P.J. Dunphy (Norton)
6th	W.D. Ivy (Monard)

Almost every rider at Mallory Park put his signature to a protest which was handed to the ACU during the meeting. This protest concerned the way place money had been allocated, particularly in the thousand guinea (£1,050) Race of the Year.

As Charlie Rous explained in *MCN's* Paddock Gossip column after the Mallory meeting: 'Bill Ivy, who finished in sixth place in the Race of the Year, on Geoff Monty's Monard, found himself winning £10. There was no prize money below sixth place. And yet before that race new tyres had to be fitted (even at a special price) – at a cost of £11 16s 10d and fuel costs were 10s. After a 40-lap race the tyres were useless and most of the fuel had gone.'

Monard

The Monard (MONty and wARD) 500 and 650cc Triumph-powered racing motorcycles were derived from a combination of the cycle parts previously used on the 250 BSA Gold Star-engined GMS (Geoff Monty Special) machines, ridden by both Tommy Robb and Geoff Monty himself, and tuned pre-unit Triumph engines.

In originally creating the BSA-powered GMS duo, Geoff Monty employed 2¼in 16-guage steel tubing to provide a composite backbone frame together with Manx Norton components such as hubs, brakes and suspension.

As on the Swiss Egli design of almost a decade later, the engine unit (both BSA single and later Triumph pre-unit twin) was underslung behind a pair of front downtubes manufactured in Reynolds 531, the nearside (left) component carrying lubricant for the primary chain. A feature of the GMS/Monard machines was the lack of any frame bottom rails, together with a long, box-section swinging arm assembly.

Another feature was the sturdy engine plates, these being made from 5/16in duralminum. There was also a rear sub-frame, to which the upper ends of the twin Girling-sourced shock absorbers were bolted. This layout not only provided a lower engine fitment but also, usefully, reduced weight.

As detailed in the main text, Geoff Monty first came into contact with Bill Ivy via Honda's successful 1962 Maudes Trophy attempt at Goodwood, where the latter was one of a team of riders who circled the Sussex track for seven days and seven nights on a trio of 50cc Honda machines.

Following this venture, Geoff was ultimately to renew his acquaintance with Bill to the mutual benefit of both parties. Besides riding Yamaha, Norton and Cotton machinery for Geoff, Bill was also the pilot for both versions of the Monard twin.

In creating the Monards, Geoff converted the 250 GMS into the 500cc Monard – embracing a 498cc pre-unit Triumph Tiger 100 engine and Manx Norton close ratio racing gearbox. The engine was the responsibility of Geoff's business partner Allen Dudley-Ward. Initially the 500cc Monard had simply a carefully tuned motor, with standard bore and stroke dimensions. However, later this was replaced with a special 71 x 62.5mm short-stroke version sporting a one-piece Laystall crankshaft, high compression pistons, higher lift cams, together with a reworked cylinder head, nemonic valves and steep downdraught inlet tracks. At the same time the four-speed Norton 'box was replaced by a new Swedish-made Aargard assembly, although a Norton clutch was retained.

With the tuned short-stroke unit, maximum rpm rose to 9,000 – providing the up-and-coming Bill Ivy with a serious rival to the all-conquering Manx Nortons and Matchless G50s, which had previously ruled British short circuit racing unchallenged.

Significantly, the additional tuning/engine revolutions did not adversely affect the short-stroke five-hundred Triumph's reliability. And together with the larger 649cc Bonneville-engined (still pre-unit) machine, it played an important role in Bill Ivy's progress as a rider during his time as a protégé of Geoff Monty.

The Monards were relatively small machines (they had begun as 250/350 bikes), but Bill's small frame, when tucked away behind the fairing, gave an impression that they were large. Both Monards used shortened Manx Norton Roadholder forks, although the smaller model was race-tested with the Reynold's leading-link type on at least one occasion.

Another reason why the Monards were smaller than a standard Manx Norton was Geoff Monty's use of 18in – instead of 19in – rims and tyres.

Importantly, from a business point of view, the Monards were not simply racing machines, Geoff also employed them as mobile test beds for the range of Monty and Ward tuning goodies; such components including higher capacity oil pump, finned sumps and alloy pushrods, together with lightened rockers and timing gears.

At one time serious consideration was given to producing Monard replicas for general sale, but in the end this idea was not followed up – maybe affected by Bill Ivy's departure to ride for rival Tom Kirby in spring 1965.

After Bill came a string of riders for the Monard, including John Blanchard, Ray Pickrell and later Roy Francis, Martyn Ashwood and John Taylor.

Eventually, Geoff lost interest and instead focused on developing the firm's 8-valve 750cc Triumph conversion. The last man to race the Monard (now in 750cc guise, but still with a 4-valve head) was Keith Martin in 1972 and in a one-off ride in 1975, Barry Homewood.

New Monard

At Mallory, Geoff Monty revealed that he hoped to have two Monard 500s at Oulton Park the following Saturday. Bill would be practising on the new bike, which was fitted with a special short-stroke engine (see boxed section). Geoff told Charlie Rous that if both bikes went well in practice he was 'almost certain' to lend one of them to someone else at the meeting to race it.

Excellent Performances at Oulton

Continuing his ever improving form, Bill certainly impressed at Oulton Park on 4 October 1964. First he won the 125cc event. Then mounted on the Monty Cotton he came home fourth in the 250cc race. But it should be mentioned that the first two men home, Mike Duff and Tommy Robb, were aboard works Yamahas. Behind them Bill and Derek Minter fought out a 'battle royale' for the remaining rostrum position; Derek eventually getting the verdict on the works model.

Then in the main race of the day, the 500cc Bob McIntyre Memorial Trophy event, Bill chased Minter and John Cooper (Norton) home. *Motor Cycle News* capturing the moment: 'for sheer determined effort, the race was Bill Ivy's on Geoff Monty's Monard Special. Ivy had all his work cut out to oust Joe Dunphy and then went a stage further to joust with Dave Croxford and then pass him. In third place, he finished six seconds behind Cooper, who in turn was seven seconds down on Minter.'

Results and Finals at Brands

By now people were beginning to take notice of our hero. For example, *Motor Cycle News* dated 14 October 1964 had this to say: 'Pint-sized he might be but 24-year-old Bill, from Maidstone, Kent, who started racing on 50cc machines, has made tremendous strides this year. Riding anything from 50s to 650s, he must rank as one of Britain's most versatile riders.'

In that very same issue of *MCN* came reports from the final Brands Hatch meeting of the year; Bill's name being prominent in all the solo races, except the 50cc class which he did not enter! The results were as follows: 125cc first, 250cc second, 350cc sixth and 1000cc fifth. As such it was probably Bill's most consistent performance to date – five finals, five finishes in the top six.

Besides his mandatory victory on the Chis Honda, Bill finished runner-up on the Monty Cotton to Tommy Robb, the latter piloting one of the 1963 works Yamaha RD56s. His sixth place in the 350cc race came on Geoff Monty's 350 Norton, while the two other results, fifth and sixth in the 500 and 1000cc classes, came aboard Monards.

250cc Brands Hatch – 8 laps

1st	T. Robb (works Yamaha)
2nd	W.D. Ivy (Monty Cotton)
3rd	D.F. Degens (Aermacchi)
4th	D.W. Minter (works Cotton)
5th	R. Everett (Broad Yamaha)
6th	G. Keith (Orpin Greeves)

Over 70mph for 250 Miles

Although Bill had decided to quit the 50cc class before joining Geoff Monty, he made a one-off return on 7 October 1964, when, together with co-rider Paul Latham, he won the 250-mile (402km) Racing 50 Club's Snetterton Enduro.

The machine the pair rode was a Honda CR110 production racer, which proved faultless from the start at 12 noon to the finish 3 hours 35 minutes later. The pair averaged 70.32mph (113.14km/h).

But Bill and Paul did not have it all their own way. For most of the 93 laps that the winners covered, they were hotly challenged by another Honda CR110 ridden by Charlie Mates and George Ashton.

However, 12 laps from the finish the Mates/Ashton bike ground to a halt with suspected valve gear trouble; although they still managed to finish fourth overall and third in their class.

50cc Racing 50 Club Enduro, Snetterton – 93 laps – 250 miles

1st	W.D. Ivy/P. Latham (Honda)
2nd	A. Hutchins/R. Scivyer (Honda)
3rd	D.A. Simmonds/M.J. Simmonds (Tohatsu)
4th	G.F. Ashton/C. Mates (Honda)
5th	G. Bedford/V. Dedden (GBS)
6th	B. Goldthorpe/M. Sampson (Kreidler)

The 1964 Season Ends

And so the 1964 racing season ended. Later that month the ACU (Auto Cycle Union) announced the final positions in its Star Championships. Besides being victorious in the 125cc class, Bill also finished third in the 250cc category with 41 points.

As a thanks for the great help they gave throughout the year, the Brands Hatch organisation gave two parties at the circuit for marshals, officials and riders. These took place in December 1964 in the lead up to the Christmas festivities. Some 400 people were invited to the two occasions. Among the celebrities present were Bill Boddice and his wife Iris (who had driven down from their Birmingham home), Derek Minter, Joe Dunphy and Dave Degens, plus scramblers Vic Eastwood and Johnny Giles.

A New Season Begins

The 1965 British short circuit racing season got under way at Mallory Park on Sunday 7 March. And Bill Ivy started very much as he had finished the previous year, by appearing in all four solo events. After winning the 125cc event (on the Chis Honda) came the 250cc final. Earlier in the day Bill had won the second heat on Geoff Monty's Cotton. As for the final, John Cooper (riding a Greeves) made a meteoric start and grabbed a 150-yard lead from Fred Launchbury (196 Bultaco) with Derek Minter (works Cotton) third. Soon both Minter and Dave Simmonds (Honda twin) were past Lanchbury. Dave Degens (Aermacchi) had also moved up the field. Bill had made a poor start and it took him time to work his way towards the front, eventually finishing fourth behind Minter, Degens and Simmonds.

In the 350cc final, riding Geoff's Norton, he rode extremely well, bringing the machine home third – in front of Derek Minter.

350cc Mallory Park – 10 laps – 13.2 miles

1st	J. Cooper (Norton)
2nd	P.J. Dunphy (Norton)
3rd	W.D. Ivy (Monty Norton)
4th	D.W. Minter (Norton)
5th	R. Butcher (Norton)
6th	P.J. Phillips (AJS)

The main race of the day, the 15-lap 500cc final, was dominated by John Cooper. But as the *Motor Cycle News* race report said: 'If Cooper provided the speed, the spectacle came in an exciting duel between Derek Minter and Joe Dunphy, and further back Dave Williams, Rex Butcher, Dave Degens, Bill Ivy and Dave Croxford. The latter eventually fell back and Ivy, on the Geoff Monty Monard, disappeared when a valve dropped.'

For most of Bill's time with Geoff Monty his mechanic was David Adby.

Bill is pictured here with the Monty Cotton on the Brands Hatch programme cover, dated Sunday 21 March 1965. He had first raced the machine on 26 July the previous year.

Five Classes at Brands

At Brands Hatch on Sunday 21 March 1965 Bill took in five solo classes – 125, 250, 350, 500 and 1000cc. Once again he won the 125cc race. In the 250cc on Geoff Monty's six-speed 'works spec' Cotton, he 'streaked into the lead' (*Motor Cycle News*), hotly pursued by the pack. But, sadly, after a few laps the Villiers-powered bike slowed, allowing three riders to get past – Derek Minter (Cotton), Dave Degens (Aermacchi) and John Blanchard (Aermacchi).

In the 350cc class, Bill was fifth on the Monty Norton, while in the 500cc Redex Trophy race on the smaller Monard he was eighth. On the 650 Monard he put in a much better performance, coming home a creditable third behind Dave Degens (650 Dunstall Domiracer) and Derek Minter (500 Norton).

Bill with Geoff Monty's 350 Norton at Snetterton, 28 March 1965; he finished fourth.

A Snetterton Double

Bill scored a double victory at Snetterton on 28 March, winning the 125cc race (Chis Honda) plus the 250cc final on the Monty Cotton. Bill shot into an immediate lead. And with Derek Minter's Cotton retiring with engine trouble, Bill scored a comfortable victory.

250cc Snetterton – 6 laps – 16.26 miles

1st	W.D. Ivy (Monty Cotton)
2nd	D. Simmonds (Honda)
3rd	T.F. Phillips (Aermacchi)
4th	P.J. Dunphy (Aermacchi)
5th	D.L. Croxford (NSU)
6th	V.D. Chatterton (Yamaha)

Besides these results, on a pair of Nortons supplied by Geoff Monty, Bill came fourth in the 350cc race and fifth in the 500cc class.

The Easter Weekend

The 1965 Easter motorcycle racing weekend began on Good Friday, 17 April, at Brands Hatch. In several instances Bill led his respective races, but except for a by now rare outing in the 50cc (on the CR110 he had won the 250 mile Enduro with the previous year) was denied victory.

50cc Brands Hatch – 5 laps – 13.25 miles

1st	W.D. Ivy (Honda)
2nd	C. Mates (Honda)
3rd	B. Smith (Derbi)
4th	D. Simmonds (Tohatsu)
5th	R. Smith (Honda)
6th	P. Horsham (Honda)

Bill with the 500cc Monard, Brands Hatch Good Friday 16 April 1965; one of his very last meetings for Geoff Monty.

In the 125cc race he also won (Chis Honda). Then came the 250cc event. Here Mike Duff rode a works Yamaha to victory. But the great surprise was the 'terrific' (*Motor Cycle News*) performance by Reg Everett on Ted Broad's production Yamaha TD1A, who pulled away from Bill (Monty Cotton) and Dave Simmonds (Honda). Reg had looked all set to make it a Yamaha benefit, only to fall off on the final lap at Druids Hill hairpin. He remounted to finish eighth.

250cc Brands Hatch – 8 laps – 21.2 miles

1st	M. Duff (works Yamaha)
2nd	W.D. Ivy (Monty Cotton)
3rd	D.A. Simmonds (Honda)
4th	D.W. Minter (works Cotton)
5th	T. Robb (Bultaco)
6th	P. Inchley (Villiers)

In the 350cc race, at the end of the first lap Bill (Monty Norton) led from Paddy Driver and Mike Hailwood (both riding Tom Kirby AJS 7Rs). But Bill's lead was to be short-lived. He was forced back to ninth with rear suspension gremlins.

The 500cc Redex Trophy race was won by Derek Minter, but as *Motor Cycle News* commented: 'The most striking performance was put up by Bill Ivy, who finished a strong second.'

500cc Redex Trophy, Brands Hatch – 10 laps – 26.5 miles

1st	D.W. Minter (Norton)
2nd	W.D. Ivy (Monard)
3rd	D.F. Degens (Dunstall Domiracer)
4th	P. Driver (Matchless)
5th	D. Croxford (Matchless)
6th	J. Smith (Norton)

The oil patch which had claimed Reg Everett in the 250cc race also took out Bill during the early stages of the main race, the King of Brands 250–1000cc.

At Snetterton two days later, Bill scored his usual 125cc victory but otherwise had something of an off-day, finishing fifth in the 250cc and sixth in the 500cc. He did not feature in the 350cc event.

On the following day, Easter Monday 19 April, Bill was at Oulton Park. Here he was runner-up in both the 125 and 250cc races, and fourth in the 350cc class.

The 1965 Easter programme included a Tuesday (20 April) meeting at Mallory Park, which was wet and windy – and attracted few spectators.

After winning the 125cc race, Bill led the 250cc event from the start, but was eventually overtaken by Dave Simmonds (who went on to win) with Bill runner-up and Tommy Robb (Bultaco) third.

Bill dropped the Monty Norton at the hairpin, while leading the first heat of the 350cc class, and, as *Motor Cycle News* commented in its race report: 'Although he turned out in the 500 was obviously not feeling too confident, for he pulled in.'

Switching Camps

After competing in some 20 races at four meetings over Easter, it could be expected that Bill was somewhat tired – and the crash at Mallory on the 350 had badly bruised an arm. Even so, sponsor Geoff Monty detected something was not right and before leaving Mallory Park Bill told him that he did not wish to compete on the big machines any more. Geoff said he was 'astonished by this news'. Knowing Bill's character, Geoff found this hard to believe – as he would have been 'the last person to be put off by a crash'.

So, Geoff said: 'you've knocked yourself about a bit today, and you have had a hard weekend. You don't want to make rash decisions now. Go home, get a good night's rest and see how you feel tomorrow. Then give me a call tomorrow evening.'

The following evening, as agreed, Bill rang Geoff, and after discovering Bill was 'OK', Geoff asked Bill if he had made up his mind about what he was going to do. And as Alan Peck described in his 1972 book *No Time To Lose*: 'There was an uneasy silence, then came a stammered reply which shook him rigid. "I'm sorry," Bill said, "but I won't be able to ride your bikes any more...I'm going to ride for Tom Kirby"!'

To say Geoff was angry would be an understatement. This was primarily because although Bill had signed a contract to ride for him in 1964, for 1965 Geoff had decided that it would not be fair to make Bill sign another contract which might prevent him getting a works ride. Geoff was of the opinion that how Bill was progressing this would only be a matter of time. But to lose him to another British sponsor was a bitter pill. However, as events were to prove, from a purely racing point of view on the career move Bill had made the right decision.

Chapter 5

Tom Kirby

During the 1960s, the name Tom Kirby shone brilliantly as one of the biggest and best names in British motorcycle racing. As a sponsor, 'Uncle Tom's' bikes were campaigned at various times by the very top names in the sport, including Mike Hailwood, Phil Read and Bill Ivy.

For a fuller picture of the man himself, readers are advised to consult the separate boxed section within this chapter. Here, in the main text, we are solely concerned with Tom's involvement with the subject of this book, Bill Ivy.

Bill made his debut on Kirby machinery at Brands Hatch on 9 May 1965, winning the 500cc race on the G50 Matchless.

Jumping Ship

As is revealed at the end of the previous chapter, following a hectic 20-race Easter schedule which comprised a quartet of meetings (Brands Hatch, Snetterton, Oulton Park and Mallory Park), Bill eventually broke the news to his then current sponsor in the 250, 350 and 500cc classes, Geoff Monty, by saying: 'Sorry, but I won't be able to ride your bikes any more...I'm going to ride for Tom Kirby.' Obviously, Geoff was none too pleased. As Alan Peck recalled in his 1972 book *No Time To Lose*, Geoff was angry and rather bitter about the whole business. It was not that Bill had left him without warning that annoyed him as much as the excuse he had made about not wanting to ride the big bikes any more. Prior to Easter, the 'grapevine' had buzzed with rumours of Ivy practising on Kirby's machines at Brands Hatch, but Geoff had not believed them at the time. Only when Bill revealed that he was leaving to join Kirby's team did he realise that they must have been true.

Press Reaction

When news of Bill's move from Monty to Kirby broke, the motorcycling press was divided in its approach to the issue. *Motor Cycle News* in its 28

Bill with the victor's laurels after winning the 500cc event at Snetterton, 16 May 1965.

The Tom Kirby 350 AJS 7R short-stroke pictured in summer 1965. Development took from 1964 through to 1967. Bill struggled with the machine in comparison with the much more competitive Matchless G50 five-hundred.

April 1965 issue carried the simple headline: 'Ivy Joins Kirby.' Going on to say: 'Bill Ivy, the five-foot-nothing jockey with stamina to ride as many bikes in as many classes and events as he can (he rode 50, 125, 250, 350, 500 and 650 at Brands Hatch on Good Friday) has severed his very successful sponsorship with Chisholm's and Geoff Monty and is joining Tom Kirby's AJS and Matchless camp.'

Meanwhile, *Motor Cycle* were more sympathetic towards Geoff Monty – their headline reading: 'Shock for Monty – Ivy joins Kirby.' It continued: 'Twickenham sponsor Geoff Monty had a nasty shock last week. For, only a day after his highly successful weekend, his rider Bill Ivy rang Geoff to say that he wouldn't be riding for him anymore. He'd decided to race Tom Kirby's machines. This means that bang in the middle of the busiest racing time of the year, Geoff is left without a pilot for his very successful machines. Naturally, he's not exactly delighted: "I think I might have been given a bit of warning. The first I knew was when Bill rang me" he said ruefully.'

As for Bill, he was on record as saying: 'I don't like upsetting anyone, but I want to race an AJS and a Matchless, and I want to do the TT.' Geoff Monty, it has to be said, had been unable to supply Bill with three machines for the TT on cost grounds.

As Alan Peck says in *No Time To Lose*: 'Bill was slightly out of favour at the time, and even some of his fans didn't think much of his actions.'

The Kirby Debut

When the Kirby debut meeting came – at Brands Hatch on 9 May – much of the controversy was overshadowed by what went on on the track. *Motor Cycle News* having this to say: 'Pint-sized Bill Ivy, out for the first time on Tom Kirby raceware, turned giant-killer at Brands Hatch on Sunday to shatter the big bike stars at their own level. In blistering form, he streaked home ahead of a furiously scrapping 500cc "Redex Trophy" field including Minter, Cooper, Driver and Dunphy. Added to this, he scored his traditional win in the 125 race and gained a superb third place in the 1,000, 350 and 250cc races.'

500cc Redex Trophy, Brands Hatch – 10 laps – 26.4 miles

1st	W.D. Ivy (Kirby Matchless)
2nd	J. Cooper (Norton)
3rd	E.G. Driver (Matchless)
4th	P.J. Dunphy (Norton)
5th	D.L. Croxford (Matchless)
6th	D.W. Minter (Norton)

The Kirby team in 1965, left to right: Mike Hailwood, Tom Kirby, Bill and Paddy Driver. Mike rode for Tom at selected meetings if his works MV or Honda contracts allowed.

Tom Kirby

Tom Kirby was born in 1922 and it was grass track racing which was his original passion. In this he was following in his father's wheel-tracks, Tom Snr, having taken part in the very first speedway meeting at High Beach (in Epping Forrest) when dirt track racing came to Britain in 1928, with Tom Jnr himself racing on the grass for the first time in 1938 when he was 16.

Tom's machine was a three-fifty Big Port AJS, and with this he won the first race that season – with a set of spanners as the prize. When he began racing, Tom joined the Ilford Amateur MCC, remaining in the club for many years. He was eventually to become its president.

His job as an apprentice motorcycle mechanic came to an end when the war came along. He joined the Royal Air Force and was soon posted to the Far East – via South Africa, India, Burma and Singapore. As Tom later recalled: 'Being with a Motor Transport unit, we didn't have things too bad, and when things quietened down out there we were even able to get on with a bit of racing!'

After the conflict, Tom went back into the motorcycle trade, and in 1947 he decided it was time to branch out on his own, opening a dealership in Romford.

Tom told journalist Charlie Rous in 1964 that: 'I've always felt that active participation in competitions must help business,' and throughout his business career he followed this principle. The first rider Tom sponsored was Ron Allan, who won the 250 Eastern Counties Championship title on Tom's Rudge.

Next he teamed up with Gordon 'Maxie' Miller, who raced a 350 BSA B32 on the grass, and later took part in short circuit road racing at Cadwell Park and Brands Hatch. Sadly, 'Maxie', who was to remain a close friend of Tom's, died while piloting an aircraft in 1962.

Next came a young medical student by the name of Peter Ferbrache. After this came the legendary Alf Hagon, who Tom began helping in 1951.

Kirby team bikes at Snetterton in September 1964; ridden that day by Roger Hunter.

Tom Kirby in conversation with Bill and AMC development engineer Jack Williams (with pipe); Brands Hatch, 9 May 1965.

His first machine was another BSA B32, fitted with Kirby's home-made swinging arm rear suspension. This machine, as Hagon began to make his presence felt on the tracks, was later fitted with a 350 JAP engine which took the rider to a vast number of victories, including a sensational 71mph (114km/h) lap record at the Leicester Query Club's Kirkby Mallory (Mallory Park) grass track.

Together, Tom and Alf put their heads together and conceived their first speedway-style grass bike, and in the process they set a new trend in that discipline of motorcycle sport.

The Kirby-Hagon partnership lasted for a whole decade before the latter decided to branch out into business on his own. This also signalled the end of the famous Kirby specials, and for Tom, his long interest in grass track racing.

Ernie Wooder worked for Tom at this time, and in 1961 Tom began his love affair with road racing. Ernie had been competing since 1956 and was always a competent rider. So Tom decided to help him further his career and ordered a new AJS 7R and Matchless G50 for the 1962 season.

In 1962, Robin Dawson also came under Tom's wing – the result being victory in the Junior Manx Grand Prix that same year. In 1963 the Kirby race team moved up a gear. As Tom later recalled: 'Things happened so quickly that I could hardly keep time with myself.' Much of this was due to the London-based AMC factory approaching him to foster the running of their works development machines. And he soon found himself running a team of no less than *eight* bikes with four riders – Alan Shepherd, Paddy Driver, Roger Hunter and Lewis Young.

In recalling the 1963 season, Tom was to say: 'We had a great year together, highlighted by Alan's second place in the World Championship, but a big disappointment was Roger's retirement in the Senior Manx GP – when he ran out of petrol on the last lap while in the lead.' Other highlights that year were Paddy Driver and co-rider Joe Dunphy's win on an AJS 650 CSR in the Bemsee 1,000 Kilometre endurance race and Alan Shepherd beating the Gileras at Mallory Park.

For 1964, the team was joined by even more riders, including, at selected events, the likes of Mike Hailwood and Phil Read. As is described in the main text, the Kirby team was joined by Bill Ivy in spring 1965. Right from the off Bill proved a big hit on the Kirby machines, particularly the larger G50-engined bike. Probably the highlights, of many, on the Kirby machines were the 1965 500cc British Championship title (at Oulton Park) and winning the 'King of Brands' title in 1966.

Eventually, of course, Bill moved on to become a full works-supported Yamaha teamster, while Tom continued to help riders on the British scene, even after the AMC factory closed. Later still Tom became involved with his friend Vic Camp (the Walthamstow, East London, Ducati specialist). Vic had opened a successful racing school at Brands Hatch; and in the late 1960s this became the Camp-Kirby Racing School. The machines used for this purpose remained 250 Ducatis.

At one time Tom Kirby's motorcycle dealership at Roneo Corner, Romford, held agencies for no less than 14 different makes of machines and was known throughout the British Isles – and overseas. Tom had been correct in his belief that involvement in motorcycle sport can bring success in the showroom. But did his vast expenditure on racing reap equal records in the profit and loss column?

Snetterton

In previewing Bill's next meeting, at Snetterton on the following Sunday, *Motor Cycle News* had this to say: 'Will Bill Ivy continue his giant-killing act at Snetterton? His switch to Tom Kirby machinery seems to have given him the incentive he desired and after winning the 500cc race at Brands Hatch at the weekend he is brimming on confidence.'

After taking his usual 125cc victory on the Honda (he had not left Chisholm's as reported), Bill once again impressed on the larger Kirby bike. *MCN's* race report is worth repeating: 'Bill Ivy followed up his breathtaking Brands win a week earlier by repeating the dose in the 500cc race on the Kirby Matchless. What's more, he finished the race with a wobbling rear wheel due to a collapsed bearing. Old favourites Minter and Cooper each had a lap at the front before Ivy steamed into the lead on lap three and stayed there right to the flag.'

Bill also put up the fastest lap at 94.17mph (151.51km/h) – slightly slower than his quickest circuit when winning his heat earlier in the day.

500cc Snetterton – 10 laps – 27.1 miles

1st	W.D. Ivy (Kirby Matchless)
2nd	R. Watmore (Matchless)
3rd	J. Cooper (Norton)
4th	D.W. Minter (Norton)
5th	P. Williams (Norton)
6th	D.L. Croxford (Matchless)

Even More Convincing

Then at Mallory Park seven days later, continuing his 'rapid rise to stardom' (*Motor Cycle News*), Bill scored what was seen as his most impressive performance yet, with convincing victories in the 125, 250 and 500cc races on 23 May. In winning the 500cc final on his Kirby Matchless, Bill set a new 15-lap race record of 86.65mph (139.41km/h) in his pursuit which swept him past John Cooper (Norton).

Not only had the day been his most successful meeting yet, but he also took home the lion's share of 'Memories of Donington' awards; those being magnificent trophies from the famous pre-war circuit, which were presented to Bill by the riders who had last won them way back in 1939!

As before, the 350 Kirby AJS did not match its larger Matchless-engined brother and so Bill could only finish third – the only race he did not win that day. The two men in front were the winner, Derek Minter, and runner-up John Cooper, both riding Nortons.

Of course, it was the 500cc final which grabbed the headlines. The pace was set from the very start by circuit specialist Cooper, who held Bill off for 16 of the 20 laps, but once our man got ahead there was 'no holding him' (*Motor Cycle News*) and he went on to win with ease.

500cc Mallory Park – 20 laps – 27 miles

1st	W.D. Ivy (Kirby Matchless)
2nd	J. Cooper (Norton)
3rd	D. Degens (Dunstall Domiracer)
4th	P. Williams (Norton)
5th	R. Chandler (Matchless)
6th	D.W. Minter (Norton)

Bill's Sponsors

It is worth pointing out to readers at this stage that, since having joined the Kirby camp, many racegoers were confused as to just who Bill's other sponsors were. As was already known, his involvement with the Hornchurch, Essex, dealer was for the larger classes only. Bill's 250cc machine was a Cotton provided by Frank Higley, while the 125 Honda was owned by Chisholm's of Maidstone. But this picture became even more confused when he was provided with works-supported Yamaha machines for the Isle of Man TT (125 and 250cc); this final aspect of Bill's varied machinery at that time is fully covered in Chapter 7 – Signing for Yamaha.

TT Experiences

As we know, Bill cited the Isle of Man TT as the main reason why he moved from Geoff Monty to Tom Kirby. However, the Yamaha connection gave Ivy's 1965 TT an entirely new dimension. But even though he had four races he only finished one, the Ultra Lightweight (125cc) event on the Yamaha (fully described in Chapter 7). In the Lightweight (250cc) he amazed everyone by having a sensational ride on an RD56 air-cooled disc valve twin. In fact, for two laps he was lying second and had lapped at over 98mph (158km/h), a tremendous performance on a strange machine. Unfortunately, his race came to a premature end when he fell off in the Mountain mist at Brandywell, breaking off a carburettor and touring back to Douglas to retire.

As for his Junior (350cc) and Senior (500cc) rides on Kirby machinery, these had an even less successful outcome. In the former event after fighting his way up the field, he was eighth at the end of lap four. Then, at Barregarrow on the next lap his chain came off and he was forced to retire. Then came the Senior race but again Bill was out of luck, with a broken con-rod on his Kirby Matchless engine.

Bill with the Kirby AJS 7R short-stroke during the 1965 Junior TT. Over the measured 176 yards at the Highlander, the machine clocked 120.4mph (193.7km/h).

Luck Returns at Mallory

If he had been out of luck in the TT, Bill's fortunes soared back at the Post TT international at Mallory Park on Sunday 20 June. The *Motor Cycle News* headline said it all: 'Ivy's a giant at Mallory!' going on to explain: 'Giants like Mike Hailwood, Jim Redman and Phil Read could not overshadow him! Brilliant riders such as John Cooper, Joe Dunphy and Mike Duff finished behind him – Bill Ivy was the hero of the all-star Mallory Park international.'

After concluding his by now usual 125cc race win on the Honda CR93, Bill put in two magnificent performances – finishing runner-up to Redman (Honda 4) in the 350cc race and the same position to Mike Hailwood (MV Agusta) in the bigger class. And in both cases Bill was mounted on single-cylinder bikes! In fact, in the latter, Mike Hailwood was so impressed by Bill's performance that on the victory lap the two riders rode their respective bikes and Mike gave his winner's laurels to Bill. As *Motor Cycle News* pointed out: 'Less than two years ago, Bill was an almost unknown 50 Itom rider; today he can mix it with the greatest.'

Bill, with other members of the winning team from the Relay Race; Brands Hatch 27 June 1965. Left to right: Jim Curry, Dave Croxford, Tommy Robb and Wee Bill.

350cc Mallory Park – 15 laps – 20.25 miles

1st	J. Redman (Honda 4)
2nd	W.D. Ivy (Kirby AJS)
3rd	P.J. Dunphy (Norton)
4th	M. Duff (AJS)
5th	D.F. Shorey (Norton)
6th	D. Ainsworth (Norton)

500cc Mallory Park – 20 laps – 27 miles

1st	S.M.B. Hailwood (MV Agusta 4)
2d	W.D. Ivy (Kirby Matchless)
3rd	J. Cooper (Norton)
4th	P.J. Dunphy (Norton)
5th	R. Chandler (Matchless)
6th	C.R. Conn (Norton)

More of the Same

After a one-off ride in the Dutch TT at Assen on Saturday 26 June (finishing fourth on a works 125cc Yamaha), Bill was back in England the following day at Brands Hatch. Here, it was more of the same. *Motor Cycle News* takes up the story: 'Giant-killer Bill Ivy (Matchless), already tipped for world stardom, notched another major success when he beat Derek Minter (Norton) in the main 500cc race at Brands Hatch on Sunday.'

Besides this, he also won the 125cc event and finished runner-up (to Minter) in the 350cc event, before rounding off a great day by winning the decisive leg of the first team relay race on a British circuit (on his five-hundred Kirby Matchless).

Out of Luck

Snetterton on Sunday 25 July was the scene for the Eastern Sidecar Championship races. However, there were two solo events – for 50cc and 250cc machines. But it was an unlucky day for Bill. First he was forced to retire on Frank Higley's Cotton in the 250cc practice (with a broken steering damper) and so was a non-starter in the race itself. Then, riding a Honda CR110, the machine seized up when he was leading the 50cc event.

Then came more misfortune, when after winning the 250cc race on the Cotton at Thruxton on 1 August (and also setting the fastest lap), Bill came off his Kirby AJS during the 350cc event after only four laps. He suffered a badly bruised hand, which put him out of the meeting; but, luckily, no bones were broken so he was expected to be fit enough to ride in the Hutchinson 100 at Silverstone in two weeks' time.

Derek Minter

When Bill Ivy won the 'King of Brands' crown at the famous Kent circuit in April 1966 the man he deposed was Derek Minter, who to many will always be the true 'King of Brands' having dominated proceedings (certainly in the larger capacity classes) after John Surtees had joined MV Agusta, for a decade until that day in the spring of 1966.

D.W. (Derek William) Minter was born in the tiny village of Ickham, some four miles from Canterbury in rural Kent on 27 April 1932.

Upon leaving school, Derek's first job of work was at the East Kent Bus Company, based in Canterbury, as an apprentice electrician. His original mode of transport from there to his home was a pedal cycle. However, as Derek says: 'I soon got tired of this' and with his savings he purchased his first motorcycle, a brand new BSA B31 three-fifty from Canterbury dealers Hallets in 1948.

In late 1949 Derek left his job with the bus company and joined Hallets as a mechanic. Then, in 1950, upon reaching 18 years of age, Derek was called up for National Service, joining the Royal Air Force. Upon his demob in 1952 he took up where he had left off in civilian life, working as a mechanic for Hallets.

As for the beginning of his racing career, this began at Brands Hatch on 14 May 1953. To enable him to go racing Derek had exchanged his B31 for a new BB34 five-hundred BSA Gold Star, purchased, like his previous model, from Hallets.

By the end of 1955 Derek had begun to put in some impressive performances on the Gold Star, to such an extent that he received an offer from Ron Harris to ride MV Agustas in the lightweight classes – and also a job with Harris selling the Italian machines.

As for the Gold Star, this was by now using a later big-fin DB34 engine tuned at the BSA works by Roland Pike.

Derek's big break came during 1957 when he was sponsored on a couple of brand new Manx Nortons (tuned by Steve Lancefield), by Wincheap Garage.

Derek Minter standing beside the works 250cc Bianchi twin he rode in the 1960 Lightweight TT.

After gaining several victories – and also a rostrum (third) position in the 500cc Belgian Grand Prix, Derek decided to go full-time professional for the 1958 season, after quitting Wincheap (where he also worked). This proved an excellent decision as he went on to win the 350 and 500cc British Championship titles at Thruxton that same year. In fact, Derek never looked back and soon came under the wing of Steve Lancefield himself (at Wincheap it was a different liaison, with the company simply paying Lancefield to prepare the engines, whereas now it was a direct connection).

This Lancefield-Minter alliance brought a period of real achievement, including firmly establishing himself as 'King of Brands' and also, in 1960, becoming the first man to lap the Isle of Man TT circuit at over 100mph (161km/h) on a single-cylinder machine. This period also brought the first works rides, including rides for MZ, Morini and Bianchi.

But following the 1961 TT, where Steve Lancefield was not invited to official Norton celebrations for Minter's 100mph lap the previous year, the relationship with the famous south London tuner came to an end. In Lancefield's place the Norton factory took Derek under their wing. During the next few months (the second half of 1961 and the first half of 1962) he rode works development Nortons, including the 350cc Low Boy machine and Domiracer twins.

Nineteen-sixty-two was without doubt Derek Minter's best-ever year. Everything he touched turned to gold. On his Nortons he was virtually unbeatable on the British short circuits, while riding a 1961 Honda 250 four he won every race he entered, including the TT where he beat the entire factory Honda squad. But sadly, after an offer from Honda to go to Japan, he turned it down because the company could not guarantee that he could ride 'his' four. He was also triple British Champion that year (250, 350 and 500cc).

At the beginning of 1963 he signed to ride for the Geoff Duke Scuderia Gilera team. At Silverstone in April that year, Derek gave Gilera (after six years away) their first victory. However, his undoubted world-class potential was never to be realised. Only a few weeks after the Silverstone successes (and others at Oulton Park, Brands Hatch and Imola) a fateful race curbed hopes of Grand Prix glory. Riding a Ray Petty-tuned Norton, the setting was Brands Hatch in May 1963. An up-and-coming youngster named Dave Downer was aboard Paul Dunstall's 650 Domiracer twin, which challenged Minter with its superior acceleration. As journalist Charlie Rous was to recall: 'It was the fiercest two-bike battle I ever saw and in a last lap collision Downer died.'

Derek, although badly injured, ultimately recovered from spinal injuries and other damage. But even though he was to retain his 500cc British Championship title at Oulton Park in August, he was sidelined during the main part of that year's Grand Prix races and so any chance of success aboard the Gilera in these events was lost.

In 1964, riding his own Nortons (still Petty tuned) plus a 250cc works Cotton he again won the 500cc British title, plus the 350 and 250cc ACU Star series.

Although many more victories were to come his way over the next three seasons, somehow the old sparkle was not quite there. Even so, in 1965 he was at last officially crowned 'King of Brands'.

Derek winning the 250cc British Championship title at Oulton Park in August 1962, riding the 1961 ex-works Honda four, loaned to him for the season by the then Honda importers, Hondis Ltd.

But Derek was still able to go out in winning style, with victories in the 350 and 1000cc races at Brands Hatch on 22 October 1967. Although he did come back to share (with Reg Everett) a ride on Vic Camp's 340cc Sebring in the 500-mile Production event at the Kent circuit on 14 May 1968; the pair finished fourth in their class.

With the arrival of the classic scene at the end of the 1970s Derek got to parade some of his old machines on occasions. This was followed, during the 1990s, by regular appearances on Summerfield Nortons. However, all this came to an end one day in October 2000 when he suffered a brain haemorrhage at Darley Moor. Although his life was saved, this event signalled the end of Derek's post-racing riding career.

Silverstone

Although he was to finish runner-up to Mike Hailwood's MV Agusta in the 500cc race on his Kirby Matchless, Bill was definitely not at his best during the international meeting at Silverstone on Saturday 14 August 1965.

Inevitably for the Northamptonshire circuit, it rained on race day – steadily and miserably for most of the afternoon. But not before a tremendous crowd had gathered around the 2.93 mile (4.71km) Grand Prix circuit.

The previous day's practice, in stark contrast, had been held in glorious sunshine – that day every lap record was unofficially broken.

Besides that runner-up spot behind Hailwood in the 500cc event, Bill's other results were as follows: 50cc fourth, 125cc third, 250cc sixth and 350cc sixth. There is little doubt that our hero was still suffering the effects of his Thruxton get-off.

Back to form

Even though he had been below par at Silverstone the day before, the next day, Sunday 15 August, Bill suddenly got back into the racing groove with a series of top line performances at his local Brands Hatch circuit. This was the scene for a national meeting on the 'old' 1.24 mile (19.95km) circuit, used for the first time since 1961.

Although he probably had other things on his mind – not helped by being out of luck in the 250cc race when after leading on a works Yamaha he struck plug trouble and eventually came home seventh – he still managed to win the 125cc event (then sponsored by Liverpool dealer, Bill Hannah). While on the Kirby machines Bill managed a third on the AJS in the 350cc event and recorded another victory on the Matchless in the main race of the day, the 500cc Redex Trophy.

It was generally agreed that this race was, as *Motor Cycle News* described, 'quite fantastic.' After five laps, just one and a half seconds covered the first six riders – Derek Minter, John Cooper, Paddy Driver, Griff Jenkins, Dave Croxford and Bill.

But the Kirby rider had his sights on the lead and soon it was Minter and Ivy out front by themselves. The crucial moment in the race came when Minter got into a great wobble, this allowing Bill to make his bid to get past at the Druids Hill Hairpin. Once in the lead he drew away and in the process set the fastest lap of the race at 77.50mph (124.96km/h).

It was also around this time that Bill had his first laps in a single seat racing car (a Formula 3) at Brands Hatch, *Motor Cycle News* in its 25 August 1965 issue reporting: 'Bill has been training on four wheels for a few

Bill had his first laps in a single seat racing car (a Formula 3) at Brands Hatch in August 1965, the car belonging to the circuit's race school.

weeks now and having lowered his lap times to around 55 seconds on the short circuit, is considered as a good future motor racing prospect.' But *MCN* went on to add: 'Bill has no plans for motor racing just yet but is looking forward to the future.'

British Champion

August Bank Holiday Monday, 30 August, saw the ACU international meeting – with races to find the new 1965 British Champions. And the main race of the day, the Avon Gold Cup 500cc event held over 19 laps of the 2.71 mile (4.36km) Oulton Park circuit, was a cracker. It was certainly Bill's greatest moment up to that time. Derek Minter had been the British 500cc Champion for the previous few years. And it was to be Bill and Derek who stood head and shoulders above the rest of the field.

Minter was unfortunate to make one of his legendary slow starts, and while Bill was dashing off building up an appreciable lead, the 'Mint' was having to carve his way through the pack.

With the victor's garlands after winning the 500cc British Championship title at Oulton Park, August Bank Holiday Monday 1965.

Few reckoned he had any hope of success. But one by one he cut down the lead, setting the fastest lap of the meeting in the process at 90.36mph (145.38km/h) – and looked set to catch and pass Bill. It was quite incredible. But equally amazing after such a pursuit, as *Motor Cycle News* said: 'The diminutive Ivy was able to pull something from the bag and recapture the lead from Minter on the final lap, holding it to the end by a length.' And all this in a race with a distance of 52.46 miles (84.40km)!

The 350cc British title went to Dan Shorey (Norton) ahead of Minter, with Bill in third place. Certainly, the smaller Kirby machine never seemed as competitive as its larger brother.

The Final Two Months of the Season

Then came the final two months of the British short-circuit racing season. This began for Bill on Sunday 5 September at Snetterton in Norfolk and ended on Sunday

January 1966 and Bill is pictured here receiving the 125 and 500cc Brands Hatch Shields, after topping both sections during 1965 at the Kentish circuit. Also in the picture are Tom Kirby to Bill's right and the circuit boss, John Webb.

31 October at Mallory Park, Leicestershire. Discounting heats, this totalled no less than 31 races. Besides the previously named two circuits, others were Cadwell Park, Oulton Park, plus two races on Yamahas at the Japanese Grand Prix at Suzuka.

The undoubted highlights as regards his Kirby rides were victories on the 500cc Matchless at Snetterton (5 September), Oulton Park (2 October), Brands Hatch (10 October) and Mallory Park (31 October). He also finished third in the Race of the Year at Mallory (26 September) and runner-up in the Race of the South at Brands Hatch (10 October).

A full listing of Bill's results for these two hectic months can be found in the Results appendices at the rear of this book.

Man of the Year

As *Motor Cycle News* said in its issue dated 17 November 1965: 'It is all happening for Bill Ivy! British 500cc Champion works rider for Yamaha and now, to cap it all, he has been voted "Man of the Year" by thousands of *Motor Cycle News* readers.' It continued: 'You've taken the giant-killer to your hearts. It could be that 13 is Bill's lucky number, for that was his placing in last year's *MCN* popularity poll. Good omen it must have been, for even mighty Mike Hailwood has taken second place to our Champion '65. Bill has arrived!'

In the same copy of *MCN*, Robin Miller did a 'Man of the Year' profile, entitled 'Just William'. In this Robin said: 'It is easy to understand why Ivy is so poplar with the fans. His stature for a start. English people always like to see the little chap putting it over the big 'uns – and that he has done in no uncertain fashion. His unruly mop of fair hair and big grin, not to mention his slightly bandy legs, make him a great favourite with the girls. Their boyfriends, on the other hand, like his dash and tenacity. If there is a scrap going on, little Bill is more than likely to be in it. And this season he has come out on top more often than not.'

Nineteen-sixty-six began in fine style for Bill, when *Motor Cycle News* organised a special night in his honour at Brands Hatch on Wednesday 5 January. On that evening, in the Brands clubhouse, he was officially presented with his 'Man of the Year' trophy – and an accompanying cheque.

Bill also received another cheque from Grovewood Securities (owners of the Brands Hatch group of circuits at that time), the organisation reckoning that the 23-year-old Maidstone rider was their Man of the Year as well.

During February 1966 Bill was at Brands Hatch on several occasions testing the brand new Rickman Metisse machines which Tom Kirby would be running in the forthcoming season.

The Rickman brothers Derek and Don in their new Milton, Hampshire, factory with one of the new Metisse road racers.

The Rickman Metisse

During February 1966 Bill was at Brands on several occasions testing the brand new Rickman Metisse machines which sponsor Tom Kirby would be running in the upcoming season.

Don and Derek Rickman had only decided to build racing machines just before Christmas, and Derek had set about the project in the true technical style by drawing a complete set of plans.

As the development progressed so the Rickman's adapted its production facilities to cope with this new sector of the sport; having previously specialised almost exclusively in motocross machinery.

Admittedly, they did not have to design and build an engine and gearbox, or forks or wheels, but they had completed the first two prototype machines

Inside the Rickman factory, spring 1966. The photograph shows a complete AMC-engined Metisse, plus a part assembled one and a number of frames.

ready for the track in less than six weeks. This was, as one commentator said at the time, 'something the major companies of this country have not been able to do for years.' The Rickmans were quick to acknowledge that this effort had only been possible thanks to BP (British Petroleum), who had supported the project from day one.

These first two prototypes were also produced exclusively for Tom Kirby and included a rather special 350, a one-off 7R with different (shorter-stroke) measurements to standard. This machine – the development of which is reported to have cost Tom Kirby a significant amount of money – also used special materials, notably titanium, and it also had a five-speed gearbox. The other bike used a Matchless G50 engine. The team were already satisfied with the performance of the latter power unit. It was hoped that the stroke-stroke engine would at last provide a competitive performance for Bill in the 350cc class.

Teething Troubles

Like any new project, at first there were a few changes to be made in light of testing. In the Rickmans's case, the only real trouble was that the brothers had not been aware of the terrific pressure which circulated the oil of 7Rs and G50s (some 65lb/square inch). And oil was forcing its way out of the breather pipe in the frame (the Metisse employed the frame, rather than a separate tank, to store the engine lubricating oil). However, this was soon cured and the tests were able to continue by draining approximately one pint from the 6.5-pint capacity.

Another change which went hand in hand with this was the introduction of a small header-tank that was intended to relieve the pressure and solve the problem permanently.

An unexpected discovery was that the BP oil with which the machines were lubricated ran at 30 degrees centigrade cooler than with a conventional under-the-seat tank.

The only other snag which showed itself was a tendency for the three-gallon (13.5 litre) Mitchenhall glass-fibre fuel tank to move forwards, but this problem was soon solved by Doug Mitchenhall, who was on hand during the testing.

The Debut

The first race for the new bikes was to be at the Mallory Park season-opener, on Sunday 6 March 1966. And what a debut it was too for the Metisse framed bikes – the larger-engined model in particular.

This is what *Motor Cycle News* had to say: 'The new Kirby-Rickman Metisse, built in a matter of weeks, bounded past the pedigrees at Mallory Park on Sunday for a great start to the 1966 season. Ridden by British 500 Champion Bill Ivy, the Metisse clinched two records in winning the 500cc race. Ivy set up a new figure in one of the all-too-brief three-lap heats, and in the 15-lap final he shattered Bob Anderson's seven-year-old time by almost 25 seconds.'

Bill winning on the five-hundred Kirby Matisse at the Mallory Park season opener, 5 March 1966. Note the then revolutionary Lockheed disc front brake.

500cc Mallory Park – 15 laps – 20.25 miles

1st	W.D. Ivy (Kirby Metisse)
2nd	D.F. Degens (Matchless)
3rd	D.W. Minter (Seeley)
4th	G. Jenkins (Norton)
5th	J. Cooper (Norton)
6th	C.R. Conn (Matchless)

As for the 350cc race, although Bill brought the Kirby Metisse home fourth, he had been 500rpm down for almost the entire race thanks to a tight primary chain.

As for the other classes, Bill's 1966 factory Yamaha contract forbade him from riding other makes of machinery in the smaller classes – hence his appearance at Mallory on only the Kirby bikes.

First 350cc Victory

Exactly seven days later, on 13 March, Bill at last scored his first victory on a 350cc single-cylinder machine, when he won the class at Brands Hatch on the Kirby Metisse.

Racing conditions were just about perfect for the race, the opening event of the day. Bill made a slow start and at the end of the first lap was lying 12th. However, he proceeded to slice his way through the field until, on lap five, he was in the lead! Quite simply none of the other riders were able to match him.

350cc Brands Hatch – 10 laps – 26.4 miles

1st	W.D. Ivy (Kirby Metisse)
2nd	D.F. Degens (Norton)
3rd	J. Cooper (Norton)
4th	D.F. Shorey (Norton)
5th	D.L. Croxford (AJS)
6th	R. Chandler (AJS)

It is strange, then, that on the larger-engined bike Bill was not so successful – a fifth in the 500cc 'Redex Trophy' and finishing runner-up to Dave Degens (650cc Dunstall Domiracer) in the 1000cc event.

An Unfortunate Crash

On Sunday 20 March Bill suffered an unfortunate crash when he came off the 350 Kirby Metisse while leading his 350cc heat. He was severely shaken but suffered nothing more than a torn leg muscle. A fractured oil pipe covered the rear of the machine in lubricant as Bill rushed into the Esses and, as the *MCN* race report said: 'He went round feet first!'

This incident sidelined him for almost three weeks, but in the 6 April issue of *Motor Cycle News* Bill was quoted as saying: 'I hope it's my Good Friday.'

In fact, the Easter weekend was to be Bill's final fling in Britain before going on the Continent with Phil Read to race as a full-time member of the works Yamaha team. Bill said, 'in spite of a few aches and pains I'm looking forward to the four Easter meetings very much.' He continued: 'Brands is probably my favourite circuit. It is where I started riding, and I think you always have a liking for the place where you start. There used to be some very close dices with Howard German and Maurice Thomas, which was probably why I held the lap record when I was only 16.'

King of Brands

The *Motor Cycle News* headline from its 13 April 1966 issue exclaimed: 'William the conqueror!' this was in response to Bill having just beaten the best in British racing at Brands Hatch, including Mike Hailwood on the works four-cylinder Honda 350, and with it emerging victorious in the highspot of the meeting – the 1000cc 'King of Brands' race.

And what a race it was too. From the flag Bill gunned his Kirby Metisse G50 into the lead, hotly pursued by the four screaming megaphones of Hailwood's Honda. The race was jam-packed with talent, including Minter, Cooper, Croxford, Williams and many, many more. But it was to be Dave Degens' (650 Dresda Triton – with unit construction engine) who provided the main challenge to Ivy. This dice went on for lap after lap, one leading then the other.

But, finally, it was Bill who led where it mattered most, while Hailwood showed Williams and Croxford a thing or two by pipping them on the line.

Bill with Tom Kirby after being crowned 'King of Brands', 8 April 1966.

1000cc 'King of Brands' Brands Hatch – 15 laps – 39.6 miles

1st	W.D. Ivy (500 Kirby Metisse)
2nd	D.F. Degens (650 Dresda Triton)
3rd	S.M.B. Hailwood (350 Honda 4)
4th	D. Croxford (500 Matchless)
5th	P. Williams (500 Matchless)
6th	D.F. Shorey (500 Norton)

Hailwood did what everyone expected him to do in the 350cc race – he won on his four-cylinder Honda. But, surprisingly, he was challenged hard by Bill, riding Tom Kirby's 9,000rpm short-stroke 7R-engined Metisse.

350cc Brands Hatch – 10 laps – 26.4 miles

1st	S.M.B. Hailwood (Honda 4)
2nd	W.D. Ivy (Kirby Metisse)
3rd	P. Williams (Arter AJS)
4th	D.F. Degens (Norton)
5th	P.J. Dunphy (Norton)
6th	D.W. Minter (Norton)

The Snetterton Skid Pan

Easter Sunday 10 April 1966 will always be remembered as the day of the 'Snetterton Skid Pan' – aka Russell corner. And to Mike Hailwood went the dubious distinction of being the first to come unstuck in an ultra-slippery 350cc race that fateful day. As the *Motor Cycle News* reported: 'He dropped his Honda four on the exit from Russell corner, where fallen riders soon stood like so many lupins. Coated with rubber from Friday's car races, the wet hazard brought riders down like ninepins before the race was stopped.'

In fact, only intervention by Bill's sponsor, Tom Kirby, prompted organisers to red-flag the survivors after four laps of the 2.71 mile (4.36km) circuit. It later emerged that most of the ACU officials present were having their lunch!

Writing as somebody who was actually there, this day remains one of the very worst in poor management of a motorcycle race meeting that I can remember in almost 50 years of the sport.

Of the few survivors, Peter Williams was a worthy winner when the race was stopped, with Bill Ivy some 14 seconds behind in the runner-up berth.

Bill then recorded another second place in the 500cc race, behind Dave Degens (Matchless).

Then, the following day at Oulton Park on Easter Monday, Bill seemed to have a definite off-day; finishing fifth in both the 350 and 500cc races.

The Brands Hatch 500 miler, 26 June 1966. Bill prepares to take over from co-rider John Cooper on the Kirby 654cc BSA Lightning.

The Final Kirby Appearances

After suffering a couple of retirements at Mallory Park on Sunday 21 April – 350cc ignition and 500cc suspension – Bill then began his works Yamaha season.

Only two more meetings were taken in with Kirby bikes after this; both coming at his local Brands Hatch circuit, the first on 30 May 1966. But again his form on the bikes was not of the high order experienced earlier – he finished third in the 350cc and fourth in the 1000cc race on the larger Kirby machine.

The second outing came at Brands Hatch on Sunday 26 June, the day after he had raced works Yamahas at the Dutch TT. Bill shared Tom Kirby's 654cc BSA Spitfire with John Cooper in the 500 Mile Production Race, but after taking over from Cooper for his first race stint, Bill crashed the machine at Dingle Dell after a couple of laps. The damage sustained to the bike was enough to cause the team's retirement.

In the author's opinion, by then Bill was firmly tuned into his Yamaha works contract – the Kirby affair being very much a second priority. Who could blame him?

Even so, we must pay credit to Tom Kirby's time with Bill; certainly he had helped fast-track Bill's racing career, as the young rider became a star almost overnight once he came under the Hornchurch race entrant's wing.

Bill's mechanic during his time with Tom Kirby was Neil Collett. Neil also attended the 1999 Bill Ivy Day at Brands Hatch, which is described later in the book.

Chapter 6

Frank Higley and Bill Hannah

Two more of Bill's sponsors who played a role in his rise to stardom were Frank Higley and Bill Hannah. Although their time with Bill was relatively short, they are still important pieces of the Bill Ivy jigsaw. Frank Higley's role was to supply a Cotton for the 250cc class between Bill ending his relationship with Geoff Monty and signing for Yamaha; while Bill Hannah did a very similar task in sponsoring the rider during the period after the Chisholms withdrew their support and before our hero joined the works Yamaha squad as a full-time member.

An Ideal Solution

Frank Higley had been looking for a top-line rider since Tom Phillips had left to ride for Syd Lawton. So the availability of Bill Ivy, who was not only familiar with the Cotton but also a star rider, proved an ideal solution for Frank.

Bill's debut on the Higley Cotton (at that time with a four-speed gearbox) came at the same meeting as his debut on Kirby machinery (see Chapter 5), at Brands Hatch on Sunday 9 May 1965. Although he grabbed the headlines with his performances in winning the 125cc (Honda) and 500cc (Kirby Matchless) races, his debut performance on the Higley Cotton was more than acceptable.

250cc Brands Hatch – 8 laps – 21.2 miles

1st	D.W. Minter (works Cotton)
2nd	D.F. Degens (Aermacchi)
3rd	W.D. Ivy (Higley Cotton)
4th	T. Robb (Bultaco)
5th	D.H.G. Chester (Yamaha)
6th	T. Grotefeld (Aermacchi)

More Progress

After finishing fourth on the Higley Cotton at Snetterton on 16 May, Bill grabbed a front page headline in *Motor Cycle News* dated 26 May 1965. Entitles 'Ivy "League" Top Mallory chart'. This was in response to his continuing rapid rise to stardom, after scoring his most impressive performance yet, with convincing victories in the 125, 250 and 500cc races at Mallory Park on 23 May. Not only this, but he set the fastest lap in each of these events.

Bill had begun his day at Mallory by taking over Jack Ahearn's entry on the Frank Higley Cotton. And he never looked like losing this race. From a faultless start, he went straight into the lead and held it until the end.

By the time Bill joined Frank Higley, to ride the latter's Cotton, he was fast becoming a top name in the racing world, as this 1965 advertisement for *Motor Cycle News* proves.

250cc Mallory Park – 10 laps – 13.5 miles

1st	W.D. Ivy (Higley Cotton)
2nd	R. Everett (Yamaha)
3rd	D.W. Minter (works Cotton)
4th	D.F. Degens (Aermacchi)
5th	P. Inchley (Villiers)
6th	R. Pladdys (Honda)

Following his Mallory exploits came news that Bill would be riding both works Yamahas in the Isle of Man TT, following successful tests at Silverstone in late May (see Chapter 7).

While shortly after the TT was over came news that the Yamaha racing department had released an ex-works 250cc (RD56) racing machine, to full 1965 specification. This was placed in the hands of Yamaha dealer and racing sponsor Ted Broad of Ilford, Essex. The machine, which had been entrusted to him with a full set of spares, including crankshafts, was, at that time, probably the most expensive racing machine in Great Britain. The factory's racing manager, Takehiko Hasagawa, estimated the value of the bike to be at £8,000 (£120,000 in 2009).

Bill on the Higley Cotton, rounding Mallory Park's Hairpin, 20 June 1965. Note the use of Norton front forks and an Italian Oldani front brake.

How would the arrival of this machine, which had been sent expressly for use by Bill Ivy, affect the Frank Higley/Ivy relationship? Well, the answer is limited, because Bill continued to use the Cotton for the remainder of the 1965 British short circuit meetings that season.

Back to Brands

Of course, besides the TT, Bill also rode for Yamaha in the Dutch TT at Assen on 26 June. However, he was back at Brands Hatch the following day, Sunday 27 June 1965, but although he turned out in the 125, 350 and 500cc races, finishing first, second and first respectively, he was unplaced on the Higley Cotton.

So it was not until Snetterton some four weeks later that he had his next outing on the Higley bike. Even then it was not a successful ride, as he was forced into retirement with a broken steering damper.

Cotton Telstar

Winners of the 1923 Junior TT and 1926 Lightweight races in the Isle of Man, the Gloucester-based Cotton marque stormed back onto the racing stage when leading riders Derek Minter and Bill Ivy scored many victories on the Telstar 247cc (68 x 68mm) production racer during the mid-1960s.

The Telstar had made its public debut at the Earls Court Show in the autumn of 1962, being announced a month or so prior to the show itself, thus becoming the first of Britain's new generation 'Formula Junior' racers to appear. The newcomer had been sparked off thanks to the introduction of the newly released Villiers Starmaker engine, and as with the Greeves Silverstone, by the initial efforts of a private rider. In Cotton's case this was Peter Vallis, who had campaigned a 'racerised' scrambler with some success during the 1962 season.

Although the Villiers company had their own dynamometer, it was Cotton who primarily race developed the new Starmaker engine. This had begun as early as October 1962 and the Cotton staff included Fluff Brown (who later went on to run the FB-AJS concern at Andover).

Cotton's managing director, Pat Onions, signed up Derek Minter in time for the 1963 season and he responded by finishing an impressive runner-up to Mike Hailwood at the season opener at Mallory Park in March that year. However, much of 1963 was spent squeezing out not only more power but reliability too. These early engines were what one might truthfully describe as fragile.

Minter's works machine received a variety of modifications such as remote contact breakers, a single Amal GP carburettor and a more reliable rigid cylinder liner.

However, the most important of these changes came in June 1964 in the form of a six-speed gearbox, which was required to overcome the narrowing powerband of Minter's rapidly developing factory engine. Bill Ivy too with his Cotton (see main text) also benefited from these developments; including the additional gearbox ratios (at least on some occasions).

Bill Ivy with the then brand new Geoff Monty Cotton Telstar, summer 1964.

Derek Minter's (and Bill Ivy's) engine progressed from the original 25bhp at 6,500rpm to 31.2bhp at 7,800rpm. This was more or less the power available when Minter rode his machine to victory in the 1964 250cc ACU Star (British) Championship title. Both Minter and Ivy were not keen on the standard issue Armstrong leading link front forks and both riders preferred Norton (Manx) Roadholder front forks instead.

Cotton had, at that time, been manufacturing motorcycles for the previous 40 years or so and obviously knew a thing or two when it came to making them handle. The frame consisted of a full duplex layout, manufactured from seamless 'A' grade cold drawn steel tubing. The top rail and swinging arm were constructed of 1⅛in x 14swg with the cradle and subframe made from ⅞in x 14swg.

Derek Minter working on his factory-supplied Telstar (with 6-speeds); *c.*1964.

Actually, Cotton manufactured little else apart from the frame and the swinging arm: employing Armstrong leading link front forks and rear shock absorbers (later models having Girling items) to control the Telstar's suspension, on the production model.

The first Telstars were equipped with the infamous 6in (152mm) SLS British Hub Company's full-width alloy hub assemblies both back and front. However, the 6in front brake, famous for its lack of effect, was soon changed and by 1964 the Telstar, along with the Greeves Silverstone, sported the newly-introduced 7½in (190mm) TLS unit, which British Hub had produced to quell the many complaints arising from the original small brake's poor performance.

Unlike machines from rival factories such as DMW, Greeves and Royal Enfield, the Cotton was fitted with 19in wheels front and rear throughout its production life. This, if one considers modern trends, should have been a disadvantage; however this does not seem to have been the case. In fact when Robin Miller tested a Telstar for *Motor Cycle News* in its 20 October 1965 issue, he said: 'Without doubt it is the most comfortable and roomy 250 I have ever ridden!' While the *MCN* test revealed: 'Below 6,000 rpm the motor was virtually dead, but once the needle moved past that things really started happening. When the needle flicked over 8,000, it was time to change and the revs dropped to 7,000.'

MCN were testing a Higley model with Norton forks and Oldani front stopper, but only a four-speed gearbox, and they found: 'It is an unfortunate feature of the Starmaker four-speed box that the gap between first and second gears is, in my opinion, a fraction too wide. It was necessary to let the motor really buzz before cogging up, and even then there was a slight lull before the motor picked up.'

The test took place at Snetterton (with the long Norwich Straight still in place!) and *MCN* achieved an electronically-timed 104.28mph (167.78km/h).

A distinctive feature of Cotton's racer was its Mitchenhall (Avon) fibreglass ware. Upon its introduction, the Telstar was kitted out with a 2.5 gallon (11 litre) jelly-mould continental-style fuel tank and a rather awkward looking single-piece fairing. However, with the Mark II's appearance in 1964 the fuel tank, seat and fairing came in for a change and the Telstar now looked far more conventional, with the maroon coloured fibreglass components styled in the conventional British racer fashion.

The majority of Telstar production occurred during 1964–65 and by the time of its demise in 1967 over 60 examples had been produced. They found their way to various corners of the globe, with Australia at present holding the honour of receiving the highest numbered known example – machine number 66.

Victory at Thruxton

As the *Motor Cycle News* headline shouted out: 'New 250 Thruxton Lap Record'; this being in response to the first lap record to be broken at the Hampshire circuit for two years, when the South African Martin Watson (Bultaco) went round at 80.16mph (128.97km/h) in attempting to wrest the lead from Bill, mounted on the Higley Cotton. But it was to no avail, as our hero took a well-deserved victory.

Cadwell Park International, September 1965. Bill Ivy (Higley Cotton Telstar, 40) leads Derek Chatterton (Yamaha TD1B). Bill was to later crash out of the race.

250cc Thruxton – 10 laps – 18.5 miles

1st	W.D. Ivy (Higley Cotton)
2nd	M. Watson (Bultaco)
3rd	G. Keith (Royal Enfield)
4th	R. Trimnell (Bultaco)
5th	R. Pladdys (Honda)
6th	E. Page (Bultaco)

But poor Bill was not so lucky in the 350cc event, as he came off the Kirby AJS when his engine seized after four laps. He suffered a badly bruised hand but no bones were broken and it was expected that he would be fit enough to take part in the forthcoming Hutchinson 100 meeting at Silverstone in two weeks' time.

But at Thruxton, his crash ruled him out of his remaining races (the 125 and 500cc events).

By the time the big Silverstone international meeting arrived on Saturday 14 August, Bill was still feeling the effects of his Thruxton spill, and so a sixth place on the Higley Cotton against star-studded opposition was not a bad result. One has to remember that he was pitted against works entries from the likes of Yamaha (Mike Duff and Phil Read), MZ (Derek Woodman), Royal Enfield (Percy Tait), Honda (Ralph Bryans) and Cotton themselves (Derek Minter).

Besides his 250cc ride, Bill also rode in the 50cc (Latham Honda) finishing fourth, behind the works entries of Toshio Fujji (Suzuki), Chris Vincent (Suzuki) and Hans Georg Anscheidt (Keidler); 125cc (Hannah Honda) third; 350cc (Kirby AJS) sixth; 500cc (Kirby Matchless) runner-up to World Champion Mike Hailwood (MV Agusta).

At Brands Hatch the following day, 15 August, he rode a works Yamaha, as mentioned in chapter 7, so the Higley Cotton was given a rest.

Bill in an unposed moment, adjusting his goggles, summer 1965.

Bill's next outing on the Higley-sponsored bike came at Oulton Park during the ACU international British Championship meeting at the Cheshire circuit on Bank Holiday Monday, 30 August 1965; with Bill coming in fifth during the 19-lap, 52.46 mile (84.40km) event. Six days later at Snetterton on Sunday 5 September Bill finished third on the Cotton behind the winner Dave Simmonds (Honda) and runner-up Peter Inchley on the works development Villiers. As *Motor Cycle News* reported: 'eighth at the end of the first lap, Inchley – the new British Champion – worked his way through to challenge Ivy coming into Coram, and in a desperate rush to the flag, put a wheel in front – sharing the same time as Ivy.'

250cc Snetterton – 6 laps – 16.26 miles

1st	D. Simmonds (Honda)
2nd	P. Inchley (Villiers)
3rd	W.D. Ivy (Higley Cotton)
4th	M. Watson (Bultaco)
5th	R. Everett (Yamaha)
6th	K. Cass (Bultaco)

Honda CR93

The first the world saw of the CR93 was when it went on sale in Japan during May 1962. For the home market it was offered in two guises, one complete with full road-going equipment – head and tail lights, a horn, a pair of large silencers and even a rear-view mirror; the other, more well known, at least to British eyes, was the stripped-for-racing version.

The 124.8cc double-overhead-camshaft parallel twin featured 'square' bore and stroke dimensions of 43 x 43mm. The street version put out 16.5bhp, at 11,500rpm; the full racer 20bhp. Honda sources claimed a maximum speed of 84mph (135km/h) for the roadster and 102mph (164km/h) for the racer (the latter complete with dolphin fairing).

The CR93 was designed by a Honda technician called Suzuki (a common name in Japan, as Smith is in the UK). It shared the four-valves-per-cylinder layout of the then current factory racers. A conventional roller bearing big-end, 360 degree crankshaft (both pistons rising and falling together) drove the five-speed, unit-construction gearbox by helical spur gears. There was a surprisingly large primary reduction of 3.7:1. The standard Honda technique of wet-sump lubrication (with scavenge pump) was retained.

Producing maximum power at 11,500rpm, the engine was still mechanically safe at 13,000rpm. Within these limits – and with the proviso that the oil was changed after every race – it would give long life with reliability. The CR93 would rev beyond its redline but with a greatly increasing risk of mechanical failure.

When the CR93 went on sale in Britain in early 1963 it cost £609, but this was later reduced to £504. However, it remained on the British market for only two seasons.

Generally, the CR93 was an easy bike to ride and was very easy to bump into life. However, there was absolutely no power below 5,800rpm; then the power surged in suddenly, as if one had released a cut-out button. It was entirely free from vibration and would run straight up to the safe

On 1 November 1964, exactly a week before the start of the London Earls Court Show, a CR93 captured several British national speed records at Chelveston Airfield, near Bedford; the machine was ridden by Jack Terry (pictured here) and Reg Gilbert.

The 124.8cc (43x43mm) air-cooled 8-valve dohc parallel twin CR93 engine. Maximum power was 20bhp at 11,500pm.

13,000 peak. A change at this speed brought the revs down to around 9,500. Therefore, it was extremely easy to keep smack in the powerband, which was just as well because of the lack of urge and the severe 'megaphonitis' when out of it. The shallow-taper megaphones emitted a superb mellow howl, which was not too sharp but carried over a long distance.

Other interesting features of the design included a compression ratio of 10.2:1, a pair of 22mm Keihin carburettors, energy transfer magneto ignition, spine-type frame (with the engine assembly as a structural member), a light-alloy 2.2 gallon (10 litre) fuel tank and a dry weight of 279lb (127kg).

Some 40 CR93s found their way to Britain and riders such as Bill Ivy used them to score many a victory; other notable names include Chris Vincent, Derek Chatterton and Rod Scivyer. Both Bill Ivy and Rod Scivyer were to become 125cc British Champions aboard CR93s. Other notable achievements by the CR93 included capturing the British national speed record for the 125 and 175cc classes in the standing-start quarter mile and kilometre at Chelveston Airfield, Bedford, on 7 November 1965, with rider Jack Terry. Another was an overboard 182cc model campaigned in 250cc races with considerable success by Jim Curry and Ron Pladdys. When this was finally outclassed by the ever improving Yamahas, Pladdys built a 249.2cc (49.6 x 43mm) three-cylinder model. This unique machine achieved a number of victories and proved its reliability by finishing in the gruelling Isle of Man Lightweight TT.

The only real change during the CR93's production life concerned its front brake. The earliest production machines (built in 1963) were normally fitted with the works-type double-sided, single-leading shoe assembly; whereas the later (built in 1964) version employed a production-based, single-sided, twin-leading shoe component.

Although Honda also built the CR110 (50cc), CR72 (250cc) and CR77 (305cc), the CR93 was by far the most successful of the breed.

A Costly Crash

What had been a fantastic duel for third place in the 250cc race at the Cadwell Park international meeting on 12 September, involving half a dozen riders, ended dramatically when Peter Inchley and Bill collided at the Hairpin. This incident not only put him out of the race, but as *Motor Cycle News* correspondent Charlie Rous revealed: '[It] detuned Bill and lost him the chance of the big money in the [main] £1,000 race.' Although he courageously started the big race on the Kirby Matchless, he was forced out when literally sick after only a few laps.

After Cadwell came Brands Hatch a week later. Here, Bill bounced back to top form, with wins in the 125 and 350cc events. But after dicing with Derek Minter on the works Cotton, Bill's Higley-entered example expired, forcing him into retirement.

At Mallory Park, Bill brought the Higley Cotton home fourth – his last race on this machine.

A Works Cotton Ride

But Bill did have one more outing on a Cotton. This came at Oulton Park on 2 October 1965. This time he was riding the works Cotton in place of the injured Derek Minter – and was first away when the flag fell to start the race. However, when lying second at the beginning of the final lap Bill was forced to pull in with a missing exhaust expansion chamber!

That same week, Bill was reported to be travelling to South Africa for a season of winter racing there, and that he would be leaving in November. However, as is fully detailed in Chapter 7, this trip never materialised – as he signed a contract to race works Yamahas after competing in the Japanese Grand Prix at Suzuka over the weekend of 23–24 October.

The Hannah Connection

As is fully explained in Chapter 2, Bill's long association with the Chisholm brothers, Don and Bill, came to and end after his final outing on the Chis Honda CR93 at Brands Hatch on 27 June. At least their association came to a winning end, with victory in the 125cc race. Essentially, their parting had come about by a combination of Bill's increasing progress in racing – meaning more and more time off from his job as a mechanic at the Chisholms's business – and the fact that due to falling motorcycle sales the Chisholms could no longer afford to pay for the upkeep of the Honda to the standard which was required.

So, 37-year-old Liverpool dealer and former speedway rider Bill Hannah – who had previously sponsored Chris Vincent on a 125 Honda – agreed to loan a bike to Bill. However, as Roy Francis revealed to the author, it was not quite as clear cut as might appear at first glance. Why? Well, when the machine was delivered, in Roy's words, 'it was in an awful state.' Effectively it required a major rebuild, including a new cylinder head. Having got Bill Hannah's agreement on the financial costs involved, Roy and Bill rebuilt the bike – in the Chisholm workshop – which obviously goes to show that Bill and the Chisholms were still on friendly terms!

Bill winning the 125cc event at Cadwell Park International road races; 12 September 1965 on the Hannah Honda CR93.

Brands Hatch 15 August 1965. Bill pictured winning the 125cc on the Hannah Honda CR93.

It must be said that even though Bill Hannah had a reputation of being something of a hard businessman there is equally no doubt that as a racing sponsor he put an awful lot of money and energy into the sport over several years. One must, of course, point out that after the Honda involvement he went on to bankroll the Italian Paton Grand Prix squad during the late 1960s, with riders including Fred Stevens and Billie Nelson.

The Hannah Debut

Bill's debut on the Hannah Honda came some seven weeks after the final Chisholm ride. As we know, part of the reason was that the bike required a lot of work to get it into a suitable condition for Bill to stand a chance of winning.

And what a meeting to have his first ride on the bike – the international BMCRC 31st Hutchinson 100 at Silverstone on Saturday 14 August 1965.

Honda CR110

The first indication of a totally new breed of Honda came at the Tokyo Show in late October 1961. It was at this venue that the company, already Japan's largest two-wheel concern, displayed the prototype of what was to emerge later as the CR110, a 49cc over-the-counter dohc single-cylinder racer. This original prototype boasted an output of 8.9bhp at a then amazing 14,000rpm and a five-speed gearbox. At the show it was referred to simply as the Honda Cub Racer.

It was not until July 1962 that Honda announced the production version – coded CR110. Like its bigger, twin-cylinder CR93 brother, the CR110 was offered with full road-going equipment for the domestic market or as a pure racer for export.

The most significant difference between the production model and the 1961 Tokyo Show prototype concerned the gearbox – it now having no less than *eight* ratios, instead of the earlier bike's five speeds. This change came due directly as a result of Honda's Grand Prix experiences in the initial races counting towards the first year of the 50cc World Championship series.

Like the CR93, the CR110 was the work of Honda engineer Suzuki. It was introduced into Britain for the 1963 season. Relatively few (21 to be precise) were imported that year, when they sold for £330, but they were even scarcer 12 months later when their production was terminated.

Revving to 13,500 peak power speed, and to 15,000 for occasional drastic use, the 49cc (40.4 x 39mm) 'egg-cup' racer developed 8.5bhp and 3.55lb/ft of torque on a compression ratio of 10.3:1. Ball and needle-roller bearings were used in profusion, the gear-train to the overhead camshaft mechanism being a case in point. Roller-bearing big-end and mains were featured, the crankpin being formed integrally with the drive-side flywheel.

Using a cross-over, all-direct, eight-speed gearbox, the CR110 had its clutch on the offside, gear-driven directly from the engine shaft. The

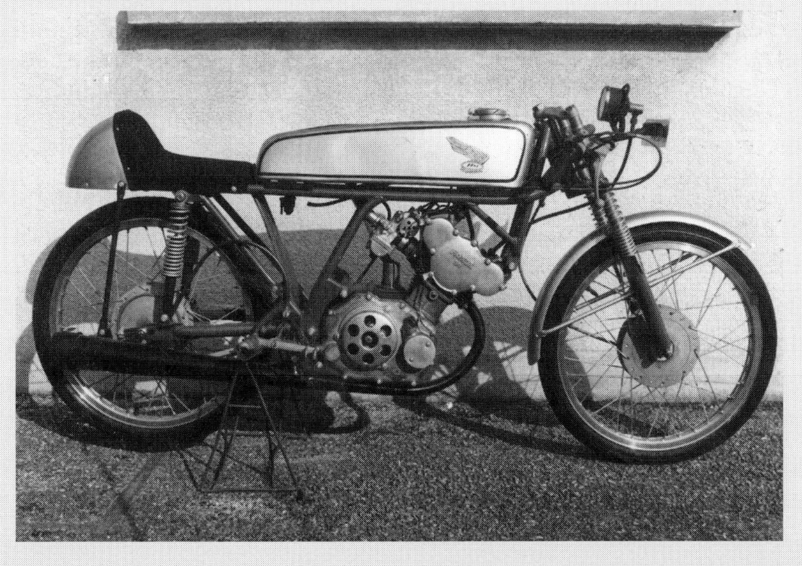

A CR110 with fairing removed showing the open frame design which used the engine as a stressed member. Note also the dry clutch and steeply angled carburettor.

A CR110 with non-standard inlet cover-mounted contact breaker and nickel-plated frame.

multiplate, oil-bath clutch was hydraulically operated. A wet-sump, integrated with the transmission, stored oil for pressurized distribution from the clutch-driven plunger pump.

A 26mm Keihin carburettor was controlled by a neat and unconventional twin-cable arrangement with the throttle wire wrapped around a pulley on the instrument. A single 10mm spark plug was fired by a crankshaft-mounted magneto. However, several owners subsequently modified their machines to battery/coil ignition to improve starting.

The cylinder was inclined 35 degrees forward, and, like the CR93, the engine unit was installed in a spine-type frame with the motor functioning as a structural member. Besides ensuring that the engine itself was mechanically sound at all times, there were two other areas of special preparation. One was making absolutely sure that the oil was changed between races and on cold days pre-warmed before being added to the sump. The other was checking rear-chain tension, which was critical. If too tight, or too loose, this would impair gear changing.

As for the gear ratios themselves, they were very close, as little as 800rpm apart on some changes. No power at all was produced below 8,000rpm and not much until 11,000. Above that, it flowed in with increasing gusto up to the recommended 13,500rpm. Once again, to exceed this would be to invite reducing the level of mechanical reliability.

The first British owner to take delivery of a CR110 in 1963 was Val Knapp of Dorking, but the list of riders to race one of these all-conquering tiny Hondas reads like a 'who's who' of the 50cc world – Dave Simmonds, Brian Kettle, George Ashton, Charlie Mates, Jim Pink – and of course the subject of this book, Bill Ivy. Perhaps the model's most noteworthy achievement was Chris Walpole's superb runner-up spot in the 1963 50cc Isle of Man TT.

As for maximum speed – in full race trim – the CR110 could exceed 80mph (129km/h).

Today, as with the CR93, CR110s command top prices with collectors of classic racing machines. And, in the author's opinion, they are best described as being like a Swiss watch – top quality.

Certainly the competition was fierce in most of the races, with a plethora of works machinery. In the 125cc race this meant Bill was lined up against a trio of works Suzuki riders (Toshio Fujji, Frank Perris and Ernst Degner). Another notable entry was Luigi Taveri on a Honda twin. Yet more star potential came in the shape of the German star Hans Georg Anscheidt, with his Kreidler-MZ special, plus UK-based stars such as Dave Simmonds, Tommy Robb and Rod Scivyer. It was, all-in-all, what could truthfully be referred to as a star-studded field.

The early leader in a rain soaked race was Anscheidt, but, after a sensational start when he surged through the field from the back of the grid, the German threw his machine away at Stowe – the very first corner!

Eventually Hugh Anderson had little difficulty in taking victory, with his teammate Fujji second. Next came Bill on the Hannah Honda – an excellent result considering the opposition.

125cc Silverstone – 10 laps – 27.1 miles

1st	H. Anderson (Suzuki)
2nd	T. Fujji (Suzuki)
3er	W.D. Ivy (Hannah Honda)
4th	L. Taveri (Honda)
5th	D. Simmonds (Tohatsu)
6th	R. Scivyer (Honda)

A First Victory and Record Lap

His first victory on the Bill Hannah Honda came the day after Silverstone, at Brands Hatch on Sunday 15 August 1965. Not only this, but he also broke Tommy Robb's race record by over 4mph at 71.03mph (114.28km/h) – beating the old record of 68.6mph (110.37km/h) by 3.8 seconds, also held by Robb. It should be pointed out that the meeting was staged over the 'old' 1.24 mile course for the first time since 1961.

Second place went to Dave Simmonds (Tohatsu) from Rod Scivyer. Roy Francis, having taken over the Chis Honda, came home a creditable sixth.

125cc Brands Hatch – 10 laps – 12.4 miles

1st	W.D. Ivy (Hannah Honda)
2nd	D. Simmonds (Tohatsu)
3rd	R. Scivyer (Honda)
4th	T. Robb (Bultaco)
5th	K. Cass (Bultaco)
6th	R. Francis (Chis Honda)

Brands Hatch 10 October 1965. The photograph shows Bill leading George Ashton in the 50cc which he not only won but also set the fastest lap. Both riders are on Honda CR110s.

At Oulton Park on Bank Holiday Monday, 30 August, the 1965 British Championship meeting took place. But although Bill won the 500cc Championship title on Tom Kirby's Matchless G50, he did not enjoy the same success in the 125cc event. This was because after leading for 11 of the 19 laps he was forced to retire with a misfire; victory going to Tohatsu-mounted Dave Simmonds.

A String of Victories

Then came the first of a string of victories on the Hannah-backed Honda, the first of which came at Snetterton on Sunday 5 September.

This, it has to be said, was easy, especially after his main challenger, Dave Simmonds, had stopped at the Esses.

This began a winning streak of five consecutive victories on the Hannah Honda – after Snetterton came Cadwell Park (12 September), Brands Hatch (19 September), Mallory Park (26 September) and finally Oulton Park (2 October).

Then it was back to Brands Hatch on 10 October. All-in-all this meeting was to be remembered for all the wrong reasons. First, Bill suffered from food poisoning. Then, at what was the last meeting at the Kent circuit that year, MZ works rider Derek Woodman, making only his second appearance at the track, won both the 125 and 250cc races. As *Motor Cycle News* was to report: 'there was no real challenge for the MZ was much faster than the private Honda.' Although leading initially, Ivy made a big fight of it by getting ahead until about half distance. But this looked more the directive of Woodman, because once he chose to move off there was nothing Bill could do about it.

Although Bill scored victories at both ends of the capacity class – 50 and 500cc – his luck was out in the 250 and 350cc events in which he posted a retirement in both.

But, sadly, the Brands meeting was marred when Florian Camathias, one of the world's greatest-ever sidecar racers, was killed after swerving off the track; his BMW sidecar passenger, Franz Ducret, also suffered serious head and leg injuries. As *Motor Cycle News* commented: 'The fatal crash put a cloud over what would otherwise have been a superb meeting.'

Then Bill travelled to Japan to ride works Yamahas in the 125 and 250cc races, before he returned with a full factory contract for the 1966 season.

This meant that the final meeting of the British season – at Mallory Park on 31 October – was also to be his last on privately entered machinery (250cc and below) as stipulated in the Yamaha contract. And so a third place, behind race winner Derek Woodman (works MZ) and Rod Scivyer (Honda), on the Hannah Honda was to be his last appearance for the Liverpool-based sponsor.

It could be said that, at least as far as the smaller classes were concerned, Frank Higley and Bill Hannah had been the final stepping stones on Bill Ivy's journey into the realms of a full works rider.

Chapter 7

Signing for Yamaha

Yamaha, one of the great four Japanese motorcycle brand names – the others being Honda, Kawasaki and Suzuki – was to be closely associated with Bill Ivy right from the very first time that he straddled one of their machines back in 1963.

This first ride on a Yamaha came, as related fully in Chapter 4, courtesy of Bill's then sponsor, Twickenham dealer and race entrant, Geoff Monty.

That First Outing

Little did Bill realise it at the time, but his initial outing on a Yamaha – a production two-fifty TD1 at Brands Hatch on 25 August 1963 – was to be the first step on the road which would, ultimately, lead to a full works contract and subsequently a World Championship.

His debut ride on the Monty Yamaha ended with Bill finishing runner-up behind Tommy Robb (Bultaco).

This photograph shows Bill's first 'works' Yamaha ride, on a 1963 two-fifty air-cooled RD56, at Brands Hatch 21 June 1964. He made the most of it too, winning the race.

Phil Read, seen here with Seki, Hasagawa and other Yamaha support staff in early 1965, was responsible for Bill being offered works bikes for the TT and Dutch rounds of that year's World Championship series.

A Pukka Works Job

Then, almost 10 months later, came his chance to ride a pukka works job, in the shape of a 1963 RD56 disc-valve twin. Again the ride came at his local Brands Hatch circuit – and again it was thanks to Geoff Monty, who at that time was handling Yamaha racing affairs (sales and service in the UK). But this time our hero went one better, scoring an impressive victory on the Japanese machine on 21 June 1964. As *Motor Cycle News* journalist Charlie Rous told readers: 'First works ride for Bill Ivy and making most of it, he won'. Bill finished ahead of Derek Minter (Cotton) and Dave Simmonds (Greeves).

Silverstone Test

It was not until the following year when first news of a possible works-factory-Yamaha ride became known. In the 2 June 1965 issue of *Motor Cycle News* the front page headline read: 'Works Yamaha For Ivy?' written by Robin Miller, the scoop story went on to reveal: 'The world was waiting

Former racer Bob Anderson (seen here Norton-mounted finishing runner-up to MV-mounted John Surtees in the 1958 Senior TT) was at the Silverstone Yamaha test described in the text but declined the offer of a TT ride.

for a word from Phil Read today that would spring a last minute surprise in the formation of the Yamaha team for the TT.' The *MCN* feature continued: 'It is confidently expected that another name will be added to those of World Champion Read and Mike Duff to ride Yamaha works machinery in the 125 and 250cc classes.' And the name which *MCN* thought most likely was Bill Ivy, who the previous week had tried out the new 125 and 250 Yamahas at Silverstone.

But although his performances had been quoted as 'very good', Phil Read had hinted to Robin Miller that Yamaha 'had more than one rider in mind.' Phil continued: 'I can't tell you any more because I will not be making my recommendation to the Yamaha team manager in the Isle of Man until Wednesday.'

A week later came news that Bill would be aboard a works 125 Yamaha in the TT – and it also looked almost certain that he would be supporting World Champion Phil Read and Canadian Mike Duff on a 250 Yamaha as well.

Yamaha RD56

The RD (Racing Development) 56 was the first Yamaha to win a World Championship, when Phil Read took the 1964 250cc title. It was also the first Yamaha racer that Bill Ivy was to ride.

The RD56 had first appeared in Europe in 1963, when Yamaha took in three meetings counting towards World Championship points – the Isle of Man TT, Dutch TT and Belgian Grand Prix.

Their star man in 1963 was the Japanese rider Fumio Ito, who had previously raced Yamahas in both Japan and the USA (the latter during the late 1950s) before then coming to Europe in 1960 to campaign (successfully) a BMW Rennsport 500cc twin as a privateer.

After taking the runner-up position in both the Isle of Man and Holland, and then going on to win the ultra-fast Belgian Grand Prix at Spa, it could have been expected that Fumio Ito would have been allowed to remain in Europe to have a full crack at the world crown. But no. He, and the remainder of the Yamaha Grand Prix squad headed by manager Hiroshi Naito, were recalled to Japan. Ito was able to race the RD56 in the final round (at Suzuka) in which he and new signing Phil Read finished second and third respectively to race winner Jim Redman on a Honda. This gave Ito a magnificent third overall in the Championship table; having contested only four of the 10 rounds!

Rather strangely, in the author's opinion, Fumio Ito was not given another race in the works team, particularly after the many years he had put in for the Yamaha cause; instead Phil Read was joined by the Canadian Mike Duff. Out also went the 1963 team boss Naito, in favour of Takehiko Hasagawa, with chief engineer Nagayasu in charge of three other engineers and five mechanics. While the actual design and development

The RD56 burst onto the world stage when the Japanese rider Fumio Ito finished second in the 1963 Isle of Man Lightweight TT.

The RD56 employed an air-cooled 249.7cc (56x50.7mm) disc-valve parallel twin two-stroke engine with the cylinders inclined slightly forward.

of the RD56 had been (as with other early Yamaha Grand Prix machines) undertaken by Makayasu Nakamura.

On the technical front, the RD56 had an air-cooled 249.7cc (56 x 50.7mm) parallel twin two-stroke engine with the cylinders inclined slightly forward. During 1963 the engine had developed around 40bhp, but in Read's 1964 Championship-winning season, this had been increased to around 47-52bhp (development being very much an on-going process at the time).

Much work had taken place over the winter of 1963–64 into engine efficiency, and to increase reliability, which of course often meant a conflict of interests.

The compression was left at 7.8:1, with the combustion chamber being semi-spherical for improved efficiency. One of the three-ports for each cylinder was larger than the other two, while the floating disc-valve was

Yamaha team mechanics together with a number of RD56 machines at the Japanese Grand Prix, October 1964.

lubricated by an oil pump, as was the crankshaft bearing. Formerly, Yamaha had experienced many problems with carburation, so Mikuni had modified their instruments to prevent frothing (which caused misfiring and, in the most serious examples, entire engine cut-outs). The twin crankshafts were independent of one another, each transmitting power through its own gears to an idler shaft. The small-end bearing was of the needle roller type.

Ignition came from a Mitsubishi-made magneto set above the gearbox and aft of the cylinders. The gearbox had seven ratios and there was a dry, multi-plate clutch. An oil tank was located under the gearbox and featured a complex separator built into it. The lubricant was fed to an adjusting device. The all-steel frame was of the double cradle variety and was manufactured for Yamaha by the Kuromori concern.

There was also a 252cc version of the RD56, this being built to enable riders to contest the 350cc class; the increase in capacity being achieved simply by increasing the bore size by 1mm.

The RD56 was finally replaced by the RD05 liquid-cooled four-cylinder model, which made its racing debut at the Italian Grand Prix at Monza in September 1965.

However, while researching this book, the author uncovered an intriguing fact that someone else came very close to riding the third Yamaha 250 at the TT. This was the former racing motorcyclist and, at the time, racing car driver Bob Anderson. Bob had been at Silverstone testing his car, when the Yamahas and Bill were there for the test session described earlier, and Phil Read had let Bob have a ride on one of the old 250s.

The staggering result was that Bob Anderson had broken Jim Redman's 250 Honda four-lap record for Silverstone by three seconds – and was subsequently offered a machine for the Isle of Man. But this was declined – Bob saying he could not compete because of his racing car commitments!

TT Practice

TT practice for the 1965 series began on Friday evening, 4 June. But while Bill's new teammates were already in the island, he had not arrived in time and his first session was not until Monday morning, 7 June; and even then this was not on a Yamaha but Tom Kirby's Matchless.

And so it was not until the Monday evening's practice that Bill made his debut aboard one of his new Yamaha mounts. However, as the 9 June 1965 issue of *Motor Cycle News* was to record: 'The practice was sad for Bill Ivy's works Yamaha debut. He stopped during the opening lap on the 125 and was unable to return to the pits for an outing on the 250.'

In fact, Bill did not have the best of practice weeks on the Yamahas. Another quote from *Motor Cycle News* (regarding the Friday 11 June

Bob Anderson broke Jim Redman's (pictured here) 250cc Silverstone lap record during the Silverstone test, made prior to the 1965 TT.

session): 'Yamaha hopes for the 125 class received a set-back when Read's water-cooled twin became a "single" at Ballaugh and Ivy's air-cooled motor seized its magneto on the Mountain climb.'

However, not all had been bad news, because on Wednesday morning, 9 June, Bill had headed the 250 leader board on his first outing with a 1965 Yamaha, clocking a speed of 93.43mph (150.32km/h) ahead of Jim Redman (Honda), Derek Woodman (MZ) and Tarquinio Provini (Benelli).

The Races

As for the races themselves, his first appearance on one of the Japanese bikes came in the Lightweight (250cc) event. This took place on Monday, 14 June. It began with Phil Read becoming the first man to lap at over 100mph (161km/h) on a 250 over the Mountain circuit – and he achieved this from a standing start! But this performance proved too much for his machine and on the next lap he retired with a broken crankshaft. This left Honda's Jim Redman (riding one of the new six-cylinder models) in the lead.

Bill had been in third behind these two riders at the end of the first lap and Phil's departure moved him up to second, behind Jim; a position he was to hold on laps two and three.

This is how *MCN*s Charlie Rous described the action: 'With Read out of the race, Yamaha's hopes now lay with Bill Ivy, who started 3 minutes 40 seconds behind Redman on the road, and Mike Duff.' Rous continued: 'Ivy was 14.6 seconds down in second place at 98.22mph [158.03km/h] with Duff well down at 96.22mph [154.81km/h].' Later in the report – at half distance in the 226.38 mile (364.24km) race – the *MCN* feature revealed: 'Ivy at this stage was 62 seconds behind and averaging 97.87mph [157.47km/h] – a great race by this little Kent rider who had never raced one of the 1965 Yamahas before.'

But then disaster hit the Yamaha camp for a second time. Bill came off at Brandywell (the highest point on the course) trying to avoid a slower rider

Opposite: A smiling Bill astride the RD56 he rode in the 1965 Lightweight (250cc) TT. He impressed everyone by holding second position, until a crash forced him to retire.

DANGER
45
YAMAHA
45

in thick mist. Luckily he was unhurt and managed to get his bike going again. However, the machine had suffered a broken-off carburettor (the instruments being mounted on the side of the disc-valve two-stroke engine) and after motoring slowly down the Mountain, he was forced to push in from Governor's Bridge and retire.

With this turn of events, Jim Redman was left with a comfortable victory – his third successive TT victory in the class. Bill's teammate Mike Duff finished the race as runner-up.

A couple of days later, on Wednesday 16 June, came Bill's other Yamaha TT race. But riding one of the old air-cooled machines – teammates Phil Read and Mike Duff having the brand new, much quicker water-cooled bikes – Bill was hard pressed to live with not only the other Yamahas but also works machinery from Honda, Suzuki and MZ.

However, he certainly gave his best. Not only did he finish in seventh position, but by lapping at 93.15mph (149.87km/h) he was only just outside the existing class lap record of 93.53mph (150.48km/h) which had been set up by Honda's Luigi Taveri in 1963. However, Suzuki's Hugh Anderson smashed this during the race to go round at 96.02mph (154.49km/h).

Yamaha debuted its new eight-speed liquid-cooled 125cc twin in the 125cc TT on which Phil Read (pictured) won at record speed. Bill rode an older air cooled bike and finished seventh.

Bill and Phil Read at the awards presentation evening alongside works Yamaha staff; Isle of Man TT 5 June 1965.

Ultra Lightweight (125cc) TT – 3 laps – 113.19 miles

1st	P.W. Read (Yamaha, water-cooled)
2nd	L. Taveri (Honda four)
3rd	M.A. Duff (Yamaha, water-cooled)
4th	D. Woodman (MZ)
5th	H.R. Anderson (Suzuki)
6th	R. Bryans (Honda four)
7th	W.D. Ivy (Yamaha, air-cooled)
8th	E. Degner (Suzuki)

Dutch TT

Next came news that Yamaha would be providing Bill with a 125cc twin for the Dutch TT at Assen on Saturday 26 June. Renowned for its brilliant weather and its 100,000-plus crowd, the 40th anniversary of this famous event carried on the tradition, although strong winds kept the day fairly cool.

The 125 race over 14 laps 'really got the crowd jumping' (*MCN*). Phil Read led in the early stages but was later forced to retire; both he and Mike

The brand new RD05 two-fifty V4 which Yamaha debuted at the Dutch TT in late June 1965; although it was not raced.

Duff were aboard the latest liquid-cooled bikes, whereas Bill still had to make do with one of the old air-cooled jobs. As in the Isle of Man, there were factory entries from not only Yamaha but Suzuki, Honda and MZ. Once again Suzuki's Hugh Anderson set a new class lap record at 86.60mph (139.33km/h). But it was Yamaha's Mike Duff who eventually emerged victorious. Only the first five finishers remained unlapped.

125cc Dutch TT, Assen – 14 laps – 67.02 miles

1st	M.A. Duff (Yamaha, water-cooled)
2nd	Y. Katayama (Suzuki)
3rd	H.R. Anderson (Suzuki)
4th	W.D. Ivy (Yamaha, air-cooled)
5th	L. Taveri (Honda)

After his rides in the Isle of Man and Holland, Bill was to race a 1965 specification RD56 machine at a few British meetings that summer. As detailed elsewhere, this machine had been loaned by the Ilford (Essex) dealer and racing sponsor Ted Broad. Ted, having successfully tuned the production TD1A piston-ported machine raced by Reg Everett, was made responsible for the fettling of the works RD56 machine, provided by the factory's racing manager, Takehiko Hasagawa.

A complete listing of Bill's outings on this motorcycle is provided in the Appendices, but suffice to say his best performance was undoubtedly at Brands Hatch on 19 September 1965, when riding the bike as a '254cc' he won the 350cc event and with it the Fred Neville Trophy. Bill also had the satisfaction of setting the fastest lap at 85.94mph (138.27km/h).

A Call to Japan

On Saturday 16 October an urgent telephone call led to Bill flying over the North Pole to race works Yamahas at the following Sunday's Japanese Grand Prix. This was in response to Yamaha's request that he take over the 125cc and 250cc rides of Mike Duff, who had crashed at Suzuka while testing on Friday 15 October.

Bill had arrived in Japan late on Sunday night. With Mike Duff in hospital waiting an operation for a suspected fractured hip, and Hiroshi Hasagawa also out of action after another practice crash, the Yamaha works team had been reduced to Phil Read and Akayasu Motohashi.

It was reported in Japan that Bill's unanticipated arrival had already surprised the Honda and Suzuki opposition.

Phil Read, who had been in Japan a fortnight, had telephoned Bill on Saturday. He had eventually tracked him down to Brands Hatch, where Bill was testing a racing car. The carrot – if he needed one – was that a Yamaha works contract was very much on the cards for Bill.

The revised V4 at Assen a year later, with Yamaha riders, left to right, Mike Duff, Phil Read and Bill Ivy.

Phil and Bill were down to ride in two classes only – the 125cc on Saturday 23 October and the 250cc the day afterwards. And it was reported that they would most probably race the new four-cylinder machines, which were said to be actually better than the twins.

The following is a special report prepared by Peter Howdle (who was in Japan) for *Motor Cycle News* and is worth repeating in full. It was entitled: 'Nippon-go!'

'"Nippon-Go" is the name for the Japanese language in which it is correct to add the suffice "san" to people's surnames, as we label folk Mr, Mrs or Miss. And "Nippon-Go" also describes the speed Bill Ivy flew to Japan after Mike Duff crashed. It was 7pm in Yokkaichi (11am in London) when Phil Read rang Bill's home on 15 October. Fifteen minutes later, Phil spoke to Bill at Brands Hatch. Twenty-four hours later, Ivy-san was on his way to Japan. He's seldom packed so fast. His first job was to get a passport. On Friday afternoon his brother-in-law [David Swift] dashed to a hospital to get Bill's smallpox vaccine. Bag packed, cash collected and re-inoculated Saturday morning, Ivy was at London [Heathrow] Airport by 11.30am. With stops at Copenhagen and Anchorage [Alaska], he flew over the North

Ilford (Essex) dealer/entrant Ted Broad was made responsible for fettling the works RD56 machine which Bill rode occasionally during the latter half of the 1965 British short circuit season. Ted is seen here with Reg Everett's TDI production racer.

Phil Read (far left of picture), Bill and two Yamaha officials, Japan, October 1965.

Pole to Tokyo. He got to Yokkaichi near the circuit at 1.30am Monday [Japanese time is some eight hours ahead of GMT] and despite the loss of a night's sleep, he was training at Suzuka the same afternoon.'

The 'training' referred to by Peter Howdle began with a Yamaha sports roadster, a YDS3. Then on Tuesday Bill rode a 250 four for the first time – and what a time to ride this fearsome machine – it was raining heavily! Then on Wednesday, in superb weather, he lapped five seconds slower than Jim Redman (Honda six) – the only other riders quicker than Bill in this session were Phil Read and Mike Hailwood. Following this Bill got his first outing on the 125cc model, but after circulating with Hugh Anderson (Suzuki) this ended when the throttle jammed.

The 125cc Race

As for the races themselves, the first was the 125cc event. And at Suzuka, the big news was the race debut of Honda's brand new five-cylinder machine, ridden by the Swiss star, Luigi Taveri. This race was watched by some 25,000 spectators; but the following day (Sunday) 250cc race saw this figure rise to the 80,000 mark.

Of course, it was the first time that Bill had ridden at Suzuka. And, surprisingly, all he had prior to his race on the 125cc Yamaha at breakfast was 'a glass of pop' (*MCN*). And Bill's race was almost over even before it got under way, when Suzuki rider Haruo Koshino's machine cartwheeled up the road; Bill had to take to the grass to avoid the fallen Japanese rider. But he stayed on, eventually finishing fourth.

125cc Japanese GP, Suzuka – 20 laps – 74.61 miles

1st	L. Taveri (Honda five)
2nd	R. Bryans (Honda five)
3rd	M. Itoh (Suzuki)
4th	W.D. Ivy (Yamaha twin)
5th	Y. Yuzawa (Honda four)
6th	K. Matsushima (Yamaha twin)

Isle of Man TT

For many years, certainly during the Bill Ivy era, the Isle of Man TT was the world's premier motorcycle racing event.

First employed in 1911 (though in slightly different guise), the legendary Mountain Course measured 37.73 miles in length and comprised roads which were the normal traffic arteries of the Isle of Man. To avoid too much interference with everyday trade on the Island, therefore, the pre-race practice periods largely took place in the early hours of the morning. Closure of the roads for both practice and racing required a separate Act of the Isle of Man Parliament every year.

The start, grandstand, scoreboard and pits were situated in Glencrutchery Road high above the town of Douglas. Soon after leaving the slight rise of Brown's Hill, followed by the drop to Quarter Bridge, a slow right-hander necessitated hard braking, engagement of bottom gear and usually the use of the clutch.

Braddan Bridge was the next landmark, a spectacular S-bend over the railway and river, then on to Union Mills three miles from the start, winding and undulating, and then the course dropped down to the Highlander and through the bends at Greeba to Ballacraine (7.25 miles); a sharp right-hander.

The course was now very much out in the country, with the road twisting and turning through the leafy tunnel of the Neb Valley, past Laurel Bank and Glen Helen, then up the 1-in-10 rise of Creg Willey's Hill on to the heights of Cronk-y-Voddee. The descent of Baaregarroo before the 13th milestone section was generally held as being the fastest part of the course. It was followed by a tricky section ending with Westwood's Corner, a relatively fast left-hander.

Soon riders reached Kirkmichael (14.5 miles) with its second gear right-hander followed by a trip through the narrow village street, after which there was a winding but fast stretch to Ballaugh – with the famous humpback bridge where both wheels left the ground. Left, right, left – the trio of Quarry Bends were taken in the region of 100mph or more – the bends leading out on to the start of the famous mile-long Sulby Straight, with at its end an extremely sharp right-hand corner at Sulby Bridge (20 miles). Then came

The giant scoreboard opposite the pits was a feature of the TT for many years; this photograph dates from 1964.

hard acceleration up to and around the long, sweeping left-hander at Ginger Hall. Through wooded Kerromoar and the foot of Glen Auldyn, the circuit wound its way on to the town of Ramsey, where riders flicked right and left through Parliament Square in the very middle of the town. Then came the beginning of the long mountain climb, the road rising up May Hill to the testing Ramsey Hairpin (24.5 miles) and up again to Waterworks Corner and the Gooseneck.

Still climbing, riders passed Guthrie's Memorial and reached East Mountain Gate (28.5 miles) where the long gruelling ascent at last began to flatten out. A further mile on led to a quartet of gentle bends at the Verandah section, followed by the bumpy crossing of the mountain railway tracks at the Bungalow. The highest point on the course was at Brandywell, a left-hand sweep beyond the Bungalow, and from there the road began to fall gently through the aptly named Windy Corner, a medium fast right-hander and the long 33rd milestone bend.

Kate's Cottage (300 yards past Keppal Gate) marked the beginning of the flat out, exhilarating sweep down to Creg-ny-Baa (34.5 miles). Still dropping, the course swept towards the left-hander at Brandish Corner and down yet more to the fast right-hander at Hilberry.

With less than two miles to the finish there followed the short climb of Cronk-ny-Mona and the sharp right-hand turn at Signpost Corner. Bedstead Corner and The Nook followed in swift succession and within a quarter-of-a-mile it was a case of hard on the brakes for Governor's Bridge, an acute hairpin, which was the slowest corner on the course. The short detour through the hollow was a link to earlier days when it formed part of the main road. Once out of the hollow, riders accelerated into Glencrutchery Road less than half-a-mile from the grandstand and pit area.

In essence the course remains the same today, when at the beginning of the 21st century the TT has long since lost its World Championship status. However, it still remains one of the most famous venues in motorcycle racing, attracting huge crowds every June. It was also the setting for some of Bill Ivy's greatest-ever triumphs; including his sensational 100mph 125cc and 105mph 250cc record laps aboard works Yamahas in 1968.

The Swiss star Luigi Taveri won the 125cc race at the 1965 Japanese Grand Prix, held at Suzuka; Bill was fourth. Later Luigi and Bill were to become best friends.

The 250cc Race

A day later Bill was out on one of the new four-cylinder models. Even though Jim Redman had been forced out due to a bee-sting the previous day – his face swollen so much that he could hardly see out of his right eye – the competition Bill faced was still extreme.

But he coped supremely well to finish an excellent third – even better when one realises that, racing a Yamaha four for the first time, he lost a lot of ground early on when he was forced to stop for a change of spark plugs. And he sliced through the field to such an extent that he claimed third spot from his teammate Hiroshi Hasagawa with a lap to go. Unfortunately, shortly after that Hasagawa's bike died and he had to push in.

250cc Japanese GP, Suzuka – 24 laps – 89.54 miles

1st	S.M.B. Hailwood (Honda six)
2nd	I. Kasuya (Honda six)
3rd	W.D. Ivy (Yamaha four)
4th	M. Yamashita (Honda four)
5th	H. Hasagawa (Yamaha)

The Contract

Bill returned from Japan before the end of October with a works Yamaha contract for 1966. The company outlined that he would be a full member of the factory racing team and would contest the World Championship races the following year.

Bill had dashed back after signing on the dotted line to enable him to take part in the final British short circuit meeting of the year at Mallory Park on Sunday 31 October 1965. It is also worth pointing out that a condition of his Yamaha contract was that he could no longer continue to race privately-entered machines in the 125 and 250cc categories. He therefore had to give up his Bill Hannah 125 Honda and Frank Higley Cotton rides. However, he was still able to continue with Tom Kirby on 350 and 500cc machines.

A Gift from Yamaha

In mid-November it was revealed that Bill was to receive a Yamaha scrambler – the first such machine in Britain.

Bill covers his ears from the noise being created by the Yamaha works mechanic, warming up his RD56 before the start of the 250cc race in Japan.

While Bill and Phil Read had been wandering around the Yamaha works in Japan, he had expressed an interest in buying one of their scrambles machines and was immediately given an example. Phil, on the other hand, chose a 305cc roadster.

However, although things looked bright for Phil and Bill, the same could not be said for Mike Duff and his family. Not only was Mike in hospital in Japan after his practice crash at Suzuka, but he was also laid low for some two months at least. Meanwhile, his wife Krista was in Finland, her homeland, and unable to go to see Mike. She had been taken ill with a kidney complaint and was about to go into hospital herself. And if all of this was not bad enough, to crown it all their small son, Tony, had a fall which resulted in a broken leg and he too was in hospital. It was, as one journalist was heard to comment: 'Duff luck!'

Bill taking part in a Yamaha factory sports day while in Japan during October 1965. Bill is pictured in the centre without a shirt.

Bill got engaged to Anne Happe at the presentation of his *Motor Cycle News* 'Man of the Year' award in November 1965.

Man of the Year

To cap what had been an impressive period, in November 1965 Bill was voted 'Man of the Year' by thousands of readers of *Motor Cycle News*.

He beat none other than World 500cc Champion Mike Hailwood, who had won the poll twice before, and the previous year's runner-up John Cooper. And it was no slender victory, with *MCN* saying he won 'by a convincing margin' in its 17 November issue.

But no one was more surprised than Bill himself, who said: 'I was certainly not expecting this.' And: 'I am really chuffed, and I would like to thank everyone who voted for me.'

In the 1964 poll Bill had been back in 13th position. But in 1965 he captured almost 20 per cent of the total votes!

In all, 120 names received votes. The top 20 were:

1st	Bill Ivy
2nd	Mike Hailwood
3rd	John Cooper
4th	Jeff Smith (the 1964 winner)
5th	Phil Read
6th	Fritz Scheidegger
7th	Derek Minter
8th	Dave Bickers
9th	Giacomo Agostini
10th	Chris Vincent
11th	Bryan Goss
12th	Alf Hagon
13th	Malcolm Simmons
14th	Jim Redman
15th	Sammy Miller
16th =	Malcolm Uphill
	Barry Briggs
18th	Victor Arbekov
19th	Ralph Bryans
20th	Bjorn Knuttson

Before signing for Yamaha, Bill had planned to spend the winter racing in Africa (with machines supplied by Tom Kirby), but the works contract brought this trip to a halt, Bill realising that his future lay with the Japanese firm. He had also decided not to follow up his interest in car racing (he had practised at Brands Hatch in one of the racing school's Formula 3 Lotus single seaters that summer), but due to his motorcycle commitments (read Yamaha) he would not be on four wheels in 1966.

Also in November 1965 he celebrated his *MCN* Man of the Year nomination by announcing his engagement to 21-year-old Tenterden lass Anne Happe, a manageress at Butlins.

Nineteen-sixty-six

And so came 1966 – and with its arrival Bill faced the prospect of competing regularly in the Grand Prix world, with new challenges both in terms of the top rivals and Continental Europe's finest circuits. And, of course, this meant several tracks that up to then he had never seen, let alone raced on. Bill was accompanied on several Continental trips by his brother-in-law Dave Swift and younger brother John.

Of course, as is fully covered in Chapter 5 – Tom Kirby, Bill began the new season racing on the British short circuit meetings, where he gained a string of victories on the new Kirby Metisse machines.

An historic moment as Bill signs the Yamaha contract, meaning that he would be a full works rider for the 1966 season.

Phil Read and Bill with a couple of Yamaha works mechanics during training for the Belgian Grand Prix at Spa Francorchamps, July 1966.

Continental Europe

Bill's first Yamaha outing of 1966 came at Cesenatico, a street circuit on the Italian Adriatic coast. But, riding an old air-cooled RD56, he retired when in eighth spot. The race was won by Tarquinio Provini (Benelli four), from Phil Read (Yamaha) and Derek Woodman (MZ).

Much more successful was the first GP of the new season – the Spanish at Montjuich Park, Barcelona on 8 May. Here, riding one of the latest water-cooled twins, Bill not only led from the third lap, when World Champion Hugh Anderson (Suzuki) retired, to beat the five-cylinder Hondas of Luigi Taveri and Ralph Bryans but also set a new race-winning speed of 69.947mph (112.544km/h) for the tortuous Spanish course. All the Suzukis retired, but in truth Bill would probably still have won because even on the first lap he was catching the leader, Anderson, with the rest of the field already well behind this pair, so his performance was even more impressive.

125cc Spanish GP, Barcelona – 27 laps – 63.45 miles

1st W.D. Ivy (Yamaha water-cooled twin)
2nd L. Taveri (Honda five)
3rd R. Bryans (Honda five)
4th P. Read (Yamaha water-cooled twin)
5th F. Villa (Montesa)
6th J. Mendrano (Bultaco)

However, Bill's fortune in the 250cc was just the reverse, as, riding one of the four-cylinder water-cooled machines, he (like teammate Phil Read) was forced to retire. After smashing the lap record by three seconds in practice, Mike Hailwood (Honda six) was favourite to take the victory. But teammate Jim Redman had no intention of being left behind and he simply rocketed away from the start. Disaster struck after half a lap. On a tricky downhill

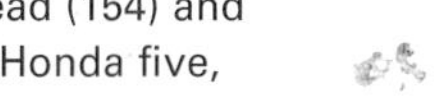

East German Grand Prix, 17 July 1966. Bill (181) leads Phil Read (154) and Luigi Taveri (Honda five, 177).

right-hander with a hump in the middle, Jim crashed and the machine (a six like Hailwood's) burst into flames! Mike, who by then was close on Jim's tail, only just managed to avoid the carnage, but from then on it was as *Motor Cycle News*'s race report said: 'A one horse race.'

And so to the West German Grand Prix on Sunday 22 May 1966, with a multitude of 'sun-soaked' (*MCN*) spectators who had packed the newly-constructed stands on the equally new twisty section of the 'sawn-off' Hockenheim circuit.

In the 125cc race Bill was forced to pull into the pits after only two laps with clutch trouble, but this was only a temporary cure and he was soon in more trouble with his clutch – this time terminal. Things were better in his other event, the 250cc race, where Bill came in third behind the six-cylinder Hondas of Mike Hailwood and Jim Redman. The rival-team riders set an equal average speed of 109.17mph (175.65km/h) for the 23-lap, 96.66 mile (155.52km) race, with Mike being adjudged the victor. Bill averaged 108.67mph (174.85km/h).

Clermont-Ferrand

The third round in the World Championship trail took place a week later round the torturous five-mile (8km) Clermont-Ferrand high in the hills of central France. Like the first two GPs, Bill had never raced on this circuit before. In France it was doubly difficult as there was no 125cc event – so Bill's

Bill enjoys a chat with Mike Hailwood, summer 1966.

only ride was on the 250. After a slow start, he fell from his V4 mount on the very first lap of the race on a tricky right-hand hairpin within full view of the packed start and finish area. Before this Bill had streaked through to fourth place, but as *Motor Cycle News* said: 'Even Dunlops have a limit and he found it.' He toured back to the start on three cylinders and with a damaged carburettor (as with the RD56 twin, the V4 had its carbs mounted on the side of the crankcase and was thus prone to damage in the event of a spill).

British Practice

To give Bill additional track time, the Yamaha factory had provided him with the use of some air-cooled ex-works models for selected British short circuit meetings. The first of these came at Brands Hatch on Whit Monday, 30 May (the day after his French crash!) and Mallory Park three weeks later on Sunday 19 June.

Actually, as one period newspaper report said of the Brands Hatch meeting: 'The Continental circus came to Brands on Monday and left our home performers gasping.' The 'circus' stars included Mike Hailwood (Honda), Phil Read and Bill (Yamahas), Frank Perris (Suzuki) and Fritz Scheidegger (BMW Sidecar) – and all went home race winners. The only non-GP competitors who won a race were Peter Williams (Arter Matchless) and the 1,300cc sidecar victor, Owen Greenwood (Mini).

Riding in the 250, 350 (both on Yamahas) plus Tom Kirby's G50 Matchless (see Chapter 5), Bill had a pretty successful day. After finishing fourth in the 1000cc event (Kirby Matchless) and third in the 500cc Redex Trophy (on the same machine), Bill came home third in the 350cc race on a 251cc Yamaha (behind Phil Read and Mike Hailwood, the latter on a four-cylinder Honda).

But the big question before the start of the 250cc race was: could Jim Redman on a Honda twin provide any sort of challenge for the Yamahas (air-cooled RD56 twins) of Phil Read and Bill? The answer soon became abundantly clear: no! It was simply a Yamaha duel between Bill and Phil as Sean Wood said in his *MCN* race report: 'Little Bill got the verdict, but the lap record now stands to Phil.'

250cc Brands Hatch – 10 laps – 26.5 miles

1st	W.D. Ivy (Yamaha)
2nd	P.W. Read (Yamaha)
3rd	T. Robb (Bultaco)
4th	D.W Minter (Cotton)
5th	J. Redman (Honda)
6th	R. Pladdys (Yamaha)

The first three finishers in the 125cc East German GP, 17 July 1966; left to right: Toshio Katayama (Suzuki), the winner Luigi Taveri (Honda) and Bill runner-up.

Both Phil and Bill were entered on 125 and 250 Yamahas for the Mallory 19 June meeting. It was the first time that the works 125s were raced on British short circuits. And as there were works Suzukis to be ridden by Hugh Anderson and Frank Perris, it promised to be a competitive race.

The Pre-TT Meeting

This meeting was, until the infamous seaman's strike of that year, known as the Post TT International – but of course, now with the TT having been rescheduled for late August, it was the one and only time it could be labelled the Pre-TT meeting!

The Mallory gathering certainly generated a huge amount of publicity. As *Motor Cycle News* commented in its 15 June 1966 issue: 'Attention frustrated TT fans: Never fear, works men are here!'

And Bill scored a Mallory victory – this coming in the 125cc event after the Japanese rider Akayasu Motohashi had made a great start by leading the race for the first two laps before being overtaken by teammate Bill – both riders being mounted on water-cooled twin-cylinder models. Bill also set the fastest lap at 83.22mph (133.90km/h) and a new class race record speed of 81.11mph (130.50km/h).

125cc Mallory Park – 10 laps – 13.5 miles

1st	W.D. Ivy (Yamaha twin, water-cooled)
2nd	A. Motohashi (Yamaha twin, water-cooled)
3rd	D. Chatterton (Honda)
4th	D. Simmonds (Tohatsu)
5th	R. Scivyer (Honda)
6th	T. Fujji (Kawasaki)

In the 250cc race, Phil Read and Bill waged a private duel blowing off Jim Redman (Honda four). Read shot into the lead, giving Redman a cheeky signal as he streaked past, with Bill going past three laps later. Then Bill closed up on Phil. In fact, after that the race was not decided until the very last lap, when Read outbraked Bill at the Esses and won 'by a fraction' (*MCN*).

250cc Mallory Park – 10 laps – 13.5 miles

1st	P.W. Read (Yamaha)
2nd	W.D. Ivy (Yamaha)
3rd	J. Redman (Honda four)
4th	G. Marsovszky (Bultaco)
5th	T. Robb (Bultaco)
6th	A. Motohashi (Yamaha)

Another Continental victory

At the Dutch TT, the 125cc race was described by *Motor Cycle News* as: 'The most promising race of the day.' This was because it was in this event over the famous Assen circuit that the competition was the greatest. Not only were the works Yamaha team present (Bill, plus Phil Read, Mike Duff and Akayasu Motohashi) but so were the the Honda fives of Luigi Taveri and Ralph Bryans, the Suzukis of Hugh Anderson, Hans Georg Anscheidt, Frank Perris and Yoshima Katayama, plus the MZs of Heinz Rosner and Derek Woodman. No less than 12 full factory entries.

Although Bill had been fastest in practice, Read led for two laps, but after that Bill assumed the lead. In the end it was Luigi Taveri who brought his screaming Honda into the runner-up berth almost three seconds behind Bill. In many ways, this was Bill's best victory up to that time. It certainly was in regards to the level of competition. Again both the race and lap records were broken.

125cc Dutch TT, Assen – 14 laps – 66.90 miles

1st	W.D. Ivy (Yamaha twin, water-cooled)
2nd	L. Taveri (Honda five)
3rd	P.W. Read (Yamaha twin, water-cooled)
4th	H. Anderson (Suzuki)
5th	A. Motohashi (Yamaha twin, water-cooled)
6th	M. Duff (Yamaha twin, water-cooled)

Bill retired in the 250cc event, with Phil Read finishing runner-up to Honda six-mounted Mike Hailwood.

Yamaha

If precision engineering can be judged by the art of the clock maker, then Torakusu Yamaha could fully claim this distinction. Born in Nagasaki during 1851, the young Torakusu, at the age of 20, took a 10-year apprenticeship under the guidance of a British clock maker. This was to provide an excellent basis for a working life in the field of engineering.

Not content with this decade of learning, Yamaha then took up another apprenticeship in the field of medical equipment at Osaka, and it was during this period that he decided to move to the Hamamatsu area. This was 1883 and four years later, in 1887 – now self-employed as a general engineer – Torakusu Yamaha was asked to repair an organ at the Hamamatsu Primary School.

It was this task which was to change his life and eventually lead his company, Nippon Gakki, to become one of the world's foremost manufacturers of musical instruments. Before the turn of the century, the company was not only a major supplier on the home market but had

Yamaha's very first production motorcycle was this YAI single cylinder two-stroke, which was clearly derived from the German DKW RT125; mid-1950s.

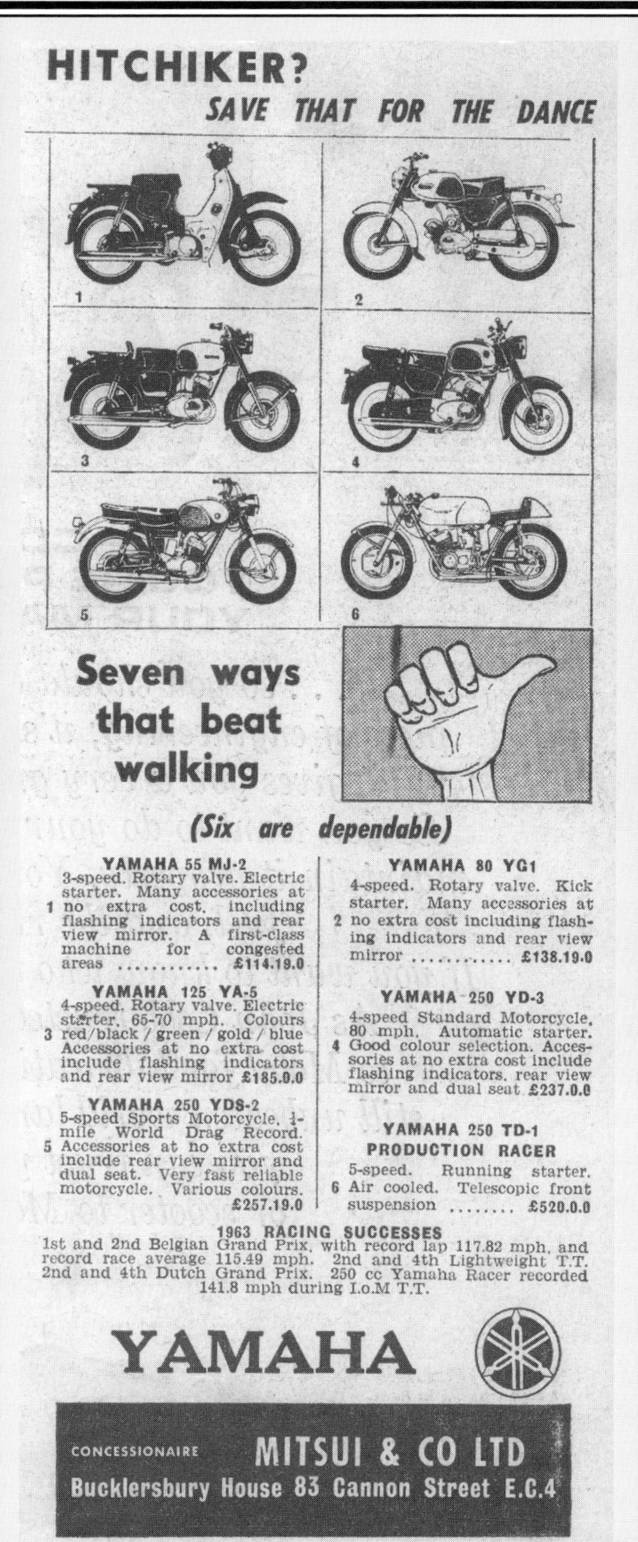

A March 1964 Yamaha advertisement, showing the six-model range available in Great Britain at that time via London-based importers, Mitsui.

already begun an export drive, which included shipping some 80 organs to Great Britain.

Expansion continued unabated, but in 1916 Torakusu Yamaha died at the age of 64. By then, however, Nippon Gakki was firmly established. The next man at the helm was Chiyanu Amano, but a series of problems in the early 1920s, including strikes and the Kanto earthquake of 1923, created severe financial problems. These were only solved in 1926 when a new president, Kaichi Kawakami, was appointed.

Compared with Amano, whose dictatorial regime had largely created industrial unrest, Kawakami went out of his way to combine both the management and workers into an effective team – it worked and has since become standard practice in Japanese industrial relations.

After the fortunes of the company had been rebuilt, the rise to power of the military regime in Japan posed another problem for Kawakami during the late 1930s. By 1940 the army had taken control of the plant, which during the war years manufactured aviation products, including fuel tanks and propellers. As for musical instrument production, this was allowed to continue to a very limited degree until 1944, when the authorities issued a total ban.

In early 1945 many of the Nippon Gakki production facilities were badly damaged by Allied bombing, and following the end of hostilities the road back to corporate health was long and hard. However, by 1948 things were improving with the resumption of musical instrument manufacture. Another advantage was that owing to Kawakami's support and active help from his employees over the years, Nippon Gakki was unaffected by the series of strikes which brought several Japanese firms (including Suzuki) to their knees during this period.

During 1950, Kawakami, who had suffered from ill-health for some time, passed the presidency to his 38-year-old son, Gen-ichi Kawakami. This was to prove the vital step towards the emergence of the Yamaha motorcycle marque. One of Kawakami's first moves was to take a long, hard look at the company, and during his investigation he decreed that wartime machinery, which had been locked away since the end of the conflict, should be utilised. The big question was for what purpose? The decision, like so many other industrial-based companies in Japan (and Germany and Italy, too), was to enter the field of powered two-wheelers.

Unlike many, however, the Nippon Gakki president wanted above all else a quality product. One which would provide the same level of satisfaction as had already made the company's musical instruments and organs so respected.

The biggest problem was deciding on the type of machine. It was finally decided to concentrate upon a motorcycle based around the highly successful German DKW RT125 design. This had first appeared in 1935, and in the post-war era it was destined to be copied by not only the Japanese company but also BSA, Harley-Davidson and the Soviet Moska factory, among others.

After an extremely comprehensive development programme and rigorous testing – including personal involvement in the latter by president Kawakami – a new factory was constructed at Hamamatsu for the express purpose of manufacturing the new bike. In addition, the enterprise was named in honour of the company's founder – hence Yamaha, rather than Nippon Gakki, was to adorn the new motorcycles's tank sides!

The success of this first effort, known as the YA1, was helped considerably by its domination of the Mount Fuji and Asama races of 1955. By the end of that year, some 200 YA1s were leaving the factory each month and work had begun on a larger model. Again, this was based around a DKW – the RT175 – and this made its debut at the end of the year.

However, the next machine was to provide Yamaha with a motorcycle of significant importance for the future, and to enable it to compete with the established marques Yamaha felt it had to be a 250cc. Originally another DKW was considered as a base, but this was a single, so another German machine, a twin-cylinder Adler MB250, was imported for evaluation.

At the time, the Adler was considered by many to represent the ultimate in two-stroke development, so when the Yamaha development team, headed by Zenzaburo Watose, informed president Kawakami that it preferred to follow its own design route this was a bold move indeed. Furthermore, Kawakami must be applauded for giving the green light to this plea. The result was a trend-setting machine. Coded TD1, the newcomer's only real Adler influence lay in the construction of the crankcase assembly – and, of course, the fact that both were 54 x 54mm piston-ported, two-stroke parallel twins.

And it was from that first YD1 that Yamaha was to rise to being leaders in two-stroke technology during the next decade, the 1960s, and they would, of course, play such an important role in the story of Bill Ivy.

Trouble with the Law

Even before the following weekend's Belgian Grand Prix at Spa Francorchamps, Bill was in trouble. However, this time it was not machine related but was instead with the local police. This occurred when he was reportedly involved in 'a scuffle' (*MCN*), while attempting to enter the circuit for practice on the Friday. This occurred because he was not able to produce passes, although he was carrying his racing leathers. Quite simply, the police demanded that he should produce a pass or could not go in.

Bill alleged, and was backed up by other witnesses including Frank Perris, that he was pushed to the ground and kicked. He was then frogmarched by two burly gendarmes to a police vehicle, presumably with the intention of arresting him. But, luckily, the police were dissuaded and Bill was allowed to go free. At the time it was widely reported that Norman Dixon, chairman of the ACU, said he thought it would be a matter for the legal department of the RAC. But in fact no record can be found of anything coming of this. The truth is more likely that the matter was handled by Bill's employers, Yamaha.

The 8.76 mile (14.09km) Spa Francorchamps circuit saw Bill suffer plug trouble from the start. The race, run in scorchingly hot weather, was a straight fight between Phil Read and Mike Hailwood, with the latter coming out on top. As for Bill, after having to stop to change a plug he eventually finished in sixth position.

Sachsenring

Next came Bill's debut at the Sachsenring; the home of the East German Grand Prix. As will become clear later, this circuit was to hold all the wrong memories in the Bill Ivy story, but on Sunday 17 July 1966 this was all very much in the future.

The 125cc race was the first of the day, and Bill suffered a moment of panic just prior to the traffic light start as all were set for action. This came about because a screw was loose in his fairing! Yamaha team mechanics quickly set about resolving the problem. This seemed to act as a spur, because immediately as the lights went green Bill was away at the head of the pack, in front of teammate Phil Read. However, on the very next lap Luigi Taveri screamed his high revving Honda past the Yamaha pair; obviously the five-cylinder Honda being quicker than the Yamaha twins. But the surprise man in the race was Suzuki's Yoshima Katayama, who 'riding on the limit and very courageously' (*MCN*) caused a stir by forcing his Suzuki into the runner-up spot.

125cc East German GP, Sachsenring – 12 laps – 64.2 miles

1st	L. Taveri (Honda five)
2nd	Y. Katayama (Suzuki)
3rd	W.D. Ivy (Yamaha)
4th	P.W. Read (Yamaha)
5th	F.G. Perris (Suzuki)
6th	R. Bryans (Honda five)

In the 250cc race Bill suffered another retirement on one of the fast (but fussy) V4s, this time with carburation glitches.

Czech Grand Prix

In a steep learning curve, Bill's next new course was the tricky 8.9 mile (14.3km) road circuit in the hills near Brno, the scene of the Czechoslovakian Grand Prix.

Unfortunately, machine ailments struck in the Yamaha squad during the 125cc event. Within the first 50 yards, Phil Read's twin stopped with a faulty ignition coil. But teammate Bill took up the challenge, speeding into the lead. This lasted for some three miles before his twin became a single with a faulty spark plug. Luigi Taveri's five-cylinder Honda streaked past the stricken Ivy, with Hugh Anderson (Suzuki) hanging on his tail. Then on lap two the New Zealander moved into the lead himself.

After a quick plug change out in the country Bill rejoined the race and he set about making up for lost time. And after smashing the lap record – going round at 89.79mph (144.47km/h), Bill had worked his way up to third at the flag.

125cc Czech GP, Brno – 8 laps – 69.3 miles

1st	L. Taveri (Honda)
2nd	R. Bryans (Honda)
3rd	W.D. Ivy (Yamaha)
4th	H. Anderson (Suzuki)
5th	F. Perris (Suzuki)
6th	F. Kohler (MZ)

In the 250cc event, the 100,000 crowd had every right to get excited, with works entries from not only the big three Japanese factories but also the local CZ concern and the East German MZ marque. But Bill did not take part, the race being a battle between Mike Hailwood and Phil Read, which the former won.

Gearbox Problems in Finland

Imatra, in Finland, was the next stop. Again Bill had only a 125cc – Yamaha being short of four-cylinder 250s at this time. After storming past Luigi Taveri's five-cylinder Honda to take third place, the Yamaha's nine-speed gearbox became a five ratio unit and that was the end of Bill's race; the 250 V4, incidentally, had an eight-speed 'box.

Then Bill had a two week break before competing at Brands Hatch on 14 August. But this was not his lucky day, as he was to crash heavily on the Tom Kirby Metisse-framed short-stroke 350 AJS and was taken to hospital with concussion and cuts – including one to his back requiring several stitches. He also had severe bruising and a black eye. Ultimately, this incident was to kill off Bill's chance of winning the 1966 125cc world title.

According to *Motor Cycle News* dated 17 August, Bill expected to be in Ireland to ride one of the two brand new 125 four-cylinder machines which Yamaha had specially flown over for this event. Essentially, these were scaled-down versions of the existing V4 250 which had arrived earlier in the season.

The Works Yamahas – A Rider's Insight

The Yamaha 250 RD56 was an air-cooled twin cylinder two-stroke, with rotary valves and a seven-speed gearbox. Power came in at about 9,000rpm and was red lined at 11,000. Top speed was in the region of 154mph (248km/h). In its early development, carburation and spark plug selection had to be so precise. During a race, if the revs even dropped below 9,000 you would foul a spark plug. But later development and better spark plugs reduced this problem. The 250 RD56 was a nice bike to ride, although handling sometimes was lacking. But it was predictable. Down through Masta 'S' at Spa at 152mph (244.5km/h), it always shook its head once at the transition from left to right. The first time it was somewhat frightening, but it was always the same so it became acceptable. I once sat in a chair and went through the Isle of Man TT in my head and calculated that I made a gear change on an average of once every three seconds for two hours and 10 minutes; fortunately, it had both an indestructible clutch and gearbox.

The first two years I rode the RD56 in the Island it frightened the hell out of me in so many places, but in 1966 after riding the bike as a private runner for half the season I was so used to the handling of the bike I felt confident enough to do just about anything with it.

The little 125 liquid cooled twin, the RA97, was perhaps my favourite racing bike of all time. It handled, it steered, it stopped, was fun to ride and had a gear for every occasion. Top speed was in the region of 136mph (219km/h) and a red line at 14,500rpm, had nine speeds to play with and was easily the fastest bike in the class in 1965. But it lacked reliability and would self-destruct in less than 100 miles.

I only rode the 125-4, the RA31, once, and that was in the Isle of Man. However, it only did 14 miles before breaking. But it was phenomenal, with 10 speeds, unlimited revs (17,500rpm) and was like riding a turbine.

The first of the 250-4, the RD05, was the worst motorcycle I have ever ridden. It was so top heavy, the mechanics would tape 35 pounds of lead weight inside the fairing to lower the centre of gravity. This made the bike almost rideable. It had eight speeds and was the only bike I have ridden that had too much horsepower. The first model was manufactured in 1965 and replaced the RD56 from 1966 onwards. In later years the factory narrowed the engine by up to three inches, which allowed it to be much lower in the frame and transformed it into probably the best and most sophisticated racing motorcycle ever built up to that time. It was clocked at Fuji in 1968 at 168mph (270km/h) but achieved another 500rpm after passing the timing device. The factory guesstimated its top speed at around 172mph (277km/h). Not bad for a skinny tyred 250 in 1968!

Michelle 'Mike' Duff

Bill had told his mother from hospital on the day following his Brands accident: 'Pack my bags and get my tickets ready. I'll be on the plane to Ireland tomorrow [Tuesday 16 August].' However, Bill was not allowed to race – his place in the Yamaha squad at Dundrod was taken instead by local boy Tommy Robb. However, this was to no avail as neither Tommy or Phil Read could beat the Hondas of race winner Luigi Taveri or runner-up Ralph Bryans. Yamaha were not pleased and instructed Bill that he was no longer allowed to ride Tom Kirby's bikes. This was understandable, as his crash had been caused when an oil pipe fractured on the Kirby 350 machine.

A Late Isle of Man TT

Because of the national seaman's strike, the Isle of Man TT was held in late August instead of June that year. And after his non-appearance at the Ulster GP only days previously, Bill was given a check-up at Nobles Hospital on Monday 22 August. Given the 'all clear', he was then ready to turn out for practice as Yamaha prepared their new 125 four-cylinder models for battle after Phil Read's problems during the Ulster GP. Bill was reported to be a little stiff and still had stitches in his back, but he was looking and feeling much better.

The Lightweight (250cc) TT was run on Sunday 28 August, and Bill, together with his Yamaha teammate Phil Read, put up 100mph (161km/h) laps on the four-cylinder models before retiring – Bill's problems really beginning towards the end of the third lap when he overshot his pit and, with his machine apparently running on only two cylinders, had to change plugs. Even so, he was in third position behind the Hondas of Mike Hailwood and Stuart Graham. And it should be pointed out that he had been holding second spot until the plug trouble.

At the end of the fourth lap, Bill came in again – running on two or three cylinders. His mechanics gave it a quick look over and it was wheeled away. The official reason was given as 'a broken carburettor.' It is also interesting to reveal that Bill's machine was the fastest through the *Motor Cycle News* speed trap – at 149.4mph (240.4km/h). He had actually topped the 150mph barrier during practice!

A Great Performance

The 7 September 1966 issue of *Motor Cycle News* said: 'Yamaha team men crush Honda fives.' Going on to say: 'Honda were given the thrashing of their lives and their best performer was Mike Hailwood, who finished sixth.' But the star performer was Bill, who *MCN* said: 'Rode the race of his life.' He not only took the victory in the Ultra Lightweight (125cc) TT but also

76
KAWASAKI
76

smashed the race and lap records for the class; the latter being raised to 98.55mph (158.56km/h). Not only this, but Yamaha also collected the team prize with Phil Read runner-up and Mike Duff fourth.

It was Bill's first TT win and one he richly deserved but almost did not make. As Robin Miller described for *MCN*: 'His opening lap was a trifle hairy to say the least. He misjudged his braking at the Gooseneck, a bottom-gear right-hander leading up to the Mountain, and scraped along a stone wall as he ran out of road.' Fortunately only his fairing was damaged, but he lost precious seconds and lay behind Phil Read at the end of lap one.

The Kawasaki factory sent Toshio (Known as 'Tosh') Fujji to Europe during 1965 and 1966. Sadly he was to be killed during practice for the Isle of Man TT in August 1966; the TT having been delayed by the seaman's strike that year.

Twins Rather Than Fours

Yamaha had chosen to use their twins in preference to the fours for all their riders, and this proved a wise decision. Mist on the Mountain on Wednesday 31 August delayed the start of the race and when Hugh Anderson (Suzuki) and Fred Stevens (Honda) pushed off it was 2pm and they were three hours behind schedule.

Again, as on the 250 machine, Bill's 125 Yamaha was fastest, recording 130.9mph (210.6km/h) in the race. In practice he had been recorded at an even faster speed, 132.4mph (213.1km/h). *MCN*'s speed trap was located on the drop between Creg-Ny-Baa and Brandish.

The start of the 250cc Junior (for production-based machines) at the 1966 Japanese GP at Fisco. The machines are a mixture of Yamahas, Suzukis and Kawasakis.

Ultra Lightweight 125 TT – 3 laps – 113.19 miles

1st	W.D. Ivy (Yamaha twin)
2nd	P.W. Read (Yamaha twin)
3rd	H. Anderson (Suzuki)
4th	M. Duff (Yamaha twin)
5th	F. Perris (Suzuki)
6th	S.M.B. Hailwood (Honda five)
7th	R. Bryans (Honda five)
8th	L. Taveri (Honda five)

Two Victories Needed to be Champion

After his TT victory, Bill needed to win the final two GPs, in Italy and Japan, to become 125 World Champion. Could he do it? Unfortunately, the answer was no.

The first of the two events came at Monza in Italy on Sunday 11 September. Here his Yamaha (still a twin) was slow to fire up and refused to run cleanly on both cylinders until he reached the Grande Curve, nearly a mile from the start. He was never to make up this disadvantage, actually finishing third in front of teammate Phil Read.

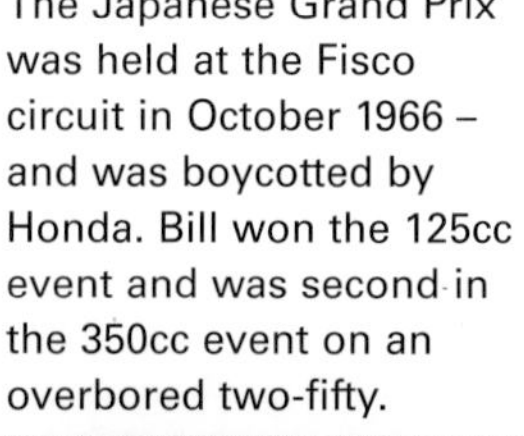

The Japanese Grand Prix was held at the Fisco circuit in October 1966 – and was boycotted by Honda. Bill won the 125cc event and was second in the 350cc event on an overbored two-fifty.

The new 125 four, pictured at the Japanese GP in October 1966. With this machine Yamaha and Bill were set to dominate the class the following year.

Strangely, Yamaha did not contest the 250cc event, with only Mike Duff on a 'private' air-cooled RD56 taking part. This was notable as Mike used a non-standard disc brake – the works machines exclusively employing drum assemblies.

Mallory Park

Then, prior to the final Grand Prix of the season in Japan the following month, Bill took part in the annual big money Race of the Year meeting at Mallory Park.

Riding one of the old air-cooled RD56 two-fifty twins, he caused something of a sensation by finishing runner-up to Giacomo Agostini's three-cylinder 500 MV Agusta in the main race.

Race of the Year, Mallory Park – 30 laps – 39 miles

1st	G. Agostini (MV Agusta 500 three)
2nd	W.D. Ivy (Yamaha 250 RD56 air-cooled twin)
3rd	M. Duff (Yamaha 250 RD56 air-cooled twin)
4th	P. Williams (Arter Matchless G50 500)
5th	J. Cooper (Norton 500)
6th	R. Chandler (Matchless 500)

At Mallory, Bill confirmed that he would continue riding for Yamaha in 1967, saying: 'I haven't signed a contract yet, but I expect to when I go to

Bill rode a Yamaha YDS3 sports roadster, like the one pictured here in his first training session at the Fisco circuit in October 1966.

Japan'. He also added: 'I would very much like to win the 125cc World Championship, but I would also give consideration to car racing.'

Another Grand Prix Victory

And so to the final Grand Prix of the 1966 season, and with a victory in the 125cc race – his fourth in the class that year – Bill completed a highly successful debut season as a full Yamaha works rider. This win also made him runner-up in the Championship table. In fact Yamaha virtually cleaned up, winning every class they contested over the four-mile (6.4km) Fisco circuit, built on the volcanic ash of Mount Fuji. This venue was reputed to be capable of holding more than 300,000 spectators.

The meeting was held over Saturday and Sunday, 14–15 October. The first day had seen Bill finish second to Phil Read, both riding overbored V4 models in the 350cc event. But in truth there was little opposition, as Honda had sulked because the organisers had chosen Fisco instead of their own Suzuka circuit. So, although Suzuki and Kawasaki took part, Yamaha did not have much opposition, and certainly not in the 350cc race (the biggest engine size at the meeting).

350cc Japanese GP, Fisco – 25 laps – 93.2 miles

1st	P.W. Read (Yamaha four)
2nd	W.D. Ivy (Yamaha four)
3rd	A. Pagani (Aermacchi)
4th	B. Black (Aermacchi)
5th	K. Miromashi (Honda)
6th	K. Andersson (Husqvarna)

The following day, Sunday 15 October, although Bill retired in the 24-lap, 89.5 mile (144km) 250cc event on his four-cylinder machine, he was unbeatable in the 125cc class. In this race there was competition from Suzuki and Kawasaki. Besides Bill, Yamaha also had some domestic Japanese riders aboard their works bikes. Kawasaki, like Yamaha, had a number of local riders, plus the British pair of Chris Vincent and Dave Simmonds, with Suzuki headed by New Zealander Hugh Anderson. Phil Read was another entry, but no one could match Bill and he gradually pulled ahead to win, setting the fastest lap at 102.85mph (165.48km/h).

125cc Japanese GP, Fisco – 20 laps – 74.6 miles

1st	W.D. Ivy (Yamaha)
2nd	Y. Katayama (Suzuki)
3rd	M. Itoh (Suzuki)
4th	A. Motohashi (Yamaha)
5th	T. Asaoka (Kawasaki)
6th	D. Simmonds (Kawasaki)

New Yamahas

While in Japan, Bill learned that Yamaha would have a lighter, lower and generally smaller four-cylinder 250 for the following year's Championship series. Their 1967 125 would also be a four-cylinder model.

Phil Read and Bill would lead the attack and a third rider 'might be chosen', but it was uncertain if this rider would be Mike Duff or someone new.

Certainly, it seemed that the Japanese factory was gearing itself up to offer a bigger challenge in both classes than it had done in 1966, when the new V4 250 had shown potential but had proved a difficult bike. And, of course, Yamaha was also equally keen to do well in the 125 category. In any case, Bill Ivy's name was certainly likely to shine even brighter in 1967.

Chapter 8
World Champion

Just to prove that Bill had not forgotten his origins on his way to stardom are two examples from the lead-up to the 1967 season.

Not Forgetting His Origins

The first came in January that year, when it was reported that Bill was financially assisting grass-track sidecar ace Ron Waters (passengered by Graham Croucher) when Ron attempted to break into road racing during the coming season. Bill, it was said, had purchased a complete, proven outfit for Ron to begin his tarmac career – the ex-Barry Lock 649cc Triumph machine. Actually, the truth was that Bill had suggested his name should be used to generate publicity: Bill's actual sponsorship related only to tyres and chains. Friends for many years, Bill and Ron were near neighbours and first met when they began riding motorcycles on the road.

Bill pictured 'off duty' in spring 1967.

The other story relates to a test day outing at Snetterton in late February – a final sort-out for many riders getting ready for the season ahead. And although he was no longer allowed to race bikes for Tom Kirby (who had organised the session), Bill, together with many others, journeyed up to Snetterton for the event.

Also on hand were Kirby riders Dave Degens, Pat Mahoney, Lewis Young and Terry Vinicombe, plus John Hartle, Mike Hailwood, Frank Perris, Alf Hagon and Chris Conn together with scramblers Andy Lee, Dave Nicoll and Jim Aim.

For Alf Hagon (famous as not only a builder of his own machines but also for his grass track and sprinting feats) it was his first outing for many years when he completed a few laps on one of Kirby's G50 Matchless machines.

Bill did a couple of laps on the same bike and also sampled Jim Aim's 500 Matchless-Metisse scrambler.

Title Favourite

When reviewing the prospects for the 125cc class in the forthcoming GP season, Mick Woollett in his 'Sports gossip' column in the 25 March 1967 issue of *Motor Cycling* pointed out that although Honda had withdrawn from the class (and also the 50cc category), it still left not only Yamaha and Suzuki but also works machines from Kawasaki, Bultaco, Montesa, MZ, Derbi, FB Mondial and, possibly, EMC.

Mick went on to say: 'Favourite to win the 125cc title must now be Bill Ivy who chased Luigi Taveri on the five-cylinder Honda so hard last season.'

And as Mick also pointed out: 'Yamaha got as far as trying their "four" out during practice for the Ulster last year.' And: 'Suzuki, who have been playing about with their four for several seasons now, have confined its trials to Japan.' He ended by saying: 'Both suffer from having all the power at the top end and little else – and both are considerably heavier than the twins.'

Getting the Season Off With a Win in Italy

Like other stars including Mike Hailwood and Giacomo Agostini, Bill got his 1967 season off to a start in Italy, taking in meetings at first Riccione and then Cervia.

At the former, held on Sunday 5 April, in fine weather, with a huge crowd lining the two-mile street circuit of this Adriatic seaside resort, Bill got off to a winning start. And in the process beat the 1966 class World Champion, the Swiss star, Luigi Taveri. The race had developed into a three-sided battle between Bill, Luigi (by now a close friend) and the German Suzuki works rider and 1966 50cc Champion, Hans Georg Anscheidt.

Then, on lap 12, Anscheidt retired and Bill pulled ahead of Luigi to win by some 10 seconds.

The RA31A disc-valve V4 model which won the 125cc world title in both 1967 and 1968.

Bill riding a twin cylinder works Yamaha in the 125cc race at Cervia on 12 April 1967; although he did not win, he did have the satisfaction of setting the fastest lap.

125cc Riccione – 20 laps – 40.5 miles

1st	W.D. Ivy (Yamaha)
2nd	L. Taveri (Honda)
3rd	F. Villa (FB Mondial)
4th	A. Nieto (Derbi)
5th	G. Lombardi (Montesa)
6th	A. Burlando (Honda)

Second Best at Cervia

A week later came Bill's second Italian meeting, at Cervia on 12 April. In the 125cc event, Germany's Hans Georg Anscheidt (Suzuki) fought a tremendous duel with Bill, the lead changing constantly. But at the end Bill came off second best, even though he had the satisfaction of setting the fastest lap at 63.31mph (101.89km/h).

Heavy rain began just prior to the start of the 250cc race, and the works Yamahas of Bill and Phil Read both stopped within a few laps with electrical problems.

A few days later Bill revealed that he was not too happy to have found out that Yamaha had decided to exclusively use four-cylinder models in both the 125 and 250 World Championship races in 1967. He told Mick Woollett: 'Everybody thought I'd win the World Championship, now I'm not so sure. I've never raced the four [125] and I'm not even going to get a warming-up ride on it before the title races start. So I'll have to learn to race it at the Spanish GP – and the twisty Montjuich Park circuit isn't a good place to learn to ride anything.'

The new 125 Yamaha was a water-cooled, disc-valve two-stroke constructed on the same lines as the 250cc four, with the vee-configuration engine arranged so that one pair of cylinders was near vertical while the other pair pointed forward horizontally.

Meanwhile, it was learnt that Yamaha engineers had done a tremendous amount of work on the 250 V4 – and that it was a very different motorcycle from the 1966 version.

Phil Read (16) and Bill during the 250cc race at Cervia in April 1967; Bill retired with electrical bothers on his four-cylinder machine.

Dave Simmonds' works 125cc water-cooled Kawasaki twin pictured at the Spanish Grand Prix, 30 April 1967. After many frustrating experiences with this bike, Dave eventually became World Champion in 1969.

Sunny Spain

The first round of the 1967 Championship series was held at Montjuich Park, Barcelona, on Sunday 3 May. Run in glorious sunshine over the tricky, twisting and hilly 2.3 mile (3.7km) circuit overlooking the city, it was a good day for Yamaha, with the marque winning both the 125 and 250cc races. Although, as we know, Bill was openly worried as to the suitability of the new four-cylinder 125, this proved foundless as he easily won, repeating his success at the same venue a year earlier.

Not only that, but the new machine proved extremely fast, with Bill knocking over two seconds off the old lap record for the class with a circuit of 73.82mph (118.77km/h). And with Phil Read on a second four just beating Yoshima Katayama (Suzuki) for second place, there were many smiles in the Yamaha team. This was equally because of Bill's victory and the fact that the fours had come through this test with flying colours.

125cc Spanish GP – 27 laps – 63.59 miles

1st	W.D. Ivy (Yamaha four)
2nd	P.W. Read (Yamaha four)
3rd	Y. Katayama (Suzuki)
4th	S. Graham (Suzuki)
5th	F. Villa (Montesa)
6th	J. Mendrano (Bultaco)

So slick was the organisation that no sooner had the last of the 125cc field crossed the line than the machines for the 250cc race were being wheeled out. Riders competing in both were faced with another 33 laps of this demanding course, with hardly enough time to even have a drink.

In practicing, Mike Hailwood had set the pace, but as the race began Bill was the early leader, heading the pack up the hill for the first time. But, as the 250 fours had done so many times the previous year, Bill's machine faltered on the first lap and he was forced to call at his pit and change plugs. However, when this failed to cure the misfiring, he retired.

Problems in Germany

Signs of the pressure associated with being a full-blown works rider surfaced at the second round in the World Championship series when Bill collapsed in Mike Hailwood's caravan at Hockenheim, the scene of the West German Grand Prix, on Sunday 10 May 1967. He was ordered to rest by doctors. Earlier the same day, both Bill and his Yamaha teammate Phil Read had crashed without apparent injury in the 125cc race, when the two riders they

West German GP at Hockenheim, 10 May 1967. At this time Bill and Phil Read were on the best of terms, but things were not to remain like this in the latter half of the following season.

Bill leading Barry Smith (170), Lothor John (181, MZ) and other riders during the 125cc event at Hockenheim, 10 May 1967. After setting a record lap Bill was forced to retire after a crash.

were about to lap fell right in front of them. Before that, Bill had set a new class lap record with a speed of 106.55mph (171.43km/h).

Following this incident, both Yamaha stars turned out for the 250cc race, Bill again setting a new class lap record, this time at 111.49mph (179.38km/h), before being sidelined with gearbox trouble.

The previous day, Bill had fallen off his 125 Yamaha during practice, and a week previously, in Spain, he had also suffered another fall during training. A week before this he had crashed at high speed at Brands Hatch, when the 250cc Yamaha he was testing seized its engine.

After his collapse at Hockenheim he was taken to a local hospital where he was advised to stay in for four days to recover from delayed shock.

Italian Difficulties

Seven days after Hockenheim, on Sunday 17 May, Bill ran into yet more bother in Italy when he was involved in a scuffle with a spectator at Rimini which resulted in police intervention.

As we know, Bill had been taken to hospital suffering from delayed shock after the previous Sunday's West German Grand Prix. But he had disregarded the German doctor's advice to stay in hospital for a few days rest. Instead, he had travelled down to Rimini to watch Sunday's racing.

At Rimini he was besieged by autograph hunters and in the crush one female fan received a black eye. This had angered the girl's boyfriend, who later started kicking the side of Bill's car. Bill's subsequent protests led to a fight which was broken up by an Italian journalist and a photographer. The police were called and took statements. It was later stated that Bill was taking legal action against the Italian for damaging his car.

A Stunning Comeback

Bill made a stunning track comeback, when a week after the Rimini incident he scored a dramatic, brilliant Grand Prix double victory, when he won the 125 and 250cc races at Clermont-Ferrand, the scene of the 1967 French Grand Prix. Considering he had not completed a single lap in a race at the venue previously, this success was even more remarkable.

In the 125cc event he slashed no less than 12 seconds off reigning class Champion Luigi Taveri's time for the tortuous five-mile (8km) mountain circuit, lapping at 78.72mph (126.66km/h).

In contrast, Bill had been extremely fortunate to finish the 18-lap 250cc race, let alone win it. As *Motor Cycling* said in its 27 May 1967 issue: 'It

Here Bill (4) leads Ralph Bryans (1) and Phil Read (3) during the 1967 250cc Italian GP. After setting a record lap, Bill followed his teammate Phil Read home, with Ralph Bryans third.

Clermont-Ferrand on 24 May was the setting for the 1967 French Grand Prix. Bill won both the 125 and 250cc races; setting a record lap in the former.

was one of the most trouble-plagued races ever seen at a Continental "Classic". For Hailwood's Honda six and the Yamahas of both Read and Ivy all came near to retiring.' Early on in the race, both the Yamahas were slowed, Read's by an inoperative clutch and Bill's by constant misfiring which all but forced him to abandon the race. Meanwhile, Hailwood, raising his own absolute lap record for the circuit to 83.42mph (134.22km/h), built up a tremendous lead. But then the Honda struck its own problems, suffering gearbox gremlins, and the Yamahas soon overtook him to join in their own private battle – which was eventually won by Bill.

125cc French GP, Clermont-Ferrand – 15 laps – 78.14 miles

1st	W.D. Ivy (Yamaha four)
2nd	P.W. Read (Yamaha four)
3rd	Y. Katayama (Suzuki)
4th	S. Graham (Suzuki)
5th	D.A. Simmonds (Kawasaki)
6th	J.L. Vergnais (Bultaco)

250cc French GP, Clermont-Ferrand – 18 laps – 90.09 miles

1st	W.D. Ivy (Yamaha four)
2nd	P.W. Read (Yamaha four)
3rd	S.M.B. Hailwood (Honda six)
4th	R. Bryans (Honda six)
5th	D. Woodman (MZ)
6th	H. Rosner (MZ)

An Altogether Unlucky TT

Everyone had expected Bill to achieve the first 100mph TT lap on a 125 during the 1967 Isle of Man races. But instead his entire fortnight was to turn out to be a real nightmare. Not only did he retire from both races – with engine problems on the fourth lap of the Lightweight (250cc) race on 15 June, while two days later on 17 June his machine lasted an even shorter time, with a retirement at the pits after completing only a single lap!

However, if he thought this would be the end of his misfortunes he was to receive a nasty shock. Less than 24 hours after his first race he was driving his month-old Ferrari sports car with his friend Mike Hailwood as passenger, when the car left the road and hit a wall at the tricky left-and-right kink at the end of the fast straight past the Highlander pub. Bill said at the time that a tyre had 'burst'. The nearside of the car received extensive damage – said to have been approximately one fifth of its value. But the real shock for Bill came later. When checking his insurance documents after the races, he discovered that the insurance was comprehensive only in Italy, where it had been taken out. In other countries the cover was third party only. This meant that Bill would have to meet the cost of repairs himself.

And so the Ferrari was returned (by sea) from the Isle of Man to Liverpool and then transferred to a ship which would take it to the Italian port of Genoa. From there it was taken to the Ferrari works in Modena to be repaired.

Bill's Ferrari 275GTB which was badly damaged in the Isle of Man accident (detailed in the main text) with Mike Hailwood as a passenger. Bill later discovered that his Italian insurance did not cover its use outside Continental Europe.

Yamaha teamster Akayasu Motohashi finished third in the 1967 125cc Isle of Man TT, behind the winner Phil Read (Yamaha) and Stuart Graham (Suzuki); Bill retired at the pits on lap one.

A minor consolation was to come once he left the island and returned to the mainland, where at the International Post TT Mallory Park meeting Bill not only won the 125cc event but also pushed the class lap record from 83.50mph (134.35km/h) – set by Alan Shepherd some three years earlier on an MZ – to 85.56mph (137.66km/h). He won the race on one of the previous year's twin-cylinder Yamahas.

The Dutch TT at Assen, June 1967. This photograph shows Yamaha team bikes under preparation.

A Hive of Activity

Then came a hive of Grand Prix activity. First at Assen on Saturday 28 June Bill finished runner-up to Phil Read in the 125 race and Mike Hailwood (Honda six) in the 250cc class.

Next came Spa Francorchamps in Belgium on Sunday 5 July. Here, with only a 250cc race for the factory Yamahas, Bill not only won but also set the fastest lap; this time beating none other than Hailwood himself!

Next it was a couple of Iron Curtain rounds. The first at the Sachsenring, East Germany, on Sunday 16 July 1967 saw Bill not only win the 125cc race but also set a new class lap record. This was followed by a second place finish behind teammate Phil Read in the 250cc event.

A week later the team was at Brno, Czechoslovakia, where precisely the same results were garnered – a 125cc victory and runner-up (again behind Phil) in the larger capacity class.

Bill taking his machine to second place in the Dutch TT at Assen, 28 June 1967.

Finnish Aquabatics

The 1967 Finnish Grand Prix held at Imatra on Sunday 6 August was a day in which the vast majority of riders, officials and the 30,000 spectators would have wanted to forget. Soaked to the skin through almost continuous rain, the only interlude in the weather was in time for the 125cc event. However, although it was not raining it certainly brought no luck for Bill. For despite getting a relatively good start he was soon in trouble, and at the end of lap one he was forced to call at his pit to change a plug. Then, halfway around lap two another plug went and he was again forced to pull in to his pit.

Effectively that ended whatever chances Bill had of winning his fifth 125cc GP race that year. His only satisfaction was to be the honour of setting the fastest lap – 0.7 seconds slower than Luigi Taveri's 1966 figure, but brilliant considering all his problems. As it was, Bill finished the race runner-up behind Stuart Graham (Suzuki), with Kawasaki-mounted Dave Simmonds third.

Bill also finished runner-up (to Mike Hailwood) in the 250cc event.

Mike Hailwood

Many consider S.M.B. (Stanley Michael Bailey) Hailwood to have been the greatest motorcycle racer of all time. He was born in Oxford on 2 April 1940, the son of a self-made millionaire motorcycle dealer. His father, Stan, had competed pre-war on two, three and four wheels, before going on to build up the largest grouping of dealerships seen up to that time in Great Britain.

Mike began his racing career aboard an MV Agusta 125 single overhead camshaft production racer loaned to him by family friend Bill Webster (also a close friend of Count Domenico Agusta). This debut occurred on Easter Monday 22 April 1957, at Oulton Park in Cheshire, only a few miles from Webster's base.

In stark contrast to Bill Ivy's early racing days, there is absolutely no doubt that Stan Hailwood went about buying success for his son, with the best bikes, the best tuners and a huge media hype. However, in fairness, Mike did not really need this vast support as he had natural talent in abundance. An example of Stan Hailwood's methods is displayed by a story concerning the NSU Sportmax Mike rode during the early part of his career. In 1955, John Surtees had raced the new German bike thanks to his employers Vincent (who were the British NSU distributors). John was given a bike, plus a spare engine. Then, towards the end of 1957, John received a phone call from Stan asking: 'Can we borrow the NSU for Mike to use in South Africa this winter?' John agreed, and the machine went to the Hailwood equipé. Later another call from Stan: 'Can we have the engine too?' Again John was approached and agreed to lend the spare engine. Now Stan had both bike and engine – and John was never to see either again because Stan conveniently became an NSU dealer. The 'deal' with the new London-based importers meant that King's of Oxford would

Mike Hailwood, seen here in the mid-1960s with Lord Montague of Beaulieu during the presentation by the Honda Motor Company of a 250 four to the National Motor Museum.

only become agents if Stan could keep the racer and the engine – even though it had been given to Surtees!

In many ways, Mike was embarrassed by his father's wheeler dealings, and as soon as he could he became self-sufficient – his race results giving him freedom from his father's overpowering attention. In fact, Mike nicknamed his father 'Stan the Wallet'. But this was not before Stan had bought bikes such as a 125 Paton, a 125 Grand Prix Ducati, various Desmo Ducati twins and singles for the 125, 250 and 350cc classes, a couple of ex-works FB Mondial 250 singles, a squadron of Manx Nortons and an AJS 7R. In 1958 Mike was able to score a trio of British ACU Star titles (125, 250 and 350cc).

Mike's first Grand Prix victory came aboard a factory 125 Ducati Desmo single during the 1959 Ulster – the man he beat that day was none other than his future teammate at MV Agusta, Gary Hocking (riding an MZ). That year he also won all four ACU Stars – adding the 500cc to the classes he had retained for a second year. He repeated this feat the following year and it is one which no man before or since has equalled.

For 1961, Mike rode 125 and 250cc works Hondas, plus a 350cc AJS 7R and a 500cc Manx Norton. He gained his first world title, the 250cc, on the four-cylinder Honda, took the 125 and 250cc Isle of Man TTs and the Senior race on his Norton. On the latter machine (tuned by Bill Lacey) Mike averaged over 100mph for the six-lap, 226-mile race.

At the end of 1961 he signed for MV Agusta – going on to win the 500cc world title four years in a row (1962–65). In 1964, Mike set a new one-hour world speed record (at Daytona), thus breaking the existing record set by Bob McIntyre on a 350cc Gilera four at Monza in November 1957.

In 1966 Mike rejoined Honda, winning both the 250 and 350cc classes on the new six-cylinder models, equalling this feat the following year before switching his attention to four wheels. But even he could not tame the wayward 500cc four-cylinder Honda, with MV (ridden by Giacomo Agostini) retaining the title.

Mike racing Ralph Bryans' Honda 297cc six to victory in the Race of the Year at Mallory Park, on 17 September 1967.

Mike Hailwood & Bill Ivy; 1967. The two men were great friends off the track.

For more than a decade Mike largely stayed away from bikes (except for a couple of outings on BSA and Yamaha machines) before making a historic comeback TT victory on a Ducati v-twin in 1978. The following year, 1979, he rode a Suzuki to a final TT victory. Then he retired once more, becoming a partner in the Hailwood & Gould business (with fellow World Champion Rod Gould). By a twist of fate, the premises they used had formally been the home of the Birmingham branch of King's of Oxford (part of his father Stan's dealership chain).

Mike died tragically (with his younger daughter Michelle) while driving home in his Rover car after collecting a fish and chip supper on 14 March 1981.

Back-to-Front Hutch

On 13 August 1967, the British Motor Cycle Racing Club ran its annual international Hutchinson 100 meeting in the reverse direction of the 2.65 mile (4.26km) circuit for the second year running. And Bill, riding one of the 1966 twin-cylinder Yamaha's, won the only race he contested that day – the 12-lap 125cc Championship event – from Stuart Graham (Suzuki) and Derek Woodman (MZ). But in truth, even though Ralph Bryans on a five-cylinder Honda was also entered, it proved a relatively easy victory.

First Time at the Ulster

Six days later, on Saturday 19 August, Bill competed in his first-ever Ulster GP at Dundrod. In 1966, Bill had crashed spectacularly when riding one of Tom Kirby's bikes in the Hutchinson 100 350cc race the Sunday before the Ulster, and although he travelled over to Dundrod he was not fit enough to race.

Bill at the Gooseneck before retiring his 250cc Yamaha in the 1967 Lightweight TT after experiencing engine problems.

Naturally, Bill was keen to learn the circuit, seen by many as the most difficult in the World Championship series except for the longer TT lap. However, torrential rain during the first day's practicing, on Wednesday, did not help.

Bill commenting: 'I didn't learn a thing. It was raining so hard I couldn't see where I was going.'

During Thursday, however, dry slots allowed Bill to get cracking, resulting in the third-quickest 250cc lap. Afterwards he set the fastest lap in 125cc practicing at over 96mph (154.5km/h). This was 2mph (3.2km/h) quicker than Ralph Bryans' record set a year before on a five-cylinder Honda.

A Fortunate Victory

Bill had good fortune for once, as he was able to win the 125cc Ulster, despite the fact that the cooling system of his four-cylinder Yamaha was empty halfway through the race and the engine was overheating badly. Interviewed after the race he said: 'I saw the temperature gauge go up from the normal 70 to 115 degrees – and that is as high as it goes. I think a cylinder head had cracked. All I could do was to try and coast as much as possible to keep the temperature down.'

With the win, Bill was virtually certain of becoming the 1967 125cc World Champion – and thus the first Briton to take the class title since Cecil Sandford (MV Agusta) won it some 15 years earlier in 1952. In fact, the only man with a chance of outscoring Bill was his own teammate, Phil Read. But to do that, Phil would have to win all three of the remaining rounds, and, even then, Bill would still be champion if he were to finish second in all three.

125cc Ulster GP, Dundrod – 11 laps – 82.0 miles

1st	W.D. Ivy (Yamaha)
2nd	P.W. Read (Yamaha)
3rd	S. Graham (Suzuki)
4th	K. Carruthers (Honda)
5th	K. Cass (Bultaco)
6th	W. Molloy (Bultaco)

Another aspect of the races in 1967 was the record 80,000 crowd, who were enjoying the first fine-weather Ulster GP for many years. And although Bill did not win the 250cc event, by finishing third behind the winner Mike Hailwood and Ralph Bryans (both aboard six-cylinder Hondas), his performance was still impressive – remember that this was his first ever Ulster!

A factory mechanic at work on an RA31A 125 model during the 1967 season. This liquid-cooled, disc-valve, 70-degree V4 put out a claimed 37bhp at 14,000rpm.

Bill scored a magnificent victory in the 250cc Belgian Grand Prix at Spa Francorchamps on 5 July 1967; he also set the fastest lap.

Race of Aces

Then, in-between GPs, Bill took in the international Race of Aces meeting at Snetterton.

His only event was the 125 race. But as competitors lined up on the grid, the question was: where is Bill Ivy? Bill was, in fact, taping up a split carburettor mounting on his Yamaha twin. Perhaps readers may consider this was to be a disadvantage, but it did not seem to affect Bill at all, as he joined the grid and, when the flag went down, he was soon out in the lead and in the process shattered Martin Carney's Bultaco lap record by a massive margin. He simply left runner-up Kel Carruthers (Honda) and third-place man Walter Scheimann from West Germany (Honda) far behind.

125cc Snetterton – 4 laps – 10.84 miles

1st	W.D. Ivy (Yamaha twin)
2nd	K. Carruthers (Honda)
3rd	W. Scheimann (Honda)
4th	M. Carney (Bultaco)
5th	R. Scivyer (Honda)
6th	V.D. Chatterton (Chat Honda)

Champion

Then came Bill's greatest day, when at Monza he not only won the 125cc event but also achieved a life-long ambition of winning a World Championship title. But it was certainly a nail biting victory, as shortly before the end of the 18-lap 64.31 mile (105.5km) race distance Bill was forced to make not one, but two pit stops for water – which was not available anyway – for an overheating engine. The deficit put him behind Hans Georg Anscheidt (Suzuki), whom he repassed only in the final sprint to the finish line. Bill also set the fastest lap at 111.46mph (179.38km/h).

125cc Italian GP, Monza – 18 laps – 64.31 miles

1st	W.D. Ivy (Yamaha)
2nd	H.G. Anscheidt (Suzuki)
3rd	L. Szabo (MZ)
4th	W. Scheimann (Honda)
5th	G. Burlando (Honda)
6th	F.J. Curry (Honda)

At the Czech Grand Prix, Bill scored his fourth 125cc Grand Prix victory of the 1967 season. Here he and teammate Phil Read prepare to overtake an MZ rider. Bill also set a new class lap record for the Brno road course.

This superbly evocative photograph shows the top three finishers after the race in the 250cc Italian GP at Monza on 3 September 1967. Phil Read can be seen putting his arm on Ralph Bryans' shoulder to almost say, 'you did your best'. Bill had earlier won the 125cc event.

A 250 Lap Record

Obviously Monza agreed with Bill, as not only did he garner his race win in the smaller class but he also impressed in the 250 category as well. Easily the fastest in practice, Bill was expected to rocket straight into the lead, but at the end of the opening lap he was tucked into Mike Hailwood's slipstream. Then came Phil Read and Ralph Bryans. No more than 2.7 seconds covered all four, who were already well ahead of the MZs of Derek Woodman and Heinz Rosner.

One of the fiercest-ever battles ensued between the two Yamahas and the two Hondas. Then Hailwood retired – his engine dead and dripping oil. Phil Read needed to win to keep alive his chance of winning the 250cc title – from Hailwood. But Ralph Bryans was determined to finish ahead of Phil. As for Bill, he needed to protect his teammate so that Phil could gain maximum points.

In the end, only 0.8 seconds separated the three riders – and it was Read, Ivy and Bryans in that order. Bill had also set the fastest (a record) lap at 121.69mph (195.79km/h), in what had been a truly breathtaking race.

The Monza meeting had taken place on Sunday 3 September. Thereafter Bill returned to Britain, taking part at Cadwell Park on 10 September and Mallory Park on 17 September. At both these meetings he rode twin-cylinder Yamahas; his best result being a win at Cadwell in the 125cc event – and a record lap.

The Canadian Grand Prix

Mosport Park, Ontario, was the setting for the newly-introduced Canadian Grand Prix. Situated some 50 miles (80km) from Toronto, the Mosport Park circuit measured 2.46 miles (4km) to the lap. It was constructed especially for racing – its name being a contraction of the words 'motor sport' – and it included a series of steep climbs and descents.

In near-artic weather conditions, Bill scored yet another 125cc race victory, with the *Motor Cycle* race report saying: 'Race day was dull, overcast, freezing cold and generally miserable.' The 125cc race came first on the programme. As there was little racing for this class at the time in North America, the majority of the field was made up of race-kitted, twin-cylinder 100cc Yamahas. So despite having to stop twice for more water to compensate for coolant lost through a leaking head gasket, Bill carried on to score yet another 125cc success. And he was followed home by five Yamaha twins, thus making it a clean sweep for the Japanese two-strokes.

The weather was so cold that there was talk of cutting the race distance for the 250cc race which followed. But after some discussion with the FIM representative, Henri Lenfranc of Belgium, it was decided to stick to the original 32 laps (78.68 miles – 126.60km).

The start of the 250cc race at Monza on 3 September 1967. Bill is number 4, Mike Hailwood (Honda six) 2, Phil Read 3, Ralph Bryans (Honda six) 1 and Heinz Rosner (MZ) 15.

Mallory Park 'Race of the Year', 17 September 1967. Bill signs his autograph for a fan.

From the start Mike Hailwood shot into the lead, followed by Bill, while Read and Bryans made slower starts.

Swapping places two and three times a lap, Mike and Bill (who by now were close friends and flatmates) showed the few spectators who had braved the cold what Grand Prix racing was all about. But sadly, only a lap from home, Bill's engine expired and Mike went on to score a vital victory; Phil Read was not close enough to do anything about it.

Only 45 minutes after the end of the racing, Mike, Phil, Bill and Giacomo Agostini boarded a helicopter to begin the first leg of their overnight trip across the Atlantic to race the following day at the Race of the South, Brands Hatch meeting.

Apart from slowing to replace a detached plug lead on the fourth lap, without losing position, Bill (Yamaha twin) never looked other than the winner at Brands Hatch in the 125cc event, though as the *Motor Cycle* commented: 'He tried to make a race of it by fluffing his start and taking nearly three laps before sweeping into the lead.'

Japanese Grand Prix

The last round of the Championship series took place at Fuji in Japan on Sunday 15 October 1967. The previous year Honda had refused to support the meeting when it was held for the first time at the Fuji circuit on the flank of the famous Mount Fuji, near Tokyo.

Honda maintained that the high speed 'wall of death' banking at the end of the main straight was too dangerous. So for 1967 a shorter, 2.7 mile

(4.4km) course was used; thus cutting out the banking. But in truth, Honda had to compete – as the 250cc Championship had not yet been decided...

Unlike the previous year, all the races were held on the Sunday, following two days of practicing. And with another victory on his four-cylinder 125, Bill's final total in the 125 World Championship points table was 56 (76 gross – as only a number of rounds actually counted!).

The actual table ended up:

1st	W.D. Ivy (GB, Yamaha)
2nd	P.W. Read (GB, Yamaha)
3rd	S. Graham (GB, Suzuki)
4th	Y. Katayama (Japan, Suzuki)
5th	L. Szabo (Hungary, MZ)
6th	D.A. Simmonds (GB, Kawasaki)

Bill Ivy – in high fashion – chats to sidecar driver Mick Boddice at Snetterton, summer 1967.

In the 250cc race, both Phil Read and Mike Hailwood retired from the race in the early stages (Phil with a broken crankshaft). This left Bill, plus teammate Hiroshi Hasegawa and Ralph Bryans (Honda six).

The two Yamaha riders pulled away from Bryans. But then, on lap 26, Hasagawa stopped with a broken crankshaft and three laps later, when leading by 18 seconds, Bill's Yamaha V4 suffered the same fate. Even so, he finished the year third, behind Read and Hailwood in the points table.

At first Phil was awarded the title, but later this was given to Mike. Actually, Phil had a higher total of points, but Mike had one more victory – and the FIM eventually crowned the Honda rider Champion. At the time this caused some considerable controversy!

Although both Bill and Phil eventually signed new contracts for the 1968 season, none of the European riders when they left Japan after the GP had put pen to paper. In fact, because of a general recession in the industry, Japanese factories were no longer as enthusiastic about Grand Prix racing as they had been in previous years.

At Mosport in Canada on 30 September 1967, Bill took the 125cc race victory; the next five finishers were all mounted on race-kitted Yamaha 100cc YL-1 twins as shown here.

First Signs of Discontent

By December 1967 there were, for the first-time, signs of discontent in the Yamaha team between Bill and Phil Read. Newspaper reports hinting that Bill would be the new first string for Yamaha certainly did not help matters between the two riders.

In the 13 December 1967 issues of *Motor Cycle* Bill said: 'I'm the happiest man in the world, everything has turned out so well for me. I've got the best car I could wish for, a nice flat and there's enough money in the bank for me to go out and enjoy myself whenever I like.' Being interviewed by Mick Woollett, Bill was talking from the comfort of a black-hide swivel chair, part of the furnishings of the luxury flat in Heston he had recently purchased from Mike Hailwood.

When he questioned Bill about the news stories which had been circulating, this is how Mick Woollett saw things: 'Obviously the new 125cc World Champion would have preferred to dodge that question! But after giving it a good deal of serious thought he evasively replied: "Well, you can certainly say that my ambition is to score a double by winning the 125 and 250cc titles. I'll be trying very hard in both classes and the factory won't mind which rider wins, so long as he's on a Yamaha".'

Mick Woollett continued: 'Not a direct answer, but one which indicated that Bill won't be shutting off to let Phil Read win 250cc races as he did this year – notably at the Czech GP and at the Italian GP.'

The same article is also interesting because of Bill's views on the latest Yamaha race machinery. This is what he had to say:

'I'd say that the latest model [250cc] as raced in the Japanese GP is the fastest, best handling and best stopping two-fifty in the world. Hardly any difference between it and the works 500cc Honda and MV, fabulous.'

He continued: 'I'd say it's the best racing motorcycle in the world and it's easy to ride now, too. You crack the throttle wide open and it flies. The extraordinary thing is that although the 125cc engine follows the same layout, its characteristics are completely different. It's hard to ride. Coming out of a corner you give it full throttle and it misfires. Then you roll the throttle back and feed in gradually until it starts to miss again or until you're on full throttle. The bike may be faster on the three-quarter than full throttle – you've got to play it along all the time. And, strangely enough, the acceleration of the 125cc four isn't so good as that of the old twin it replaced. But with the 250cc engines, it's the other way round.'

Riding one of the older twin cylinder models, Bill won the 125cc race at Brands Hatch on 1 October 1967 and in the process also set the fastest lap. It was a popular homecoming for the new 125 World Champion.

In fact, remembering the test session at Silverstone in 1965 just prior to the TT Bill recalled: 'The two-fifty handled badly. The circuit was damp and it really frightened me. I was about a second a lap slower than Phil. I did better on the little bike [the twin] and team manager Hasegawa asked me if I'd like to race for them in the Island and the Dutch TT. I accepted.'

A Third Team Member?

Speculation as to whether Yamaha would have a third member in their GP squad for the 1968 season grew when it became known that 24-year-old Paul Smart of Maidstone tested Bill Ivy's 125 works Yamaha at Brands Hatch on Wednesday 17 January. With a fastest lap of 61.5 seconds, Paul's quickest time was just over a second longer than Bill's on the same machine.

At the time Bill said: 'Paul went very, very well. Now I have to report back to Yamaha, and I expect he will be offered a ride in the TT.'

However, the following month a Grand Prix bombshell dropped, with Honda announcing that it was to quit and would not be contesting any of the 1969 title series. This came after both Mike Hailwood and Ralph Bryans had been ordered out for talks in Japan. Both riders were at first reluctant to talk when they returned home. The decision was generally believed to be the result of an economy drive. Not only that, but development work on the new six-cylinder 125cc, eight-cylinder 250cc and 500cc six had been suspended. Both Hailwood and Bryans had been loaned ex-factory bikes to enable them to race at national and international non-Grand Prix events.

However, as far as Yamaha were concerned there was now absolutely no requirement for additional riding strength. So the Paul Smart possibility went no further.

A Double Opening Success

The European racing season got under way on a circuit overlooking the Mediterranean at Alicante, Spain, on Sunday 4 February 1968. This proved to be a great day for the Yamaha team as not only did Bill win the 250cc race from teammate Phil Read but he also snatched victory from seemingly certain defeat in an exciting 125cc race. Riding a 1966 water-cooled twin, Bill took over to win the 125cc event after leader Ralph Bryans slid off his works five-cylinder Honda at a hairpin only two miles from the flag.

Then, to complete Yamaha's day, riding a four-cylinder 250 Phil Read beat Giacomo Agostini and his three-cylinder MV Agusta to win the 350cc class.

However, before all these events took place, Bill was the centre of controversy when he held up the start of the first race. For when starters for the 125cc race formed up on the grid of the 3.9 mile (6.27km) circuit at

Phil Read

Phil Read was born in Luton, Bedfordshire, on 1 January 1939 and began racing on a 499cc BSA Gold Star (encouraged by his mother) in 1957, but his big break really came when he won the Senior Manx Grand Prix on a Norton in September 1960. Then, again Norton-mounted, Phil won the Junior TT the following June. Other notable performances during the remainder of 1961 marked him out for future stardom.

During 1962 he mainly confined his racing activities to the British short circuits, winning many races, and there is little doubt that these performances, added to his victories in the Isle of Man, were responsible for prompting Geoff Duke to sign Phil to ride the Gileras following Derek Minter's serious crash at Brands Hatch prior to the first round of the 1963 World Championship series, in which the latter, together with John Hartle, had been picked to take on Mike Hailwood and the MV factory. Another factor was Phil's outstanding ride in the main (500cc) event at Silverstone, in April 1963, when he had split the Gileras

Phil Read, winner of the 1971 Lightweight TT, with his Helmet Fath-tuned TD2 Yamaha. His mechanic, Dutchman Ferry Brauer, is seated on the bike.

of Minter and Hartle in the race; it was a sensational result which was also an embarrassment to the Scuderia Duke team.

Ultimately the Gileras proved something of a disappointment (they had been mothballed since 1957), but Phil had nonetheless been able to display his talents to a wider audience. This was to provoke an offer from the Yamaha factory to race their works RD56 250 twin, Phil having his first outing for his new employer in the Japanese Grand Prix at Suzuka during October 1963.

In 1964, Phil was top man in the 250cc World Championship, giving Yamaha their first world crown. It was also the first time a two-stroke had won this particular title. Phil's victory also broke a three-year period where Yamaha's bitter rivals Honda had reigned supreme.

In 1965 Phil retained his title, then for 1966 Honda signed Mike Hailwood. This meant that both Yamaha and Honda had world-class riders in the 250cc class, and the machinery was truly awe-inspiring. Honda had a dohc six, whereas Yamaha had a brand new disc-valve V-4. Mike ended up Champion, with Phil suffering a series of teething troubles with his newly designed motorcycle.

Phil in serious mode before one of his battles with Bill Ivy.

Phil in 1973 when he was riding for MV Agusta, with his late wife, Madeline.

These problems were resolved in time for the 1967 season, and that year Read and Hailwood fought out one of the closest Championships in the history of the sport. Phil actually had a higher total of basic points, and at first was awarded the Championship. Later the FIM gave the title to Mike because he had scored an additional victory. Phil also finished runner-up to his teammate Bill Ivy in the 125cc series.

In 1968, Phil went on to win back both the 125 and 250cc titles. But even though both Honda and Suzuki had pulled out, this was no easy task, as a bitter rivalry erupted between Phil and Bill. The reason why and how all this happened is analysed within the pages of this book. But suffice to say it proved a bitter and hard fought battle between the two riders.

At the end of 1968 Yamaha quit GP 'works' racing. The reasons for this were twofold. First, their Japanese rivals had already retired from the scene (i.e. Honda and Suzuki) and, additionally, Yamaha had introduced their new over-the-counter 250TD2 and 350TR2 production racers. It was to be on one of these that Phil won the 250cc title again in 1971, on a privately owned machine tuned by the German rider/engineer Helmut Fath.

In 1972 news came that Phil would be joining MV Agusta. At first this was to ride in the 350cc class, but for 1973 this was broadened to include the blue riband 500cc category. This brought Phil into controversy once more, this time with regards to MV's number-one rider, Giacomo Agostini. As I described in my book *Giacomo Agostini: Champion of Champions* (Breedon Books): 'The move was like putting a fox into a hen house.' At that time Phil and Ago simply did not hit it off, and this was the main reason why Giacomo joined rivals Yamaha for the 1974 season after Phil had won the 500cc title the previous year. With Ago's departure Phil went on to retain the 500cc crown in 1974, but he was not to be found in the 350cc results that year for the simple fact that MV had withdrawn from the class. Instead, Giacomo Agostini took the Championship for his new team.

In 1975, a fierce battle developed between Phil and Giacomo for the 500cc Championship. Phil lost, with the Italian rider finally coming out on top, even though he had to wait until the final round to know the outcome of the titanic struggle.

Phil left MV at the end of 1975. Later, in 1977, he won the Formula 1 title in the Isle of Man on a Honda. Then came Mike Hailwood's famous comeback in 1978, with these two great riders battling it out for the F1 crown around the legendary Mountain Circuit in June 1978 – and it was Mike who was to come out on top.

There is absolutely no doubt in the author's mind that Phil had gone out of his way to invite controversy, and on the other hand that he has also been one of the truly great riders of not only his era but of all time. It is just a pity that in pursuing his quest for glory that Phil has also managed to upset so many people along the way.

10am, Bill was nowhere to be seen. He was, in fact, still in bed at his hotel fast asleep, happily dreaming that racing was due to begin at noon! A messenger, sent by the race organisers, soon woke him up and, tousled and unshaven, the 125cc World Champion formed up on the grid at 10.30am for the delayed start.

As we know, the race developed into a battle between Bill and Ralph Bryans. A massive roar went up from the 30,000 spectators as Bryans parted company at a very slippery hairpin bend. Bill picked his way through and went on to win, while the Irishman remounted to take second spot.

125cc Alicante – 15 laps – 52.97 miles

1st	W.D. Ivy (Yamaha twin)
2nd	R. Bryans (Honda five)
3rd	A. Nieto (Derbi)
4th	S. Canellas (Bultaco)
5th	R. Blanco (Bultaco)
6th	J. Mendrano (Bultaco)

Because his six-cylinder Honda arrived at Barcelona airport on Saturday, too late to be transported the 300 miles (482.7km) to Alicante in time for practicing, Ralph Bryans was forced to race an ageing Honda twin in the 250cc event. But he retired with gearbox trouble after a few laps, and it was Italy's Bruno Spaggiari on a desmodromic single-cylinder works Ducati who, surprisingly, set the pace. After two laps Bill and Phil Read on the Yamaha V4s took over and pulled away with Bill in front by just over a minute. Spaggiari held third place until three laps from the end when the Ducati spluttered to a halt with a flat battery.

250cc Alicante – 20 laps – 78.91 miles

1st	W.D. Ivy (Yamaha four)
2nd	P.W. Read (Yamaha four)
3rd	W.G. Molloy (Bultaco)
4th	G. Milani (Aermacchi)
5th	J. Findlay (Bultaco)
6th	B. Nelson (Yamaha)

Off to Japan

During early March, Bill flew out to Japan at the request of Yamaha. Before he left he said: 'I hope I'll be testing new bikes when I get there and won't get the sack.' He was obviously remembering the recent unpleasant experiences of Mike Hailwood and Ralph Bryans! Phil Read was not travelling with Bill, as he was due to race for Yamaha at Daytona around the same time as the test session was due in Japan.

Another piece of news was that not only Honda but Suzuki too had taken the decision to quit GPs. This meant that the lone Kawasakis of Dave Simmonds were to be the only other Japanese works opposition at World Championship level. Other factory entries were East German MZs, Spanish Derbis and Italian Benellis; plus of course the MV Agusta team in the 350 and 500cc classes.

Bill leading teammate Phil Read in the 250cc race at Cervia on 24 April 1968. This came only four days after the first GP of the season at the Nürburgring. On both occasions Bill beat Phil.

In Record Breaking Form

The first round of the 1968 season's 12-round World Championship series kicked off on the 4.8 mile (7.72km) southern loop of the world-famous Nürburgring in West Germany.

As the *Motor Cycle* race report reveals: 'By the time racing stated with the 125cc class on Saturday afternoon [20 April], the tortuous circuit was surrounded by the tents of thousands of German enthusiasts who were making a weekend of it.'

Phil Read and Bill tore ahead at the start, taking it in turn to lead until Bill pulled into the pits after nine of the 13 laps. A plug was changed and Bill rejoined the race; but not for long before his Yamaha stopped. When interviewed afterwards Bill said: 'It sounded expensive, but I don't know what happened.'

In the 250cc race the following day Phil made a lightning start, while Bill struggled to get his machine going. But once under way he shot through the field and easily caught Phil who was struggling with water leaking out of his machine's cooling system.

Phil's engine subsequently seized and Bill was left to win the race comfortably. As in the 125cc event Bill set the pace in terms of lap times, and in both races he set new class records.

250cc West German GP, Nürburgring – 17 laps – 81.83 miles

1st	W.D. Ivy (Yamaha)
2nd	G. Molloy (Bultaco)
3rd	K. Andersson (Yamaha)
4th	R. Gould (Yamaha-Bultaco)
5th	J. Findlay (Bultaco)
6th	H. Santiago (Ossa)

Cervia

Next Bill travelled to Italy to race at Cervia, this international meeting was run on Thursday 25 April – only four days after the West German GP had ended. And he scored an impressive double, winning both the 125 and 250cc events. Actually, as one can see from the results, this meeting was as well-supported as any round of the World Championship series.

Bill also set the fastest lap in both races. His main opposition in the smaller event came from Suzuki-mounted Stuart Graham. Then, in the 250cc event, Bill and Phil Read fought for the lead throughout. Eventually Bill came out on top on the brake-punishing seaside circuit and won by a few machine lengths.

125cc Cervia – 20 laps – 43.5 miles

1st	W.D. Ivy (Yamaha)
2nd	S. Graham (Suzuki)
3rd	R. Bryans (Honda)
4th	F. Villa (Montesa)
5th	K. Carruthers (Honda)
6th	G. Sigura (MZ)

250cc Cervia – 22 laps – 47.8 miles

1st	W.D. Ivy (Yamaha)
2nd	P.W. Read (Yamaha)
3rd	R. Bryans (Honda)
4th	R. Pasolini (Benelli)
5th	F. Villa (Montesa)
6th	S. Grassetti (Benelli)

A very happy Bill Ivy, the 1967 125cc World Champion.

Almost Missed the Boat

Even though he was the existing 125cc World Champion, Bill almost failed to get a ride in the TT, as no entry had been received from him when the ACU closed the lists on Wednesday 1 May. And it was not until Saturday 4 May that Bill's application reached the organisation's headquarters. It had been posted in Barcelona, Spain, but the date stamp was indecipherable. 'He only just made it,' commented ACU secretary Ken Shierson, who continued, 'in fact, if we hadn't provisionally reserved two entries for works Yamahas in both 125 and 250cc races, his application would have had to be refused. Although Ivy obviously posted his letter only last week, his entry form had been countersigned by Yamaha as long ago as March.'

A Double Retirement

The second round of the Championship series took place at Barcelona, Spain, on Sunday 5 May. But sadly, Bill was to score no points – having to retire in both races. The only satisfaction was setting the fastest lap at 73.27mph (117.92km/h) in the 125cc class. In that race, with a mere five laps of the 27 lap race remaining, and well in the lead, Bill's Yamaha's crankshaft broke. Then for the first half of the 250cc event Bill and Phil Read put on a Yamaha tandem act until Bill was stopped with an ignition problem, leaving Heinz Rosner (MZ), the only other rider unlapped by winner Phil, to finish in second place.

Testing at Cadwell

After the Spanish GP, Bill had entries for the international meeting at Cadwell Park on Sunday 19 May. On Friday 17 May he carried out destruction tests with a brand new 125cc four-cylinder Yamaha at the Lincolnshire circuit.

A Wolfgang Gruber portrait of Bill during spring 1968.

He completed a total of 142 laps of the 1.4 mile (2.25km) club circuit, only stopping to take on fuel. Bill said: 'The idea was to give the bike a real thrashing to try and break it. We chose Cadwell because it's a place where the power is on and off all the time. On each lap I was changing gear 32 times when it was dry and more than that when the track was wet. In all I reckon I made 5,000 gear changes that day. I was taking the engine to 17,500rpm. That's 500 over the normal limit, but it still didn't break. But my wrists were clapped.'

Setting a Record Lap

Big stars draw big crowds and that was the message which came over loud and clear at Cadwell Park's international, held two days after Bill's test session described above. Attracted by an all-star entry – all attendance records for the picturesque miniature TT course in the heart of the Lincolnshire Wolds were broken. And the star names could not have come any bigger, as not only were Bill and his Yamaha teammate there but also present were the likes of Mike Hailwood (297cc Honda six) and Helmut Fath (URS four sidecar).

Riding his new (and fully tested!) Yamaha four, Bill rocketed his machine into the lead at the beginning of the 125cc event. But Stuart Graham pushed his works Suzuki so hard on the dodgy surface that Bill could not afford to ease the pace. Then Stuart's engine went off song, allowing Bill to build up a comfortable lead which he held to the finish. He also set a new class lap record of 68.67mph (110.49km/h) for Cadwell's full 2.3 mile (3.7km) GP circuit.

In the 250cc race, Bill, after a terrible start, had fought his way through to 11th spot but was forced to retire on the third lap, his four-cylinder machine firing on only two pots.

125cc Cadwell Park – 8 laps – 18 miles

1st	W.D. Ivy (Yamaha four)
2nd	T.E. Burgess (Shepherd Special)
3rd	V.D. Chatterton (Bultaco)
4th	M. Carney (Bultaco)
5th	K. Carruthers (Honda)
6th	B. Jansson (MZ)

TT Practice

Yamaha were obviously still worried about the reliability of their bikes and so requested that Bill and teammate Phil Read go the full three-lap race distance on their 125 mounts during the beginning of Isle of Man TT practice. But although this worked out for Phil, the same could not be said for Bill – he had to walk back to the start from Union Mills where his machine had stopped with plug trouble on the very first circuit.

In an attempt to eliminate plug-fouling NGK supplied Yamaha with special spark plugs with beryllium electrodes. These were claimed to have more resistance to oiling than previous types manufactured by NGK. At the same time NGK sources claimed that Yamaha had been getting through anything up to 100 per Grand Prix! What were they doing with them – eating them? The UK arm of NGK was run by Lester Simms, assisted by former world sidecar passenger, Stan Dibben. It should also be pointed out that plug readings were necessary to get top performance and were carried out by riders snapping the throttle shut while the engine was on full bore in

On friday 17 May 1968 Bill completed 142 laps of the 1.4 mile Cadwell Park club circuit on a brand new 125 four. Then on Sunday 19 May he won the race and set a new lap record on the same machine.

21
21

Bill rounding Quarter Bridge on the first lap of the 1968 Lightweight TT on his two-fifty four-cylinder Yamaha.

top gear, this indicating to the expert whether or not the right size of jet was fitted. If the jet was too small, the engine would eventually overheat (and seize), if it was too big, maximum power was reduced.

Making History

The front page headline of *Motor Cycle* dated Wednesday 12 June 1968 said it all: 'Ivy Joins The TT History Makers.' Going on to say: 'Weight-for-weight and foot-for-foot, Maidstone's diminutive Bill Ivy must be the greatest thing that ever hit motorcycle racing. For on Monday, from a standing start, he slashed 12.4 seconds off Mike Hailwood's 250cc Isle of Man mountain circuit lap record to notch a new high of 105.51mph [169.76km/h]. And, even more sensational, during last week's practice he became the first man ever to lap the same gruelling course at over 100mph [161km/h] on a 125cc machine.'

One has to remember this was only 11 years after the great Bob McIntyre had set the first-ever 100mph lap on the TT course on his 500cc four-cylinder, fully streamlined Gilera. And on a machine with an engine size 75 per cent smaller, Bill had gone round with a speed of 100.14mph (161.12km/h) in practice!

A Record Lap – and Victory

Shattering Mike Hailwood's lap record by over 1mph from a standing start, Bill scored his first 250cc (Lightweight) TT win on Monday 10 June. All this came after a tooth-and-nail duel with teammate Phil Read in the early stages. But both Bill and his machine finished 'battered and bruised' (*Motor Cycle*).

Opposite: Airborne at Ballagh Bridge on his way to victory in the 1968 Lightweight TT.

After he had snatched a 14.2 second lead on the opening lap, Bill had been slowed after one of his exhaust expansion chambers had been shattered by exuberant cornering and he had also painfully damaged his right ankle after catching his foot under its footrest.

And so, after whittling Bill's advantage away, Phil led by one second at Ramsey on the third lap. Then, as he climbed the Mountain next time around, with the race seemingly in the bag, a fragment of flint penetrated Read's rear tyre, putting him out and letting Bill back into the lead. Yet even then Bill's troubles were not yet over. After making a second scheduled pit stop to replenish the small fuel tank of his liquid-cooled four, he caught his right foot under its rest at Milntown on lap five and badly wrenched his ankle. All the same, he continued and went on to win at an average speed of 99.58mph (160.22km/h). Which considering all his problems was truly outstanding.

Lightweight 250cc TT – 6 laps – 226.38 miles

1st	W.D. Ivy (Yamaha)
2nd	R. Pasolini (Benelli)
3rd	H. Rosner (MZ)
4th	M. Uphill (Suzuki)
5th	R.A. Gould (Yamaha)
6th	W.A. Smith (Yamaha)
7th	S. Herrero (Ossa)
8th	J.H. Cooper (Padgett Yamaha)

A miniature of Bill's works 250 four-cylinder Yamaha, built by master modeller Ian Welsh of Edinburgh.

A Wolfgang Gruber shot of Bill at the 1968 Isle of Man TT.

Interviewed after the race, Bill said that after grinding his right boot away on corners he had struck the kerb at Milntown on the fifth lap and, loosing all feeling in his right foot, thought he had broken his toes. Asked if he thought of pulling in, he replied, 'not bloody likely. Luckily I had already refuelled, otherwise I just couldn't have pushed off again.'

As for Bill's machine, the new-pattern Dunlop tyres looked as if they could have continued for several more laps. His rear drive chain was also in good condition, although burnt petrol from the broken expansion chamber had transferred itself to the rear wheel rim. Combustion chambers were said to be 'perfect.'

The 125cc Race

Yamaha's un-official team orders stated that Phil Read was to win the Ultra Lightweight (125cc) TT held on Friday morning, 14 June 1968. However, just to show who was boss, Bill led for the first 2¼ laps of the three-lap race. He also eclipsed his practice ton-up lap with an even faster speed of 100.32mph (161.41km/h) second time around. Then, with 30 miles left, he deliberately eased the pace and Read, his engine a trifle overjetted for safety, romped home winner by a margin of nearly a minute. And after the race, when questioned 'was it or was it not a matter of team orders?' Bill gave 'a slow grin' (*Motor Cycle*) in response in front of the assembled press.

Ultra Lightweight 125cc TT – 3 laps – 113.19 miles

1st P.W. Read (Yamaha)
2nd W.D. Ivy (Yamaha)
3rd K. Carruthers (Honda)
4th T.H. Robb (Bultaco)
5th G. Keith (Montesa)
6th S. Murray (Honda)
7th J. Kiddie (Honda)
8th R.J. Dickinson (Honda)

In retrospect, Bill's 1968 Isle of Man performances were not only the high point of his racing career but were also, probably, the first spark which was later to ignite into open hostilities when it came down to Championship titles; remember that Bill felt he had assisted Phil to win the 125cc race. On the other hand Phil was to say that the Yamaha mechanics had jetted-up his machine, thus restricting the revs by 1,000.

However, at Mallory Park a couple of days late after that controversial 125cc TT result there were most definitely no team orders, as both Bill and Phil battled away for victory in the 250cc race at the annual Post TT meeting on Sunday 16 June – with Bill eventually coming out on top with the victory. He was also out in the 125cc class, but though he led initially he was soon out of the running with a sick engine.

After the Mallory meeting Bill put pen to paper to the motorcycling press (something he occasionally did if he felt strongly about the subject in question). He said in that letter – published in the 26 June 1968 issue of *Motor Cycle*:

'Please, organisers at Mallory Park, give us a little bit of a chance. First you notified the time practice periods started, then altered times were written on a board in the warming-up area. This meant that someone had to be in the enclosure all the time to watch for any changes. The next part of this letter is to the official who said to my mechanic [Ron Eldridge]: "We always have trouble with that bloody Ivy." Perhaps he does not realise that our water-cooled Yamahas take about 10 minutes to warm up. Immediately they are hot enough all the plugs have to be changed – which takes about three or four minutes. After this the bike must be used at racing speed within five minutes or the whole procedure has to be gone through again. At Mallory last week we were allowed four practice sessions, each so short that there was time only for three laps. The problem for me was that I had to get straight off one bike on to the other – and I hadn't enough mechanics to cope with the warming up and plug changing on two bikes at the same time. Consequently, we did not get time to look at the plugs, let alone the jets or the gearing. About an hour later three-lap-dash practices were repeated. Please, Mr Official, don't you realise that if you gave us a chance you wouldn't have trouble with "that bloody Ivy"? And if you want exotic works machinery, you must expect to give the riders and mechanics proper practice facilities – just imagine trying to fob off a formula one car team with four five-minute practice sessions before a major international meeting!'

This letter also goes to show that Bill was not only someone who was not afraid to voice his views but also could clearly see problems when they occurred – and would present his views when many other riders would either have not been able to express themselves or would not have felt strongly enough to have compiled such a letter.

Mechanics

In his letter regarding Mallory Park, Bill brings up the issue of not having enough mechanics. It is interesting to note that the majority of the Yamaha works mechanics had returned to Japan after the Isle of Man – in fact only two were left. And for some reason, best known to Yamaha themselves, these two were supposed to supervise the work done on the bikes by Ron Eldridge and Roy Robinson, the mechanics employed by Bill and Phil Read respectively, but not to work on the bikes themselves.

Car Problems

Bill and Phil Read were to miss the early practice sessions for the Dutch TT at Assen, because Bill's Ferrari car, in which they were both travelling, suffered a broken camshaft as they were leaving Bill's London home at Heston. They eventually arrived mid-way through practicing, just when rain was bucketing down. To make matters worse, Phil's caravan, which was supposed to have been towed to the circuit by mechanic Roy Robinson, had been left in Belgium due to a misunderstanding.

Dutch TT

Of Bill's two scheduled races in the Dutch TT on Saturday 29 June, the first to take place was the 250cc event. This saw Bill and Phil put on a high-speed exhibition on their four-cylinder Yamahas, swapping places all the way and cornering side by side – a sight which really set the massed throngs of spectators (around 100,000) buzzing with excitement. Eventually, Bill nipped ahead to win, the pair of riders finishing almost two minutes ahead of Renzo Pasolini (Benelli) and Heinz Rosner (MZ) on his own in fourth place, half a minute astern of the Italian. Bill also set the fastest lap, with a speed of 89.27mph (143.71km/h).

Bill went on to not only win the race at Assen on his two-fifty but also set yet another record lap.

Leading Phil Read during the 250cc Dutch TT at Assen on 29 June 1968.

250cc Dutch TT, Assen – 17 laps – 81.38 miles

1st	W.D. Ivy (Yamaha)
2nd	P.W. Read (Yamaha)
3rd	R. Pasolini (Benelli)
4th	H. Rosner (MZ)
5th	R. Gould (Yamaha-Bultaco)
6th	S. Herrero (Ossa)

As for the 125cc race which came later, this was unfortunate for Bill. At the start his Yamaha was slow to fire and he was rammed by Sweden's Kent Andersson (MZ), who, a second earlier, had been rammed by another rider. In the confusion Bill's left foot was run over. He then did a lap but stopped and was subsequently taken to hospital with a suspected broken ankle. Although Phil Read did win the race he was very fortunate, as his Yamaha was misfiring on one cylinder.

The Bad Luck Continues

Eight days later on Sunday 7 July, the Grand Prix circus moved to Spa Francorchamps, the scene of the Belgian round. Here, in front of another 100,000-strong crowd, Bill, fighting the pain of his injured ankle, stormed into an early, commanding lead and in the process set the fastest lap at the incredible speed of 125.41mph (201.82km/h). But then he struck problems, which meant he was forced to stop at the pits and, although he got going again, he eventually was forced to retire. Again Phil Read was in luck, as at the end of the first lap he was forced into the pits – his machine down on power. A change of plug saw him get away at the tail end of the field. With four laps of the nine lap race to go, he was through to third and gaining on Rod Gould's Yamaha TD1C powered Bultaco special and race leader Heinz Rosner (MZ). As they rounded La Source hairpin and dropped down to start the last lap, Phil was right on the East German's tail and he nipped ahead as they screamed past the pits to begin the final circuit. So it was Phil and not Bill who won yet another GP. There was no 125cc race in Belgium.

Sachsenring

The next round in the Championship trail came at the Sachsenring, East Germany on 14 July: with over 200,000 people packed around the 5.35 mile (8.6km) circuit.

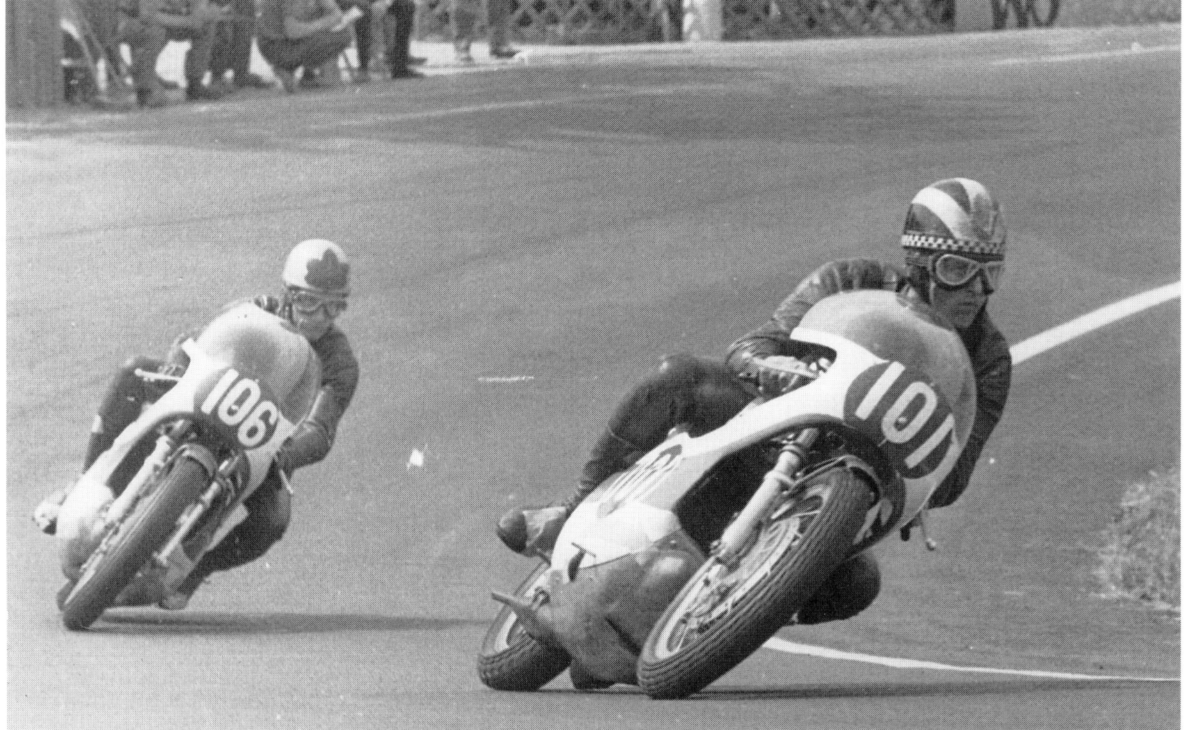

The two Yamaha works men, Phil (101) and Bill (106) disputing the lead during the 250cc race at the Sachsenring, East Germany, 14 July 1968.

Thirty-eight machines lined up for the 125cc race and 36 of these were locally built MZs. But after Heinz Rosner had led for almost a lap, the familiar race pattern of the two Yamahas took over – this after Bill had been yet again forced to stop for a fresh plug after a sluggish start – then proceeded to set a record lap of 100.25mph (161.36km/h) in his pursuit of his teammate, which although ultimately unsuccessful was nonetheless highly impressive.

As for the 250cc event, this was won by Bill, but only after Phil had himself been forced to pit – and then later went out and set a record lap himself! The *Motor Cycle* race report in the 17 July 1968 issue had this to say of Phil's actions: 'Lap eight – and there is consternation at the pits. Read pulled in for the briefest of stops and screamed off again as soon as Ivy howled by. It looked for all the world as if the situation was contrived, but lynx-eyed observers swore some water was sloshed into Read's radiator – apparently his engine was overheating.'

Bill taking his V4 Yamaha to victory in the 250cc race at the East German GP, 14 July 1968.

Bill receiving the victor's laurels after winning the 1968 250cc East German Grand Prix; Phil Read looks on.

250cc East German GP, Sachsenring – 15 laps – 80.32 miles

1st	W.D. Ivy (Yamaha)
2nd	P.W. Read (Yamaha)
3rd	H. Rosner (MZ)
4th	R. Gould (Yamaha Bultaco)
5th	W.G. Molloy (Bultaco)
6th	J. Findlay (Bultaco)

Czech GP

The Czech Grand Prix held over the 8.66 mile (139.33km) Brno circuit was probably the event which created the ill-feeling between Bill and Phil which was to only get worse as the second half of the 1968 season unfolded.

Even before the actual racing got under way many riders were complaining that the circuit was more akin to a skating rink. Bill himself commented: 'I've never been on anything like it. You can spin the rear wheel on straights in every gear. The trouble is that the chippings have sunk into the surface and all that is left is bare tar.'

Speeds were down by a vast amount – Bill was taking the fast curves through the village after the start in third gear on his 250cc Yamaha instead

Bill pictured by Wolfgang Gruber during the 125cc Czech Grand Prix before his crash...

of sixth (his big Yamaha having an eight-speed gearbox). That was in practice. As it turned out, the two-fifty race was the only dry event. As fellow rider Jack Findlay said: 'It's diabolical when its wet. You do two-wheel drifts all over the place. It's really frightening. You've just got to concentrate on staying upright, you can't race.'

But of course Bill and Phil were racing – all very serious stuff as World Championship titles were at stake. The course at Brno was a real road circuit. It weaved its way through villages, across open farmland and up and down among forests, even swooping into a suburb of the city at one point.

Race day got under way on Sunday 21 July with the 125cc event – on wet roads. And riding to Yamaha's agreed instructions Bill was following the race leader Phil Read's Yamaha, when on lap six Bill came off his machine as the two were in close formation coming into a fast uphill left-hander. Bill said: 'I saw Read's rear wheel start to slide and I thought he was coming off.' He instinctively took avoiding action but the surface was too slick and down he went. Bill continued: 'I thought that we'd both come off but when I looked round for Phil, he wasn't there.' And with an injured knee Bill was taken off on a stretcher. Even so, he was credited with the fastest lap at 87.8mph (141.36km/h).

As the *Motor Cycle* headline read: 'Rebel Read wins Bill Ivy's race.' Going on to say: 'Bill Ivy's slide off his Yamaha during the 125cc class of Sunday's Czech Grand Prix, the seventh World-Championship round of the year, may have far-reaching repercussions for, although he was fit enough to compete in the 250cc race later in the day, he could not match the speed of teammate Phil Read, who ignored Yamaha instructions that Ivy was to be first. Ivy took second place – and made no secret of his anger that Read had disobeyed "standing orders" that Ivy is to win the 250cc grands prix whenever possible, while Read takes the 125cc events.'

The facts were that, after the Czech GP, Bill led the 250cc table by two points – 38 to Phil's 36. And after Bill's mishap, Read was now 28 points clear of his nearest challenger (Bill) in the 125cc table – and only a single victory away from clinching his first Championship title in that class.

Yes, in retrospect, the 1968 Czech GP was the turning point in the Ivy-Read relationship – and the beginning of an ever-increasing war between the two both on and off the track.

...and afterwards, watching Phil Read disappear after falling from his 125 Yamaha. The incident was to spark open warfare between the two riders for the second half of the 1968 season.

After his crash in the 125cc Czech GP Bill was knocked about enough to require help by officials, as shown by this photograph.

The Storm Gathers

The gathering storm regarding the 250cc World Championship came to a head following the Czech Grand Prix, when Bill and Phil Read had disagreed on this issue.

In fact, Phil was quoted by *Motor Cycle* on 31 July 1968 as saying: 'I ride to win or quit.' He dropped a bombshell by saying that he had decided to quit the Yamaha team unless the factory rescinded an order that he must let Bill Ivy win the three remaining 250cc rounds and so take the Championship.

Cabling Read from Japan the previous week, Yamaha officials insisted on his adhering to team orders and threatened to withdraw his machines if he failed to do so. Read also believed the cable was inspired by a message to the company from Bill and the Yamaha mechanics, giving their version of the Czech incident. Phil commented: 'I thought we were riding to orders until the manufacturers' title had been clinched and that after that it was a free-for-all.' He continued: 'I'd rather not ride if I have to finish second. In fact, I shan't if Yamaha insist on my obeying their orders. I've cabled them, explaining my side of the story. Whether I ride for them again depends on their answer. Having stuck my neck out to help develop the Yamaha fours, I want an equal chance now that they're good. If Bill reckons he can beat me, let him prove it.'

When asked for his views, this is what Bill told Mick Woollett: 'I don't know what Phil's moaning about. I've let him win the 125cc title; why shouldn't he let me win the 250 class? The only reason I fell off in Czecho was that I slowed down to follow him. I only wish this business had happened earlier in the year. Then we'd have found out who was the better rider.'

Power Politics

Following these statements, all hell was let loose.

First came another row between the two riders, this time over entries for the Ulster Grand Prix on 7 August. Although initially Phil Read had arranged that he and Bill would contest only the 250cc, both later confirmed their entries for both the 125 and 250cc race. This switch followed a phone call from Bill to race secretary, Billy McMaster. The latter saying: 'Ivy told me that Phil Read had no authority to arrange his starts and said he wanted to compete in the 125cc class.' This was subsequently followed by an entry being received from Phil for the 125cc class. McMaster followed these revelations by commenting: 'It looks as though the days of Yamaha team riding are over, so we should be in for two great battles at Dundrod.'

Next the whole matter reached the FIM (the sport's governing body), with its president Henri Burik saying: 'Certainly the Yamaha cable to Read giving him instructions not to win a race is illegal as far as FIM regulations are concerned. This is conduct against the best interests of the sport and could lead to the rider being suspended if he were to obey such an order.' Burik also went on to say that, in the past, people have kept quiet about team orders, and that: 'Now we shall take the matter up with the manufacturers [Yamaha] who may not realise they cannot contravene FIM rules.'

This resulted in the FIM being contacted by Yamaha, saying: 'We don't know their statements but they will race at Ulster GP. Thanks [for] your courtesy.'

Although Bill finished runner-up in the 250cc race at the 1968 Czech Grand Prix, his performance was below par due to the battered and bruised state of his body. Here is a rostrum shot, showing the winner Phil Read, Bill and third-place man Heinz Rosner (MZ). By studying this photograph it is possible to see that Bill is not his usual confident, bubbly self.

The East German MZ rider Heinz Rosner was to put in a number of excellent performances in the 1968 250cc World Championship series; eventually finishing third overall behind the two Yamaha stars.

Well, Phil Read had managed to outsmart Bill, but ultimately the whole issue was to lead to Yamaha quitting GPs at the end of that season – so both he and Bill lost their jobs. In addition, by his actions Phil got Bill upset and this played into the former's hands. As explained elsewhere, Bill's Achilles heel was that he could become very angry and upset when he felt aggrieved. And obviously this was exactly how he felt with Phil Read.

Very quickly the two men had gone from being the best of friends to hated foes. To the author's mind, Phil *knew* the verbal agreement between himself, Bill and Yamaha regarding the Championship position; but immediately his own (125cc) title was assured, he then conveniently forgot the agreement, simply for his own benefit. Somehow, Bill, if the boot had been on the other foot, would have honoured that agreement. So Bill was angry and upset – the very things which were most likely to affect his on-track performances. Funnily enough, the outcome of Phil's actions had exactly same affect on both Bill and Yamaha. They both adhered to a similar code of conduct: an agreement is an agreement. However, Phil Read did not. Instead, his code was: win at all costs, victory is the god.

Finnish Grand Prix

Between the Czech and Ulster rounds came the Finnish Grand Prix at Imatra on Sunday 4 August, and it brought into focus the needle which existed between the two Yamaha stars.

After their clash in Czechoslovakia two weeks earlier, Phil and Bill had given the racing public an inside glimpse of power politics at the highest level of the sport.

Intrigued, the public wanted to know more and so flocked to Imatra, the tree-lined 3.74 mile (6km) circuit next to the Russian border.

First, in a tense 125cc battle, with four seconds sliced off the lap record, Read won after Ivy slowed with a worn out front brake – the linings of which had been renewed for the race. Read's victory meant that he was the 1968 125cc World Champion.

Then, on a wet track, Phil shadowed Bill in the 250cc race then went ahead and, in attempting to get back in front, Bill crashed, knocking the leg he had damaged in Czechoslovakia. An X-ray revealed a minor crack in one of the bones – but he was able to walk. However, Read's win had given him the lead in the 250cc Championship.

Phil Read and Bill – once teammates, but sadly things turned sour after the 1968 Czech Grand Prix.

Between Finland and Ulster came the Hutchinson 100 meeting at Brands Hatch – Phil took the Melano Trophy, while Bill notched a lap record. Even though strictly speaking it was a domestic British meeting, it was evident for everyone to see just what a high level of needle existed between the two Yamaha riders. In the same week as the Brands Hatch meeting, *Motor Cycle* interviewed three of the world's greatest riders to see what their reaction was to 'riding to orders'. Here is what they said:

Stanley Woods: 'The man who pays the piper calls the tune. So manufacturers who spend many thousands [read millions in today's world!] of pounds on racing must be able to demand a certain amount of discipline.'

Geoff Duke: 'From a manufacturer's point of view, riding to orders is a must. The only real point is how obvious you make it to the fans.'

Mike Hailwood: 'When you've got a team with two riders of similar ability, they must ride to orders – otherwise they'll be falling off and blowing up the bikes in their efforts to beat one another.'

This photograph typifies the intense competition between the two Yamaha riders which took place during the latter half of 1968. Both men did not want to be second best.

It was sweet revenge for Bill at the Ulster Grand Prix at Dundrod on Saturday 17 August 1968, the ninth round of the World Championship series – as he scored a magnificent double victory. He is seen here on the 250cc model.

Sweet Revenge

The Ulster Grand Prix, staged on Saturday 17 August 1968, was a special day for Bill, as after his spate of crashes and defeats he scored a magnificent double over the 7.4 mile (11.9km) Dundrod road circuit. Riding with just the right blend of coolness and dash, he always looked to have the situation under control as he fought out two great races with his Yamaha teammate and arch rival, Phil Read.

The 40th Ulster

The 1968 Ulster meeting was the 40th in the series which originated on the famous Clady circuit in 1922 before moving to the shorter Dundrod course in 1953. And the 125cc race was run in sunny weather before a record crowd of 90,000, making a promising start to the programme. Bill took the lead and for the first six laps there was nothing in it between the two Yamahas. Then Phil, in his own words, 'ran out of brakes at the hairpin.' Although he managed to get round, Bill gained a vital 200-yard advantage. Sensing that victory was his, Bill really turned up the wick but Phil never gave up and actually closed the gap slightly, though he never got to grips with his teammate. The two Yamaha men lapped all the other riders in the race at least once.

Phil Read leads Bill during their hard fought Ulster GP race, but Bill came out on top even though Phil set a record lap for the class.

125cc Ulster GP, Dundrod – 11 laps – 82 miles

1st	W.D. Ivy (Yamaha)
2nd	P.W. Read (Yamaha)
3rd	H. Rosner (MZ)
4th	G. Molloy (Bultaco)
5th	M.K. McGarrity (Honda)
6th	K. Carruthers (Honda)

But of course the 125 event was regarded by both Bill and Phil as only a curtain-raiser for the vital 250cc race which followed. Bill simply had to win to keep his Championship hopes alive. However, his chances seemed to plummet to zero when rain lashed across the Dundrod road circuit high above Belfast as they waited on the grid – as Read was considered one of the best wet-weather riders and this, coupled to his greater knowledge of the circuit, seemed to be swinging things in his favour. But Bill simply refused to be anything but positive, and even though the odds appeared to be stacked against him he sat in Phil's slipstream for five laps before going ahead. Three laps later a stone flung up from his rear wheel punctured his teammate's radiator and as coolant drained out the engine overheated and eventually seized. This left Bill leading the Championship by two points – Bill with 46, Phil with 44.

After the race, a smiling Bill said: 'Very enjoyable. Now the winner at Monza takes all.'

250cc Ulster GP, Dundrod – 15 laps – 112 miles

1st	W.D. Ivy (Yamaha)
2nd	H. Rosner (MZ)
3rd	R. Gould (Yamaha Bultaco)
4th	W. Molloy (Bultaco)
5th	M. Uphill (Suzuki)
6th	K. Andersson (Yamaha)

Double Ulster GP winner Bill Ivy in his Carnaby Street mod gear, photographed with Tommy Robb's wife Maureen.

Japanese Grand Prix Axed

At the end of August came news that the Japanese Grand Prix, the final round of the World Championship, had officially been axed. This followed persistent rumours that it would not be run. With the French GP already struck off in May, the Japanese decision reduced the number of World Championship meetings to 10, and this meant that the 250cc title, the only solo championship still to be clinched, would definitely be settled at the Italian round at Monza on Sunday 15 September.

Between the Ulster round and his trip to Italy, Bill took in two of the end-of-season British internationals at Snetterton on Sunday 31 August and at Oulton Park the following day, Bank Holiday Monday 1 September. His only victory came at Oulton, when riding a four-cylinder model he also set the fastest lap in the 19-lap, 52.46 mile (84.40km) 250cc event, with a speed of 95.39mph (153.48km/h).

Although Bill won the 125cc race at the Italian Grand Prix at Monza on 15 September, he came out second best to Phil Read in the all-important 250cc event – and thus lost the world title.

Monza

And so to Monza, and what turned out to be a miserable day for Bill in more than one respect. For a start, it was a rain-drenched affair and although he had won the 125cc race and set the fastest lap, with Phil Read suffering a last-lap crash, in the all-important 250cc Championship decider it was Read who came out on top. During practice he had been troubled by a misfire and had been over two seconds a lap down on Bill. But when the race began after the lunch break, it was Phil who had a 30-yard lead at the end of the first lap of the 3.5 mile (5.6km) circuit. Then, attempting to close the gap, Bill almost overdid things at the Parabolia and lost nearly 10 seconds. This gave Read the break he needed and thereafter Bill steadily lost ground, with Phil 20 seconds up after six laps. And so as one period newspaper said: 'Flouting Yamaha team orders, Phil Read beat teammate Bill Ivy in the 250cc class at Monza to add the 250cc world title to the 125cc Championship he clinched earlier in the year.'

With his victory, Phil Read brought his Championship tally to five wins and two second places – exactly the same as Bill's. But in a rarely-used tie-decider, Read took the title because of a lower total time in the races in which they had both finished. This gave Phil Read his first-ever double world crown; and left Bill precisely nothing – a bitter pill to swallow.

One More Chapter

However, the controversy did not stop there. Because after Read's Monza victory Bill had hurriedly scribbled a protest against the former. It ended behind closed doors after the finish of the meeting when the international jury were told that the objection had been overruled by the clerk of the course.

Bill's protest alleged that the front number plate of Phil's Yamaha, identical to his own, did not conform to FIM specification; and that Read's chain was not the make he was under contract to use.

If it had been upheld, the objection would have cost Phil the championship. For even if he, too, had been excluded because of an illegal number plate, Bill would have taken the title on his pre-Monza performances.

But the clerk of the course ruled that any protest about a machine's legality should have been made before the race and that the make of chain was immaterial.

Commenting on the incident, Bill said: 'I had nothing to lose.' Continuing: 'Before the race, Read said that if I won he would protest that I was under the FIM weight of 9st 6lb. If people say I'm a bad sportsman, being a good one didn't do me any good.'

As for Phil Read's reaction, he commented: 'I'm shattered. I can't imagine anyone making such an obviously transparent protest.'

Monza, September 1968, after the 250cc race. Bill's expression says it all – Read has won. Also in the picture is the third finisher, the Spanish rider Santiago Herrero (Ossa).

Season's End

But Monza was not the end of Bill's season, as he had already entered for non-Championship meetings at Mallory Park (22 September), Riccione (29 September) and finally Brands Hatch (6 October).

Although he took part in all three, somehow his heart did not seem to be in it. His only victories came in the 125cc class. With the 250cc Yamaha he either finished runner-up to Read or retired. However, in the final race at Brands Hatch, Bill rode a 500 Seeley in the Redex Trophy race (his only non-Yamaha appearance of 1968), finishing fourth on John Cooper's bike behind Giacomo Agostini (MV Agusta), Alan Barnett (Matchless Metisse) and Dave Croxford (Seeley).

The 'To Quit' Stories

Immediately after Brands Hatch came newspaper reports that Bill had decided to quit. Earlier, having failed to persuade Mike Hailwood to sign for them, Benelli had offered works bikes to Bill for the remainder of the season,

On 29 September 1968 Bill raced at a non-Championship meeting at Riccione in Italy. While there he had his helmet stolen and had to use Luigi Taveri's. Bill is seen here (20) leading Giacomo Agostini during the 350cc event on an overboard (251cc) Yamaha.

Bill's final race of 1968 came with a one-off outing on a 500 Seeley in the Redex Trophy event at Brands Hatch on 6 October; he finished fourth.

but this plan had been vetoed by Yamaha. Eager to ride the 350 and 500 Italian four-cylinder machines, Bill had immediately cabled the Japanese company for permission. To his disappointment they refused, even though he had no further racing commitments to them under his contract which was due to expire on 31 December 1968.

Respected *Motor Cycle* journalist David Dixon writing in the 16 October 1968 issue of that journal got things pretty well right, as the following reveals:

'In spite of confirming that he was not joking when he announced his retirement after the Race of the South [Brands Hatch], Bill Ivy may very well be racing next year. This, I hasten to add, is purely my opinion after talking to Bill last week, for the grounds on which he has retired are not the usual ones of being over the top. Apart from an odd day off, he is still in ace form and has some useful racing years ahead of him. His present frame of mind is understandable after a disappointing season in which he expected to win at least one title. Given a couple of months away from the racing scene Bill will, I feel sure, be itching to have another go. A love of racing, and all that goes with it, does not die because of a few upsets.'

David Dixon was to be proved absolutely correct in his observations. The story is fully revealed in the following chapter. The Bill Ivy racing story was set to continue into 1969.

Chapter 9

Jawa

At the end of 1968, after months of speculation and uncertainty about their plans, Yamaha finally announced that it had decided to quit World Championship racing. At the same time both Phil Read and Bill Ivy had been officially notified that their services as riders would no longer be required. It was also revealed that both Phil and Bill had been offered the loan of new 250 and 250cc twin-cylinder air-cooled production racers (the TD2 and TR2).

First Contact

As for Bill, he was, to say the least, uncertain of how to proceed. Certainly he was jobless, and he was hesitating in his decision whether to concentrate on racing cars (Formula 2) or still pursue a career on bikes – even though he had been quoted as saying he would 'never race motorcycles again.'

What actually happened was this: having been a close friend of Mike Hailwood and Luigi Taveri, he had travelled to Zurich in Switzerland to

At the end of December 1968 Bill travelled to Zurich, Switzerland, to celebrate New Year's Eve at Luigi Taveri's home. Among the other guests were Mike Hailwood (seen here with Bill and Luigi) plus Frantisek Stastny, the Czech Jawa rider.

A fun shot of Bill and Royal Air Force man Chris Conn, pictured together in Switzerland during the winter of 1968.

celebrate New Year's Eve at Luigi's home. Among the other guests was Frantisek Stastny, the Czech works Jawa rider. At that time, Jawa had on the stocks a V4 liquid-cooled 350cc racing machine. The development history is contained within a separate boxed section in this chapter, but suffice to say it had been around since 1967 and it had been tested and raced occasionally during the 1968 season. However, only a third place in the local Czech Grand Prix and fourth in the Ulster GP (ridden on both occasions by Stastny) had been worth a mention. A seven-speeder producing almost 70bhp, it had an engine layout similar to that of the factory Yamahas that Bill was so familiar with. Latest modifications to the Jawa design included a lower frame, positive lubrication for the big-ends and main bearing, and a Czech-built transistorised ignition system.

The Letter

When the ever-popular Frantisek Stastny returned home to Czechoslovakia in the early days of January 1969 he took back to his bosses a letter drafted by Bill. As a free agent, Bill wrote that he was ready to join Jawa provided, however, that the money was suitable.

Jawa V4

For well over a decade the Czech Jawa factory was racing with four-stroke dohc twins at Grand Prix level. However, by the mid-1960s it was already obvious that a more modern, two-stroke design was needed.

Early 1964 saw the first signs that Jawa was considering a switch to two-strokes, including a story in the 16 April issue of *Motor Cycle* proclaiming: 'Jawa are to race a four-cylinder five-hundred.' The engine was said to be a square-four with rotary inlet valves. *Motor Cycle* went on to say: 'Brainchild of a Jawa factory mechanic, the project was enthusiastically received by the firm who foresaw tremendous possibilities in the design when developed.'

Then, in 1965, at the season opener at the Nürburgring, an experimental 250 two-stroke twin made its debut. This had disc-valves and closely resembled the earlier air-cooled MZ design. Development of the 250 (and also a 125) continued during that year.

Influenced by the advent of the new Yamaha fours (and also the six-cylinder Hondas), Jawa pressed ahead with two-stroke development, which by 1966 included a new twin-cylinder 350. However, this did not prove successful; the air-cooled 350 twin being used for the first time during practice for the Czech GP, with disappointing results. Then, practicing for the Italian GP, works rider Franta Stastny was lucky to escape injury when the engine seized at high speed, throwing him down the road.

After this debacle it was decided to concentrate on the disc-valve 500 four-cylinder described earlier. Now liquid-cooled, with the cylinders redesigned in vee-formation, the first official hint came in September 1966 that a 350 version was also on the cards. The engines of both 500 and 350 models were reported as having two crankshafts geared together and using six-speed gearboxes.

The new 350 V4 two-stroke made its race debut at the Dutch TT in June 1967. Finished only a week earlier, it seized three times in practice and had a final seizure while being raced by Gustav Havel (second string to Stastny).

The engine followed the vee layout of the Yamaha fours – though the Jawa had in fact been thought up entirely independently. The two crankshafts were geared together – and used much of the technology gleaned by the development team from an air cooled 125 v-twin which had been constructed for test purposes.

Like the 125, the 350 used disc-valve induction, which designer Zdenek Tichy considered absolutely vital for ultimate performance (as did MZ and Yamaha). The 344.5cc (48 x 47.6mm) engine had a compression ratio of 16:1 and usable power between 9,000 and 13,500rpm. Drive to the rear wheel was by chain, via a seven-speed gearbox.

Unlike Yamaha, water-cooling was on the thermosyphon principle, and it was generally accepted that the appearance of the Czech unit was a lot tidier than the Japanese fours, although in 1967 it was not in the same performance category.

On the prototype engine there were four sets of contact breakers and four Amal GP carburettors, the latter each having their own flexible mounted float chamber.

Stastny, now back in the saddle following yet another crash, tested an example of a 250cc V4 that summer at Prague airport. He was claimed to have clocked 145mph (233km/h). This machine was very similar to the 350, but used Dell'Orto carbs. Three weeks after the Dutch TT, Jawa turned up at the East German Grand Prix with their old four-stroke 350 twins! The new V4, first used in Holland, was said to be 'under further development' back in the factory in an effort to overcome continuing main bearing failures and piston seizures.

A pump was now used in the water-cooling system, while tests were being carried out to determine if fitting an oil pump would improve engine lubrication.

Except for a fourth by Havel (in the domestic Czech GP), 1967 proved very much a year of experiment rather than results. Quite simply the new two-strokes were in need of a lengthy development period and were not yet up to the rigours of long Grand Prix-type events.

It was much the same in 1968 and it was mid-season before the V4 350 first finished a Grand Prix. This was appropriately at the home round at Brno, where Stastny, now back to race fitness, brought one of the fours home in third place despite being hampered by cramp. Stastny's average speed was 85.65mph (137.81km/h), compared to race winner Giacomo Agostini's MV Agusta of 88.86mph (142.97km/h). Stastny followed this up with a fourth in Ulster and a sixth in Italy.

At long last it appeared that the Jawa development team was getting its act together. Certainly the 350 V4 was quick, around 160mph (257.44km/h), but Stastny openly admitted to being none too sure of its reliability and it was still prone to seizures.

As we know at the end of that season, 1968, Yamaha announced its retirement from Grand Prix racing. A decision which was ultimately to lead Jawa and Bill Ivy to join forces. With this history was to be set on a new and ultimately tragic path.

The letter from Bill was presented to Josef Jozif, then general manager of Jawa's Research and Development Institute, who in turn asked the Institute's top management how to respond to Bill's request.

The factory's engineers and other technicians were enthusiastic that a rider of Bill's standing wished to pilot their machine – and assured Jozif that the bike was 'race ready and competitive.'

So in the 15 January 1969 issue of *Motor Cycle* there was a front page news story entitled 'Ivy-Jawa GP Talks.' In this it continued: 'Jawa are inviting Bill Ivy to Prague to discuss a contract for the 1969 classics after learning that the former Yamaha teamster would like to ride their four-cylinder 350 and 377cc two-strokes in the World Championships.' And that: 'The Czech company are stepping up their efforts to ready the machines.'

Dreams

Of course, the press had something of a field day. For example, Mick Woollett's column *Race Gossip* saw: 'The withdrawal of Yamaha from Grand Prix racing could prove to be a real blessing in disguise, for it means that the previously Yamaha-dominated lightweight classes are thrown wide open.' And that: 'Phil Read and Bill Ivy, two of the very best riders in the game, are free to ride other bikes.'

In fact, Read had already made his interest in the Read (no relation – dealers in Leytonstone, East London) Weslake racer project clear. And so the news that Bill had approached Jawa led Mick Woollett to do a spot of dreaming. He commented: 'So, instead of fighting among themselves in the lightweight races, there is a very real chance that these two super-stars will move up to challenge Giacomo Agostini (MV) and Renzo Pasolini (Benelli) in the big classes.' Mick Woollett concluding: 'Now it only needs Benelli to persuade Mike Hailwood to join them and the prospect for an outstanding season of World Championship racing would be very bright.'

During spring 1969 Bill was switching between bikes (Jawa) and a car (a self-financed Brabham Formula 2). Many informed observers felt that he could have made it to the very top on four wheels.

Bill at the wheel of the Brabham during the Formula 2 race at Thruxton, on 7 April 1969. He finished fourth in his heat against top line opposition, behind Jackie Stewart, Jean-Pierre Beltoise and Graham Hill. In the final at Thruxton Bill was holding a superb fifth before his engine blew up. Only Jochan Rindt had been faster in practice, and Bill had set an equal time with none other that Jackie Stewart!

Benelli, Jawa or Kirby?

For a man who had claimed to have retired from motorcycle racing, Bill Ivy was certainly acting in a strange way. Not only had he written to Czechoslovakia asking if Jawa could provide him works bikes for the season, but at the beginning of February 1969 came news from Italy that Benelli had also received a letter from Bill.

Dated mid-January, Bill's letter pointed out that he was without bikes as Yamaha had quit racing, and asked whether Benelli would be interested in his riding for them. But the Italian firm replied that it already had enough riders (Renzo Pasolini as their number one).

Yet another development had seen the MCD (Motor Circuit Development), owners of Brands Hatch, Snetterton, Mallory Park and Oulton Park, come out saying they would like to see Bill racing again – and that his former sponsor Tom Kirby 'had bikes ready if he wants them.'

But almost immediately it was revealed that Bill was expected in Prague to have talks on terms for the forthcoming season.

From Czech sources the author has been able to establish that during Bill's visit he had explained that he was 'ready to ride the bike.' However, he (Bill) added that Yamaha had paid him 28,000 US dollars a year and he was prepared to sign a Jawa contract for some 20,000 US dollars – but not less. This figure was still too much for Jawa and it began to look like negotiations would come to an end. However, the financial issue was solved in the end, with Bill agreeing to take some 250cc Jawa production racing motorcycles in lieu of money. And so the deal was done.

Bill with Franta Stastny working on the four-cylinder Jawa machine at Cesenatico, Italy, 13 April 1969.

The Agreement

Bill took delivery of five machines – selling them at once and thus receiving some cash. It was agreed that Bill would take part in the 'entire World Championship programme with the exception of the Isle of Man TT,' all appearance monies would be his and it would be up to him to obtain special parts from various suppliers outside the Communist Bloc (for example Mikuni carburettors, NGK spark plugs, Dunlop tyres etc) as well as remuneration if paid.

Testing Times

The first test of Bill on the 350cc V4 was scheduled to take place on a British circuit – Brands Hatch – in early March. Travelling with the Jawa would be chief designer Zdenek Tichy and race mechanic Jaroslav Seda. For this test the machine was to be fitted with a Czech-made transistorised ignition system, which Jawa said had passed a 'rigorous' test session at the end of February.

But before this test could take place Bill suffered a racing car crash while testing at Oulton Park during the last week of February. His Formula 2 Brabham had spun as he was accelerating away from Cascades (downhill, left-hand corner) resulting in the car leaving the track, after which it had hit a bank, deflecting it back across the track and on to the rough ground between circuit and lake. Even though the car looked badly damaged in fact this was only superficial, while Bill, strapped in with safety belts, was virtually unharmed.

Fully Fit

But if any doubts existed over Bill's fitness after this racing car accident these were soon put to rest, as in the same week the former World Champion dashed from the Post Office Tower in central London to London Airport (Heathrow) on Friday 28 February riding a 750cc BSA Rocket Three as a test for the forthcoming (May 1969) *Daily Mail* Transatlantic Air Race. The idea of the test day was to provide experience of the problems involved in reaching the airport in the shortest possible time. Cars, including a three-litre Maserati, also took part in the trials but finished well behind the two-wheelers. And to prove that Bill had lost none of his competitive spirit, he set the fastest time of all the participants.

The Test Takes Place

Finally, at Brands Hatch on Wednesday 5 March 1969, Bill tried out the latest 350 V4 Jawa. Inside two relatively short sessions the former 125cc World Champion was lapping the Kentish short circuit in 58 seconds – just outside the official record.

During the Brands test the *Motor Cycle* reported: 'the Jawa appeared to handle exceptionally well, even round the tricky Paddock Hill Bend.' And the journal also said: 'Ivy was so pleased with the bike's performance that plans to take it to Snetterton for more tests on Thursday [the following day] were abandoned.'

A Surprise for Bill

A surprise bid by Bill to have his first race on one of the 350cc V4s at Riccione in Italy on Sunday 30 March was not to be. Although Bill had made arrangements with the Jawa factory to prepare a machine for the international meeting, after spending a reported £2,660 (some £25,000 in today's values) in tempting Mike Hailwood back into action on the 500cc Honda, the organising club were unable to agree terms with Bill.

So, as originally planned, he actually made his debut on the Czech two-stroke at Cesenatico on 13 April. However, it was to prove an unlucky debut, when after clocking the seventh-best practice lap the Jawa misfired badly in the race and seized on lap 10. The race was won by Giacomo Agostini (MV Agusta three-cylinder), with Renzo Pasolini on a four-cylinder Benelli runner-up.

Back in Britain, Mick Woollett, writing in his 'Race Gossip' column in the *Motor Cycle*

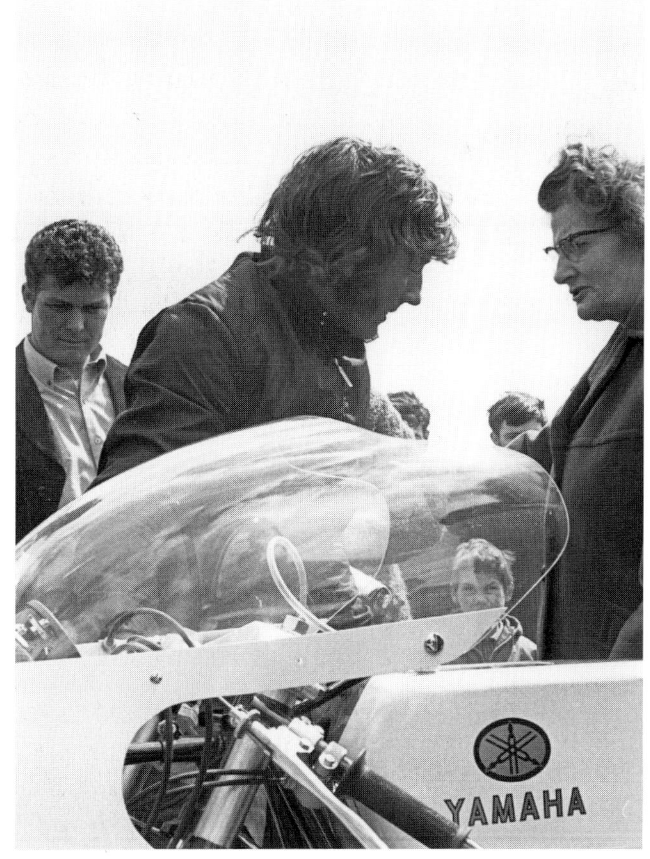

Bill with the Yamaha TR2 production racer he rode at Brands Hatch on 26 May 1969. Also in the picture is his mother, Nell Ivy, and his brother-in-law Dave Swift.

Totally unposed – Bill eating one of his favourite cup cakes!

dated 23 April 1969, went as far as saying: 'The honeymoon is over for Ivy and Jawa.' Continuing: 'I hear that Jawa were not impressed by Bill Ivy's performance at Cesenatico.' However, in many ways the Italian street circuit, with its series of walking-pace corners, was hardly suitable for such a temperamental multi-cylinder two-stroke. Besides saying that Bill had chosen to ride there, a Jawa official stated: 'It was obvious that he is more concerned with his car racing than racing with our motorcycle. When he approached us in the winter to race our machines we thought that this was a great chance but we did not realise that he was so committed to his car programme.'

More Four Wheel Problems

Later in April, while taking part in the annual Eifelrennen meeting at the Nürburgring in West Germany, Bill extensively damaged his Brabham Formula 2 racing car when he crashed out of the race.

However, luckily, Bill escaped injury and was able to telephone his mother to ask her to contact the ACU headquarters in London, to reserve an entry for the forthcoming Junior TT in the Isle of Man – to ride a Jawa or a new Yamaha TR2 production racer.

Rain in Spain

When the first round of the 1969 World Championship series got under way in Spain at the 2.12 mile (3.41km) Jarama circuit, this was not the usual sunny affair – just the reverse in fact – and certainly not the best conditions for Bill and the highly strung Czech two-stroke.

Previously staged on the magnificent Montjuich Park, Barcelona, venue, as the *Motor Cycle* commented: 'The race had been moved to Jarama, near Madrid – a miserable little artificial course crammed full of acute first-gear corners which reduced even World Champions to a crawl. To make matters worse, rain and hail lashed the first four races [which included Bill's event], flooding parts of the paddock.'

The Race

As expected, Giacomo Agostini on his MV Agusta led the 350cc event from start to finish. In the early stages he was challenged by Kel Carruthers (Aermacchi) and Rod Gould (riding one of the new Yamaha TR2s).

As for Bill, after completing the early laps on only three cylinders, but still managing to be in seventh position, when his bike finally chimed onto all four cylinders he rapidly charged up the field, passing Ginger Molloy (Bultaco) and Giuseppe Visenzi (Yamaha). Soon he had closed the gap separating him from Carruthers. But just when he had the Australian really in his sights, the Jawa struck problems – *Motor Cycle* saying the bike 'seized', while Frantisek Shulmann (son of a former Jawa race engineer) told the author recently: 'Carburettor maladies forced the unfortunate Ivy to quit the race when a podium finish was within his grasp.' Frantisek continued: 'Bill was not upset, instead he said he must approach the Mikuni people to provide him with updated carburettors for the next GP [at Hockenheim a week later].'

Chalk and Cheese

As the *Motor Cycle* race report began: 'The 1969 road-race World Championships really leapt into life on Sunday. Second race of the series, the West German GP at Hockenheim, had everything that the previous Sunday's Spanish classic had lacked – blistering sunshine, 100,000 spectators and, above all, close racing in all six classes.' The 350cc race, held over 23 laps (96.72 miles – 155.2km), began with Rod Gould (Yamaha TR2) leading from the start. This lasted for a single lap before the Japanese machine retired with a seized engine. But as *Motor Cycle* said: 'Even so, there was to be no peace for Ago as Bill Ivy showed his most sparkling and determined form and the Jawa sprouted extra long legs to help him. For four laps, Ivy pegged the gap between himself and the MV to no more than five seconds.'

Then Bill settled for second place, a position he was to retain to the end; although going into the final circuit his bike faltered. But Bill nursed it home, to discover that the hesitation had not been a warning of impending seizure. Instead his fuel tank was almost bone dry! To make it a great day for Jawa, his teammate Stastny had carved his way through the field, pushing Heinz Rosner (MZ) and Giuseppe Visenzi (Yamaha) out of third, thus giving the Jawa fours an excellent, morale boosting 2–3 success. Agostini's speed was 111.72mph (179.75km/h) compared to Bill's 110.98mph (178.56km/h). Only these two completed the full 23-lap distance.

350cc West German GP, Hockenheim – 23 laps – 96.72 miles

1st	G. Agostini (MV Agusta)
2nd	W.D. Ivy (Jawa)
3rd	F.S. Stastny (Jawa)
4th	J. Findlay (Yamaha)
5th	G. Visenzi (Yamaha)
6th	K. Carruthers (Aermacchi)

Yamaha Again

Next, on Bank Holiday Monday, 26 May 1969, Bill had his debut race on his newly purchased Yamaha TR2. However, at the *Evening News*-sponsored international at Brands Hatch his machine got sick (with ignition gremlins) after six laps. This came after he had disputed the lead in the early stages of the race with similarly-mounted Rod Gould. The event was eventually won by Phil Read, on yet another of the Yamaha production racers.

Earlier, Bill had the satisfaction of winning his heat – the other heat going to Phil.

No TT

Then came news that Bill would not be taking part in the TT, so his next outing on the works Jawa would be the Dutch TT on Saturday 28 June.

Jawa had left it to him to decide whether or not he wanted to race in the Isle of Man. They felt that the Mountain course, with its wide variations in altitude from sea level at Ramsey to 1,400 feet at Brandywell, was far from ideal for a two-stroke and so the Czech factory were none too disappointed when Bill decided against taking part.

Two bikes were being prepared for the Dutch meeting and, it was reported, they would feature newly designed, larger diameter front brakes.

The Dutch TT

And so to the Dutch TT at Assen on Saturday 28 June 1969. After arriving in Holland, first of all Bill had to counter press stories in Italy alleging that he had struck a race official at a car meeting at Monza the previous weekend.

However, as soon as practice for the Dutch began, these stories were soon overshadowed by the way Bill was performing on the Jawa out on the track as he displayed 'sparkling form' (*Motor Cycle*).

Bill himself said: 'they've got a lot more power out of the Jawa and it is handling just like a Yamaha four now.' He went on to add that stopping power had also been improved, thanks to modifications to the front brake.

Jawa staff were also impressed by Bill's performance at Assen – both in practice and later the race itself. In the race, held over 20 laps (95.75 miles – 154.06km), Bill gave Giacomo Agostini and his MV Agusta the hardest battle since the days of the Hailwood-Ago duels.

This is how *Motor Cycle* described the action: 'Urged on by a record crowd of over 150,000, Ivy hurled the Czech two-stroke around the magnificent 4.8 mile [7.7km] circuit to such good effect that he caught and passed the Italian World Champion at the end of the first lap. He clung to the lead for two laps. Then the Jawa started to misfire slightly on one cylinder. Agostini regained first place and pulled away. But the Jawa chimed back onto four pots and was in business again. With the bike flying, Ivy whittled Agostini's lead away and, gaining 100 yards a lap, flashed into the lead on lap 12. Agostini, in trouble with cramp in his throttle wrist, looked a beaten man as Ivy drew away. Not for long though. The Jawa ignition system played tricks again and, back on three cylinders, Ivy had no answer as Agostini with a record lap at 91.38mph [147.03km/h] regained the lead and went on to win.'

After a retirement (seizure) in Spain, and a runner-up spot to Agostini (MV Agusta) at Hockenheim in West Germany, Bill travelled with the Jawa to Assen for the Dutch TT.

In Holland Bill displayed his – and the Jawa's – potential by leading Agostini until slowed by a misfiring cylinder. The Italian was so worried that he requested that MV made the development of the new six-cylinder 350 an immediate priority!

With this success, Bill regained runner-up spot in the Championship table – a position he had originally gained in West Germany.

Following the Assen race, Bill was asked when he would race the Jawa again. He replied: 'I just don't know. There is no 350cc class at the Belgian and the East German organisers haven't answered my letters.'

350cc Dutch TT, Assen – 20 laps – 95.75 miles

1st	G. Agostini (MV Agusta)
2nd	W.D. Ivy (Jawa)
3rd	S. Grassetti (Yamaha)
4th	K. Hoppe (Yamaha)
5th	J. Findlay (Yamaha)
6th	G. Visenzi (Yamaha)

Giacomo Agostini

Born on 16 June 1942 (only 2½ months before Bill Ivy) at Lovere in the Bergamo region of northern Italy, Giacomo Agostini ('Mino' to his close friends, and 'Ago' to his thousands of adoring fans worldwide) got his first taste of motorcycling in his home village when, aged nine, he cadged lifts on the petrol tank of a 500 Moto Guzzi single owned by the local baker.

He pestered his father so much that, two years later, Papa finally relented and purchased Giacomo a 50cc Bianchi two-stroke. By the age of 14 Ago was racing off-road on a 125cc Parilla motocrosser. Four years later his apprenticeship was complete when he made his competition debut on the tarmac, on a 175cc Moto Morini ohv single. He finished second to the existing Italian Champion in the Trento-Bondone hill climb event.

By the beginning of 1963, Agostini was winning races all over Italy on a Morini Settebello. This led factory boss Alfonso Morini to acquire his

Spring 1967 and Giacomo Agostini (MV) leads Renzo Pasolini's Benelli four at Cesenatico, at a round of the Senior Italian Championships.

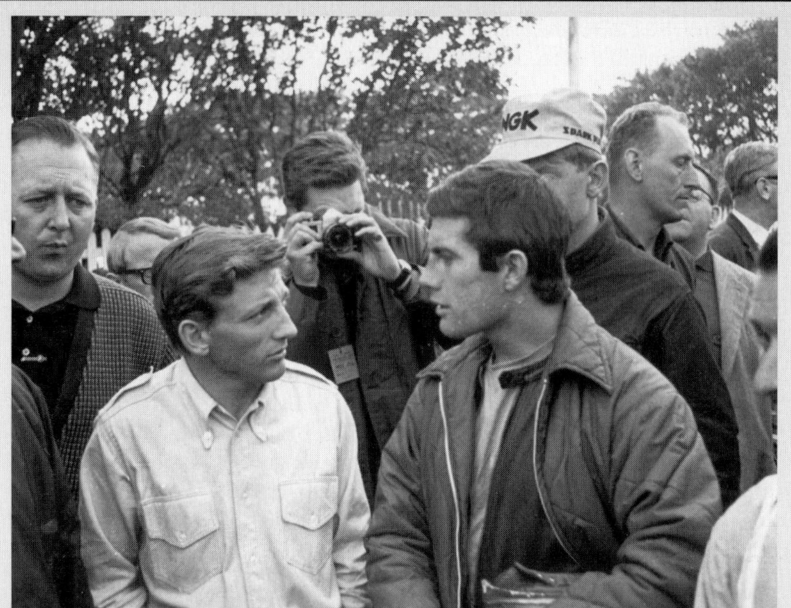

Ago talking to Bill Ivy at the Isle of Man TT, August 1966.

signature on an official works contract, making him back-up rider to the legendary double World Champion Tarquinio Provini.

At the end of 1963, Provini quit Morini and signed for rivals Benelli, with Ago being promoted to number one. Even before Provini's departure, Giacomo, now aged 21, had proved at the Italian GP at Monza in September 1963 that he had real class. He had lapped joint fastest in practice with Honda-mounted World Champion Jim Redman and MZ star Alan Shepherd.

In the race, the Morini youngster actually led in the early stages, before finally being overhauled and passed by both Provini and Redman. The following year, 1964, Agostini won the Italian Senior Championship title on the Morini.

Count Dominico Agusta had always dreamed of an Italian being able to win the blue riband 500cc world title, and his belief that Giacomo Agostini was that man led the Count to sign the gifted youngster in time for the 1965 season.

Giacomo's debut ride on the MV did not match expectations. In fact, it was just the reverse as he crashed out, but this was soon forgotten. His first victory came shortly afterwards, when he took the flag ahead of the field on one of the brand new 350 three-cylinder models at the Nürburgring in West Germany; the first round of that year's Championship series.

During 1965, Giacomo was a teammate of Mike Hailwood, but after Mike signed for Honda at the end of that year, although the two remained firm friends off the track, on it they were now fierce rivals. During 1966 and 1967 the sight of Agostini versus Hailwood duels all over Europe are now remembered as some of the greatest of all motorcycle Grand Prix races in the history of the sport.

Probably the one which most people remember was the 1967 Senior TT in the Isle of Man, which Giacomo ultimately lost by default when his final drive cried enough after some two hours of all-out action. However,

Giacomo has always maintained that to him Mike was not only the greatest rider but also a true gentleman. His achievements on the race circuit speak for themselves: a record 15 world titles, 13 on MVs, the other two on Yamahas. Added to his total of 122 Grand Prix victories, it seems like a record that will never be bettered.

Talking about Bill Ivy during the course of preparation of this book, Ago revealed that he cried for two days after Bill died, because 'he was a very nice person and very good friend.' And of course Ago knew just what a good rider Bill was too, thanks to his on-track performance, particularly their battle at the 1969 Dutch TT, when before his Jawa went on to three cylinders Bill had given Ago his hardest race since the Hailwood days.

Giacomo finally hung up his leathers at the end of the 1976 season, at the age of 35. But the ever-popular Italian superstar did not simply retire and vanish from the scene. As, during the early 1980s, he became manager of first the Marlboro Yamaha squad and later Cagiva. Later still, during the 1990s, he was deeply involved with development and subsequent launch of the new MV Agusta F4 superbike project.

Sachsenring

But, of course, the East German organisers did reply, and so Bill found himself at the Sachsenring for the next round of the World Championship.

With qualifying in full swing on a very wet day on Saturday 12 July 1969 tragedy struck the diminutive Englishman. All of a sudden the temperamental Jawa seized solid with the unfortunate Bill unable to take any avoiding action. The result was that he was thrown from the machine and skidded a considerable distance along the road, hitting an unprotected concrete post with his head. It was rumoured that Bill was busy at the time of the incident when trying to (un-)fasten his helmet, hence he was unable to engage the clutch. It is also known that Bill's helmet appeared to come off before the impact.

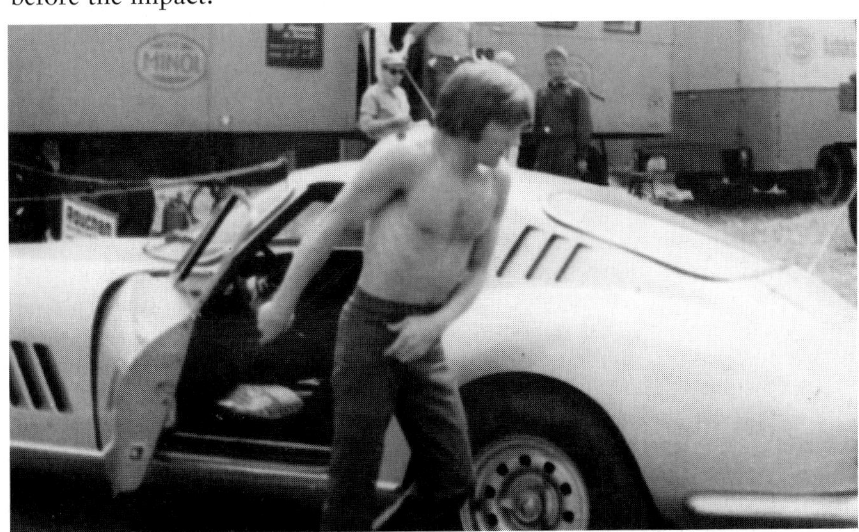

Bill at the Sachsenring, prior to the start of practicing, July 1969.

He was rushed to hospital with serious head injuries. There, doctors fought to resuscitate him with a heart massage machine, but, ultimately, these efforts proved to be in vain.

The Aftermath

Hours after the accident it was discovered, when his 350cc Jawa V4 was stripped by race officials, that the crankshaft of the two-stroke's lower nearside (left) cylinder had seized. This had occurred just as Bill shut off for a 90mph (145km/h) left-hand curve entering the town of Hohenstein-Ernstthal on the 5.4 mile (8.7km) road circuit.

The following day, on Sunday 13 July 1969, before the start of the 350cc race, the crowd of 200,000 spectators paid a moving tribute to Bill, as they stood in silence as a wreath was placed on Bill's vacant place on the grid.

One of the Jawa factory mechanics subsequently drove Bill's Maserati car from the Sachsenring to Prague where it was parked in one of the Jawa garages.

Later, once Bill's funeral at Maidstone was over, guests including Mike Hailwood, Luigi Taveri and personnel from the Jawa factory attended Bill's home, with Mrs Ivy and others.

Sachsenring, 1969. Bill preparing for the fatal practice session. Just study those faces...it was almost as if the mechanics and Bill could see into the future.

At this time it was also agreed that the Maserati would be driven to Jawa's main agent in Vienna, Austria, where Luigi Taveri would in turn take the car to Zurich to sell it. The car was registered in Switzerland and housed in Luigi's garage, because, when travelling to Continental Europe, Bill had usually flown to Zurich and continued in the Maserati.

At the same discussion which made arrangements concerning the car, Mike Hailwood told Frantisek Shulmann's father of a meeting with Giacomo Agostini a few weeks prior to Bill's fatal crash. According to Mike, Ago was very concerned by the latest developments (i.e. Bill and Jawa) and had urged MV Agusta to expedite development of new six-cylinder-engined machine otherwise he could not guarantee MV to win the 350cc World Championship that year. But Bill's premature death meant that the danger to MV's dominance had gone – and the 350cc six-cylinder bike was no longer needed.

The Tributes

As a mark of just how much Bill was loved and respected – besides being feared by other competitors on account of his fighting 'never-give-in' spirit out on the circuit – I would like to reproduce just a few of the many tributes from normal fans. Here are five such letters which were received by the motorcycle press shortly after learning of Bill's passing:

> 'I was deeply grieved to learn of Bill Ivy's death. I know that road racers and other enthusiasts will agree that Little Bill was really a brilliant rider. I remember he had an unusual way of taking the left-hander at Brands Hatch – flat out, in a two-wheel drift. It would be fitting if the corner were renamed after him.'
> *J.R. Simpson, Sidcup, Kent.*
>
> 'No rider had more guts than Bill. Remember last year's TT when he wore his boot right through to the toes? In last year's Czech GP he fell off his 125cc Yamaha but went on to compete in the two-fifty race, obviously in great pain. He will be sadly missed.'
> *Paul Gregory, Great Sankey, Lancs.*
>
> 'I would like to send my deepest sympathy to Bill Ivy's mother. He died in the sport he loved and while he was still among the top names. He will always be remembered and be listed among the greats who have made motorcycling history. Bill was my favourite international rider and I will never forget his superb riding and the things he achieved.'
> *Miss Pauline Goddard, Studley, Warwickshire.*
>
> 'Bill was a great character on and off the track. He was often criticised, but only the memories of his great rides will survive. One of his greatest was two weeks ago, when he came so near to beating Agostini in the Dutch TT.'
> *Neal Thomas, Chester-le-Street, Durham.*
>
> 'Bill and Jawa were the only threat to Agostini and MV left on the racing scene. I am sure all fans will mourn his death. Whenever Bill was racing, on any circuit, spectators got their money's worth.'
> *J.W. Folley, London W11*

Bill riding the Jawa, only minutes from disaster.

Yamaha's Tribute

Perhaps the biggest tribute of all came a few months later, when Yamaha presented Bill's mother with a brand-new 350cc TR2 production racer. And in their 12 November 1969 issue *Motor Cycle* carried the headlines: 'Butcher gets Ivy Yamaha.' Going on to say: 'Short circuit specialist Rex Butcher has been chosen by Mrs Nell Ivy to race her 350cc TR2 Yamaha – given to her by the Japanese factory after her son Bill had been killed during practice for the East German Grand Prix.' It was also stated that: 'Butcher will race the Yamaha in eight selected meetings, starting with the King of Brands in March.'

The bike was to be prepared by Yamaha-trained Ron Eldridge, who had looked after Bill's works machines in 1968, his last season on the Japanese bikes before switching to the Czech Jawa.

It was also common knowledge that Mrs Ivy's first choice would probably have been Paul Smart – a close friend of Bill's – but Paul had made it known that he was already fully committed for 1970 and so did not wish to be considered.

Chapter 10

A Place in History

So just where does Bill Ivy sit in motorcycle racing's hall of fame? Well, for a start, one has to say at the very top table. Bill was fiercely competitive in whatever he set out to do. Second best was something he never even gave consideration. In fact, he considered anything of a competitive nature to be a personal challenge.

As far as his riding ability was concerned, Bill was able to extend this capability beyond that of mere mortals to whatever extent was required, but he knew the fine line of adhesion.

He was also able to extract the very last ounce of power and speed from a motorcycle without blowing the engine to pieces – and a definite added bonus was that he possessed a good understanding of its mechanical function and weaknesses. He was thus able to analyse where faults lay – something many other would have been unable to do.

Nell Ivy with Charlie Sanby after the latter had won the Bill Ivy Trophy in 1971.

After Bill's death, Yamaha presented his mother Nell with this 350 TR2 racer. Ron Eldridge tuned, it was raced by Rex Butcher (left) and Jim Harvey (centre) under the guidance of Tom Kirby.

Bill also made the most of his physical size, which gave him an advantage regarding power to weight ratio of the machine he was riding. Not only this, but his small size was of great help in being able to tuck himself away behind the fairing to maximise streamlining and thus decrease wind resistance.

Although he was barely 5ft tall, Bill had great upper body strength and the balance and poise of a professional gymnast.

Unlike many other legendary riders, Bill Ivy did not spring to fame almost overnight. This was for several reasons. The first was that in the early days, his racing was almost always (but not exclusively) on 50cc machines; and this class received the least publicity. Then there was the fact that he was not from a well-off family. So, as a result, his early racing years were spent as a mechanic at Chisholm's of Maidstone, who were also his sponsors.

In fact, the first four seasons of his career (1959–1962 inclusive) were to see Bill only using Chisholm bikes (plus his own converted Gilera road bike). Then in 1963 he made his first move to the outside world by riding for

Frank Sheene, who was a well-known two-stroke tuner in his own right, long before his more famous son, Barry, made his entrance into the racing world.

But it was really once Chisholm's returned to the racing scene by purchasing a brand new CR93 Honda in 1964, plus rides on larger machinery that same year for Geoff Monty, did Bill's career move up a gear. From then on the pace simply took off. First with Tom Kirby from late spring 1965 and finally from the end of 1965 as a fully contracted works Yamaha rider.

The much-publicised Ivy versus Read saga during the second half of the 1968 season is probably, today, the single most remembered section of Bill's racing career, but it is only a small part. In recalling this event one needs to realise that both our hero and Phil desperately wanted to win races and both had the greatness to do so. In a way it was a pity that both men were in the same team.

Bill's mother Nell presenting awards to Paul Smart (79) and Peter Williams (7) at Snetterton; 1970.

THE 7th ANNUAL

Bill Ivy Trophy

at CADWELL PARK

SUNDAY 27th JUNE 1976

BILL IVY – World Champion
"Aviating up the Cadwell Mountain"

OFFICIAL PROGRAMME

20p

Bill's sister Marie and her husband Syd at their son Adam's graduation; also in the picture is their other son, Craig.

Had Bill lived, I am sure he would have achieved much more, not just in the motorcycle world but on four wheels too. The people who know accepted that, as one put it: 'He had both the natural ability and tigerish spirit to have ultimately matched the best car racing drivers of the world.'

Two particular tributes from the world of motorcycle racing which were made after Bill's death in 1969 are worth repeating.

The first is by journalist Charlie Rous:

'Bill Ivy was a tearaway...but in the nicest possible sense of the word, for he lived for speed and revelled in the fast life and luxury which success gave him with all the style of the swinging '60s. He was brash, even cocky. He wore fancy clothes and grew his hair long, but "Little Bill" was not a rebel without a cause – it just served to hide his dedication and determination to success. It is perhaps this side of 26-year-old Bill Ivy which is most sad for he would never accept the inevitability of his small size. But one could not believe that it was only this which drove him on with such courage and skill, for above all, Bill was sincere, and both as a rider and a man he was indeed a giant among men. So it was by motorcycle racing that he chose to fulfil his life. His ultimate success as a World Champion did not come easy. It was the outcome of a long,

Opposite: The Bill Ivy Trophy meeting, organised by the Racing 50 Club – later renamed New Era – ran annually for 30 years from 1970 until 1999. This is the programme for the seventh event, staged at Cadwell Park on 27 June 1976.

Technique

There is absolutely no doubting that Bill Ivy's technique was quite simple – to be the fastest man out on the circuit and to win races. One helped achieve the other. And he was certainly a determined, tigerish and skilful rider.

Because he had so few races in a season during his early years, it took Bill much longer than riders such as Geoff Duke, John Surtees or Mike Hailwood to reach the top. And although the Chisholm brothers undoubtedly gave Bill whatever help they could, it was not until he began branching out that he really made progress. First Frank Sheene, then Geoff Monty and finally Tom Kirby helped him make ever quicker progress. This began at the beginning of 1963 and ended in mid-1965 when he was asked by Phil Read to test 125 and 250 Yamahas at Silverstone, just prior to the TT that year. After that he rapidly achieved superstar status.

Like his great friend Mike Hailwood, Bill had that rare gift of being able to adapt himself to riding any machine and rapidly getting the best of it. The same could be said of the way he approached learning circuits. For example, in his first full GP season in 1966, well over two thirds of the circuits he had never even seen, let alone ridden round. However, this did not stop him from often battling for the lead in many of the races. In fact, as he was later to recall, when he received the call from Phil Read to get out to Japan and race at Suzuka in October 1965: 'I'd never been out of the country before except to the Dutch TT.'

That word determination often comes to the fore when considering Bill Ivy's progress, but sometimes this determination could almost be described as foolhardy. The 1966 TT is testament to this. He was still recovering from a spectacular crash at Brands Hatch during which he went through an advertisement hoarding on Tom Kirby's AJS Metisse. As Bill later recalled himself: 'I missed the first few days of practice. They finally let me out on the Wednesday morning on the one-two-five. I was getting headaches and could hardly see, but things improved when I started the race. I still must have been concussed, otherwise I'd never have gone so fast. It was sheer luck I didn't crash. On the first lap I'd just managed to catch and pass Taveri when I clouted the straw bales coming out of Schoolhouse Bend at Ramsey. Then I got on to the loose surface at the Gooseneck and clanged against an advertisement hoarding on the bank. Luigi went by as I was sorting myself out. He had a smile all over his face and that annoyed me. I caught him on the Mountain Mile. The second lap was a series of slides. The third was enjoyable. Things were back in focus. No slides, no trouble, just as fast, lovely.' He had won the race at record speed and hoisted the lap record into the bargain!

When asked whether there are any differences in racing a two-stroke or a four-stroke? Bill's reply was simply: 'None at all. People talk a lot of rot about the techniques required. Both have a throttle and that's what you've got to use. Both have a narrow power band; neither must be over-revved. You've got to keep the rev-meter needle in the power band and that's it. They're the same as far as I'm concerned. I'm not worried about a narrow spread of power as long as I've enough gears.'

Another interesting point is that many riders over the years have said how different long road circuits (such as the TT or Ulster GP) are to the average British short circuit. But as far as Bill was concerned: 'There's no real difference in riding our short circuits and the longer laps. A race is a race. You're out there on a stretch of circuit. In some cases you have to take into account the corner ahead of the one you can see – that applies whether you're on a short circuit or a long one.'

Certainly Bill's small stature was not a problem for him, because what he lacked in height and build he certainly made up for in strength. And his light weight also assisted him with acceleration and braking, particularly on smaller machines.

Mike Hailwood gave his personal insight into what made Bill tick, saying: 'He could walk on his hands for hours and was a man of immense strength in those forearms and shoulders. But despite his lack of stature he had no fear.' Continuing: 'When he was out on that wriggling ribbon of road, pitting his wits and talents against the rest of us, he was a tall as any man in the world.' Mike continued: 'His body was a criss-cross of stitch marks from some fearsome crashes but, even though he lived on the limit he never backed off a single challenge. I would not say he was fearless – no man is that – but I would offer the opinion that his margins of safety were narrower than most, and his ability to take advantage of that state of affairs was well-known by many riders who tried to follow him.'

The word 'technique' does not really sit well with the man who was Bill Ivy. Perhaps the best way of describing what drove him is the earlier mention of his 'tigerish' nature, as Mike Hailwood was to later recall, after Bill's death, was that he had fallen over about 90 times the first time he went skiing! But he didn't ever think about quitting.

So what was Bill Ivy's Achilles heel, and did he have one? The answer is yes, he did. Behind his 'race face' Bill was sensitive and emotional. This made him vulnerable and showed itself. This is how Alan Peck described things in his 1972 book *No Time To Lose*: 'He was very easily rattled, and it was easy to hurt him with words as it was with actions. Sometimes something which sparked off his temper on one occasion could send him into despondency on another. One could never be sure how he would react, and it was this ingredient in his character which made him unpredictable when things weren't running smoothly.' Of course this is precisely what happened during 1968, when all the problems arose between Bill and Phil Read. Yamaha had originally planned that Bill should win both the 125 and 250cc titles. However, Bill with his undoubted 'fairness' thought this was wrong and got Yamaha to agree to Phil having the 125cc title, while Bill would only win the 250cc crown. However, as we know, after Phil had won the 125cc title he conveniently forgot the unsigned agreement and went hell-bent on winning the 250cc title too. This then was the basis on what really happened – Bill played into Phil's hands by getting upset and ultimately rattled. Sad, but nonetheless true. Every star has a potential weak spot and Phil Read certainly uncovered Bill's.

Roy Francis (CR93, 9) and John Pitt (CB92, 8) are the current custodians of the Chisholm Honda racers which Bill rode to early success.

Opposite: The programme cover for the 22nd Bill Ivy Trophy meeting, staged at Cadwell Park on the 28 July 1991. The main race of the day was won by James Whitham, riding a Team Grant 750cc Suzuki.

hard slog by a young lad who saved his pocket-money to buy his first machine – a 1930s Francis Barnett Cruiser later sold to Roy Francis when Bill purchased his next machine, which was a pre-war Triumph Tiger 80.'

The other tribute came from sponsor Tom Kirby:

'Bill to me stood 10ft tall, not 5ft 3in as we knew him. He defied all the criticism of himself and set about proving his dedication to racing by his ability to ride well and become World Champion in the process. He enjoyed life to the full in an age of mixed opinions of how our image should be. Bill was a person of great feeling – so much so that the more anyone upset him, the more sensitive he became. He rebelled against authority because of his size, in an effort to inflate himself. Bill couldn't stand anything phoney and believed in always giving. He was always dissatisfied with himself when he could not come up to par. Bill died doing the thing he liked best – racing. His love for four wheels was just another challenge in life and he had to prove he could be as good as any before him. He rode and drove as he lived

THE TWENTY SECOND ANNUAL

BILL IVY TROPHY

CADWELL PARK

Sunday 28th July 1991

- *£1,500 to the Winner*
- *Sound of Singles Championship*
- *Battle of the Twins*
- *125cc and 250cc Grand Prix Classes*

OFFICIAL PROGRAMME £1.50

For Conditions of Admission see inside

The Bill Ivy 'Silver Helmet Memorial Trophy' presented by Bill's mother, Nell. The trophy is shown here with Bill's sister Marie and her son Craig at Brands Hatch, July 1999. Past winners:
1970 Peter Williams
1971 Charlie Sanby
1972 John Cooper
1973 Paul Smart, Barry Sheene and Stan Woods
1974 Steve Manship
1975 Steve Parrish
1976 Neil Tuxworth
1977 Kevin Richards
1978 Mick Grant
1979 Graham McGregor
1980 J. Bol
1981 Tony Head
1982 Donnie McLeod.

– spectacularly. Bill will always remain in my memory as one of the greatest riders the world has known – a true champion and a friend.'

Bill's friend, fellow racer and former workmate Roy Francis describes him as: 'Mischievous, but not malicious, and cheeky, but not rude.' And that, to my mind, tells a lot of what made Bill the character he was: the genuine article – no hyped-up image, no airs and graces, and certainly not a big-headed prima donna!

The great Mike Hailwood even went as far as saying: 'Motorcycle sport suffered an immeasurable loss for Bill, in my view, was the last of the great racing characters.' Mike continued: 'We were friends – close pals in fact – despite the fact that professionally we represented different works and, on the circuits, had to be the deadliest of rivals. That racing rivalry, with hard-fought contests every outing, never impinged on our association as two bachelors hell bent on getting the best out of life when the races were over and done with. He was a way-out character, anxious to be involved in whatever was fashionable at the time, and that meant long flowing hair and flared trousers, with garish shirts and a blinding line in neckwear! He was a cheeky little rogue and, in many ways, the little man trying to look bigger. His taste in sports cars, too, was eye-catching and, yes, you could always tell when he turned up at the circuits by the screeching of tortured tyres on the tarmac or gravel and the dust-storm that seemed to be the trademark of every spectacular arrival.'

Certainly Mike Hailwood had a great respect for Bill's racing abilities, saying: 'When he was out on that wriggling ribbon of road, pitting his wits and talents against the rest of us, he was as tall as any man in the world. The years I knew him, the races we had, and the times we spent together in the world's nightclubs, with Bill demanding steak and chips wherever we went – even in Japan – are precious to me as memories of what was one of the most enjoyable passages of my own life.' Mike concluded: 'The sad thing about his death is that the world of racing never really saw the best of Bill Ivy, but I hope we don't forget what we did see…a giant of a little man.'

With the other star riders' biographies in this series I have immediately come up with a suitable sub-title. But with Bill Ivy I was struggling – all manner of names came up and were binned. Then, one morning when the manuscript was almost completed, I was talking to my secretary, Rita, and it suddenly arrived – 'The Will to Win'. To my mind this sums up Bill's racing career perfectly, so *Bill Ivy: The Will to Win* it is.

The 30th and final Bill Ivy Memorial Meeting – 10 July 1999

Jim Parker's ambition, as founding father of the Racing 50 Club and New Era's, had always been to bring the Bill Ivy Trophy Races, mostly held at Cadwell Park since Bill's death, back to Brands Hatch, the little man's local circuit. As this was to be the 30th running and final meeting it was suggested that an extra special memorial meeting would take place. Jim contacted Alan Robinson of the TT Riders Association and myself, having been a friend of Bill and his family since schooldays, to co-ordinate getting together a representative group of riders and machines from the Ivy era. My own thought was to bring a number of 50cc and 125cc machines and riders to the grid as these marked Bill's formative years in these classes, which are so often neglected today. Contact was also made with the Oldborough Manor Community School who still present a Bill Ivy achievement award annually. A party of some 25 pupils plus were invited to attend and, time permitting, would make a lap of the circuit in a mini bus with Chris McGhan. There followed numerous phone calls from interested riders, owners of machines, letters to some 40 local clubs and contact by fans from Holland and France. Finally 10 July 1999 arrived, as near as possible with circuit hire restrictions to that fateful day 30 years ago at Sachsenring when Bill lost his life practising for the East German Grand Prix on a dismal damp day.

The weather at Brands Hatch on arrival was misty, reminiscent of East Germany in 1969, but it promised clearance to a fine sunny day. The modern-era paddock area was pretty full at 7am and scrutineering was about to start. The Bill Ivy parade riders and transport were directed to the grand prix paddock, with use of the pit garages below the control tower in the centre of the circuit. Having been allocated garage six we unloaded the ex-Bill Ivy Chis-Honda CR93 125cc, his 1964 British Championship-winning motorcycle, and noted a Frank Higley 250cc Cotton, another sponsor and machine Bill rode, was already parked in a nearby garage, as were a couple of 50cc bikes from Bill's early career. A silver van glided into the pit area, the unmistakable silhouette of a red and silver machine inside. Yes, he was attending and was the first World Champion to arrive, Phil Read complete with a 500cc MV Agusta. Early observation of other machines present showed these with breather tubes from the engine exhausted into a plastic catch tank. This had not been a requirement 35 years ago and I had overlooked fitting one to the CR93. I decided I had better fit one to meet current day regulations and searched the rubbish bins to no avail. On walking up to the modern-era machine paddock, I was able to purchase a suitable unit from a stall selling oil, tyres and parts, etc.

TTRA parade co-ordinator Alan Robinson was early on parade and set up office in the bottom of the control tower dispensing greetings, programmes and meal tickets to riders signing on. This was a very nostalgic place to be; many riders queuing to sign on had not seen each other for many years. Unnoticed by a large proportion of those already assembled, a small old car with a covered trailer slipped into position behind the garages. An elderly

Bill's younger sister, Marie, with Roy Francis; Brands Hatch, Saturday 10 July 1999 at the last Bill Ivy Trophy meeting.

gentleman and his wife emerged, released the catches to the hinged box trailer and revealed a sight never before seen at Brands Hatch, the machine that wrote Bill's final chapter, the Jawa four-cylinder two-stroke machine. Mr Zdenek Tichy had driven all the way from Prague, he was the designer and engineer of this unique machine. To one of Bill's oldest and closest friends present, this was for me the 'coming out in public' of the machine which should not be hidden away. It should be shown to all as a mark of respect both to a truly gifted and talented rider and a remarkable engineer, who were both taking on the might of the Japanese and Italian factories in the 350cc class in 1969 until fate played its wicked hand.

Riders were arriving thick and fast, Uncle Arthur Wheeler, World Championship contender in the early-1960s 'been there, done it, still riding that beautiful Moto Guzzi'. The 'little people' were now in attendance, Tommy Robb and Luigi Taveri, Tommy having brought his son and Luigi his lovely blonde daughter who confessed to having had quite a crush on Little Bill in the 1960s. From his busy world tour, Jim Redman spoke of having left home at 5am on the day before, not here to dominate proceedings on his Honda Six but to mark his respect by riding a Manx Norton, a machine his remarkable career was launched on. The garages now took on the look of those memorable days of the 1960s at Brands Hatch with Grand Prix stars mixing with the local lads. Also in attendance were Rex Butcher and Dennis Ainsworth, with Aermacchis loaned by a Dutch enthusiast. Ron Chandler appeared with an unfaired Matchless G50, also Paul Smart, although not with his Imola-winning Ducati which has pride of place in the Bologna factory museum, but with his original 250cc Cotton Telstar and a Seeley Triumph. Bob Rowe brought his immaculate Peel-fairing shod Manx Norton for John Hurlestone, legendary paddock comic, to waddle round. Unsung hero, and ever present in the 1960s and about to make an extremely generous contribution to the day, Mike Braid slipped into the champions' garage. He brought not only the beautiful John Player Monocoque Norton to ride himself but also three other famous machines for the privileged to ride; a Kirby Metisse G50, BSA Rocket 3 and a Dunstall 500cc Domiracer. Also in attendance was the evergreen John Holder with his Manx Norton and many others, all giving up their time to make this a special day. Entered in the parade but unable to drum up the kit, Grant Gibson turned up and was loaned Paul Smart's Cotton. Fixed up with my son's helmet and boots, and leathers borrowed from a modern-day competitor, he then awaited his turn on the track.

The little 50cc Pope Special, which with custodian Ray Palmer I had spent the last week making presentable from the ravages of time, took up station with its original crew in attendance. Alan Dawson, the rider together with Bill Ivy on the Chis-Itom, Howard German on the Sheene Special and Dave and Mike Simmonds on their Itoms were all big stars in the class in the early-1960s. Early in the line up sporting proudly the No. 1 plate brought to Brands by Paul Smart was the 50cc Sheene Special, the Ducson engine machine that Bill Ivy rode successfully in the Isle of Man TT. And yes, the maker of World Champions himself was present at 86 years old, driven up for the day, 'Franco' Frank Sheene, who would play a part again later in the proceedings. The area along the front of the garages was now giving the air and atmosphere of a unique occasion, with 110 machines and their riders lined up. Bikes from all classes 50cc–1000cc, many of which the 'little fella' had ridden himself.

As I was making a trip to the control tower to check on arrivals, Alan Robinson was just about to send his assistant to find me. What was to unfold left me totally 'gob-smacked'. Mr Tichy, the Czech Jawa engineer, would be unable to ride the Jawa for the final laps at the end of the meeting because of recent major surgery. Therefore a rider was required and my name had been put forward to do the memorial laps. What a request! Would I ride the machine my dear friend had last been associated with? Others in the room more famous and qualified to ride Grand Prix machinery were adding their support. In fact the atmosphere was very special. I had little hesitation in accepting, I would do it as a mark of respect to Bill and the remarkable, frail Czech engineer who had brought the machine to the memorial meeting. I would not be able to ride it in any other parades during the day except the final tribute.

On checking the tyre pressures on my CR93, I noticed the exhaust bungs were missing, these were the originals I had preserved since Bill and I uncrated the machine in 1964. Some thieving scoundrel had taken them. I hope it was in Bill's memory. Behind the pits I bumped into Peter Williams, not able to ride today because of his arm injury but present and a very welcome fellow competitor of Bill's.

Marie, Bill's younger sister, arrived on the pit wall with her husband Syd Rose and sons Adam and Craig. With a little trepidation I told her of the day's plans. I could sense her unease in the Jawa's presence but explained the day would not be complete without it. Life has gone on and Bill's ideals are still fought over irrespective of the danger, and to this we ride this day in his memory.

Having brought a MV Agusta and not a Yamaha four-cylinder, Phil Read made, in my view, a gracious gesture, forgetting the controversial confrontation as Bill's teammate at Yamaha. The controversial rider, the fatal machine, 110 machines, riders, friends, former mechanics and sponsors, this day 30 years on was taking on something special. Old workmates of Bill from the Chisholm brothers' motorcycle shop in Maidstone were playing their part. Now, as then, Fred Collins, whose daughter Emma had helped produce Bill's memorial in the Chequers Shopping Centre, Maidstone, transported myself and the CR93 to Brands with my son Keith. It was something of a role reversal for Keith as mechanic for the day, as he normally competes in SE Centre trials with me in attendance.

Maurice Thomas, senior mechanic in our Chisholm days, brought along his Gilera Saturno but not his replica Itom, which he has yet to complete. He rode with Bill in the Racing 50 Club 250-mile race at Snetterton. Peter Darwell, who worked for a neighbouring firm to that of the Chisholm brothers, was entered in the parade but was unable to find machinery and so contributed by painting my helmet to my 1960s style used when he, Bill and I rode together. I know he was savouring this day. Geoff Dear, also an ex-Chisholm mechanic, brought his enthusiasm and support to the day's programme. Don and Bill Chisholm would have loved to have been part of this special day.

The modern-day races for the Bill Ivy Trophy were now taking place. This magnificent trophy, a full size silver replica of Bill's distinctive ivy leaf design helmet on a large plinth, was being ridden for, for the last time before permanent display at Sammy Miller's Museum.

My wife Sandra and daughter Corinne arrived with family friends Jan Collins, Monica and Ken Gill, Liz Frost and Maggie Smart, along with many other familiar faces whose names fail me. In the time capsule of the track pit garage complex lunchtime arrived and people wandered off to a buffet lunch provided by the organising club. Not myself – through nerves and memories I was not hungry and gave my ticket away, as did Colin Seeley on seeing our old friend Pat Mahoney. Pat, a great competitor in the 1960s, still suffering from the crash at Paddock Hill but with an unbelievable sense of humour, a lovely man. He enjoyed meeting a lot of his old friends.

Into the pits now strode the king of the Brands' marshals at 92 years old, Ken Phillips, overseeing all those present at practice days in the 1960s. Ken was a friend of us all and it was so fitting that he should be there that day. A local lad from Maidstone, Mick Prebble, torn between competing in the trophy races and savouring the parade riders and machines, brought his copy of *No Time to Lose*, Bill's life story, and left it with me to get a few signatures while he dashed off to compete. During the lunchtime pits walkabout I noted Bill's old teacher, Mrs Colegate, among the spectators, along with Eric Dines who frequented the Staplehurst Café scene coffee bar cowboy days.

With lunchtime over the first parade was called up, 50cc and 125cc machines to go out followed by 250cc–1000cc. The show was taking off; Chas Mortimer on Jim Lilley's excellent CR93 pulled up alongside me as I warmed up the Chis-Honda in the slip road. Panic as the Simmonds Itom refuses to start and is hurried away for an extra push. Master of ceremonies Alan Robinson waves us off. What beautiful music those CR93s made as we accelerated up towards Paddock. Chas soon was really on the boil having ridden the machine earlier in June at the TT Classic Parade. He stretched the gap between us, myself riding on 25-year-old tyres and with a fragile piece of history under me, I settled for a cruise on the machine that had given Bill so much success in 1964–65 and myself TT experience in 1966. However, after three laps this nostalgic trip was interrupted by a misfire, probably sediment from the tank after many years of non-use. I stopped at the pit exit road and it appeared to clear, so I did another lap before returning to the pits, just as the larger capacity machines were lining up to go out. I had not seen him on the circuit but into view came the unmistakable figure of Charlie Mates, another fellow competitor of Bill's from the 50cc days. Charlie was right among the 50ccs, many of which had been brought over by a Dutch contingent.

The big boys were now released on to the track for their parade. Full international grid this one; Phil Read – MV, Luigi Taveri – Honda, Jim Redman – Norton, Tommy Robb – G50, Paul Smart – Seeley, Rex Butcher – Aermacchi, Arthur Wheeler – Guzzi, Ron Chandler – G50, Ollie Howe – Norton. What a sound! What a tribute!

On the pit wall numerous faces from the past, including ex-Kirby mechanic Neil Collett and AMC raceshop engineer Tom Mortimer, all added their touch to the day. Alan Peck, author of *No Time To Lose*, brought a number of the books to Brands for a special signing by himself and Marie Ivy, along with a couple hoping to make a film of Bill's life. Didier Lebeck, a French fan I had met at Montlhéry in May, to whom I sent a paddock entry ticket, brought his wonderfully unique scrapbook of Bill's racing career collected from press cuttings out of the continental press for Marie to see. With my son Keith as translator, those present saw another special tribute to Little Bill by a stranger.

On learning of my plight with the CR93, Mike Braid offered me the Tom Kirby Metisse G50 for the next parade, Tommy Robb had ridden it in the first parade but had offered to swap to the BSA 3. What a fitting addition to the day's proceedings in the presence of Rose, Tom's widow, daughter Christine and her son, accompanied by Bill's original Kirby mechanic, Neil Collett. In the 1960s I had followed on riding Bill's cast-off machines as he progressed but I never got to ride one of Uncle Tom's; polished yes, but ridden no. I felt greatly honoured to motor out for the second parade on the machinery that had given Bill his springboard to World Championship success, many wins

The programme cover for the final (1999) Bill Ivy Trophy meeting; showing Bill leading Mike Hailwood at Cadwell Park on the Yamaha V4 two-fifty.

and race and lap records. Those few laps were beyond words. Finally out of Clearways on to the main straight, flat on the tank, crowds lining the pit wall, the chequered flag. Why did it have to take a tragedy and 30 years for me to be given this opportunity? Thank you Mike Braid most sincerely for this wonderful opportunity.

My day now was taking on a roller coaster of highs and lows, exhilaration and sadness, and emotion was very difficult to control. Quiet corners sought to gain control; friends and family gave understanding looks. My daughter Corinne took custody of my helmet. My wife Sandra did not mention my being asked to ride the Jawa in the final laps, she knew, as they knew, I had to do it for myself in tribute to a very dear friend.

The day had started with me having borrowed a set of Paul Smart's leathers, soon people were calling me Paul and coming up for autographs, very flattering but embarrassing, so I taped over his name. Later as a mark of respect to Jawa in anticipation of my last ride of the day, I taped over the Honda name on the leathers. Keeping me out of the line of duty, for the next parade Mike Braid offered me the Dunstall Norton 500cc Domiracer Twin, another piece of history which reminded me very much of the Monards that Bill and I had ridden for Geoff Monty, who was sadly not present that day. Mike warmed up the machine for me and on cocking my leg over it I found it quite low unlike the Kirby G50, which I could only reach on tiptoe. Carried away by the fact I could actually touch the ground I forgot to check anything else. Accelerating away down Paddock Hill, up to Druids, I grabbed the front brake with two fingers trapping the others against the bars, just managing some control round the corner and down the hill. What a bloody awful bottom bend now! Waddling round adjusting the front brake and proceeding round Clearways on to the start and finish straight, down behind the bubble, 1968 was re-lived. Two more laps of bliss, round the Paddock again, up the hill to Druids, yellow flags were waving, a fallen rider on the entrance with marks further in across the track, a red and silver bike being pulled out of the gravel. Oh no! It's Phil Read tipped over getting back on 1960s pace, why does he try so hard? What does he have to prove? We all know how good a rider he was to win World Championships! Those who he maybe felt the need to prove it to are no longer with us. Fortunately, Phil was unhurt.

On speaking to Mr Tichy in his broken English, he had explained he would need half an hour to prepare the Jawa for the final requiem parade. The power would be between 8–11,000rpm and, although the machine would rev higher, it would be difficult to ride on the Brands Indy circuit. High gearing was fitted so maybe only three gears were usable and also the machine was fitted with the large carbs used by Silvio Grassetti at long circuits. I sat on the machine to acclimatise myself with the controls. The machine was smaller than I expected but everything was well placed. Being of Bill's stature I believed he would have felt comfortable on it and inspired by the personnel involved. I now busied myself looking at other machines in the pits and waited for the big moment. The 'get away from people' syndrome started to take over and a quiet walk and corner sought; I felt sick but knew 100 per cent I had to ride the Jawa and was prepared. The call came for all paraders to change out of their leathers except Roy Francis. Sammy Miller answered the half-hour call to help Mr Tichy start the Jawa. Instructions from the Czech engineer, Sammy, in the seat and two pushers directed to shove it along the pit road, the machine fired reluctantly 1–2–3 – 3–2–1. Silence. Knackered pushers gave way to Ollie Howe and his static starting device, a stationary engine turning a go-kart wheel jammed against the rear wheel of the Jawa on the stand. Mr Tichy maybe had not seen this method and was a little sceptical it would work. 1–2 cylinders fired, 1–2–3 – 3–2–1. Silence. No music would it make, only running for some 45 seconds, petrol pouring from up inside the carb area. Enter Mr Zdenek Tichy on baton, Frank Sheene on air lever, Sammy Miller on seat and throttle and myself on gear lever, petrol taps and stand, Ollie Howe and mate on starter. 1–2 – 1–2–3 – 1–2–3–4, four full cylinders fired, the orchestra played for some 2–3 minutes and then again started to fail, Sammy was dispatched along the pit road in an attempt to clear its throat. After a masterful turn and return, the engine again stalled, Sammy rolling to a halt with a silent patient. The team again went to work after changing the plugs and putting in more fuel. Mr Tichy lent his touch to proceedings by adding the one per cent Castrol R to the fuel in the customary dripping from the bottle method. Fragile machine, poor running, carbon hard tyres, 30-year-old reluctance to run below 8,000rpm and brakes not used for a considerable time – this was going to be some ride! Time for circuit closure was now pressing and the gathering crowd was getting uneasy at no action, so we discussed cutting short the final parade laps and just going out of the end of the pits exit, doubling back to the start line for the final ceremony. Mike offered the Kirby Metisse to do the final laps. My decision was, as Sammy had valiantly for some three quarters of an hour tried to ready the machine and had some feel of keeping it running in some sort of shape, he should attempt if at all possible to get it round to the line, some 200 yards. I would ride shotgun on the Kirby Metisse G50. Well, the Jawa fired, ran approximately 35 yards and stopped. Sammy was able to coast out of the pits exit and downhill to the start line and the awaiting crowd. The Kirby G50, moved along beside the Jawa, its single-cylinder engine echoing out between the grandstand and the pits.

In a final tribute the G50 echoed out across the circuit, then the engine was killed, the chequered flag unfurled and laid across the Jawa. A final salute to Little Bill at his home circuit.

Climbing from the Kirby G50, after the presentation and photographs, I sat on the Jawa on the start line and along with those present reflected on what might have been.

Then with another of Bill's friends and schoolmates Paul Smart, we silently pushed the machine up hill to the pits exit and I coasted it back unaided to the pit garage, where it was returned to Mr and Mrs Tichy's custody. What genuine lovely people. That day in 1969 had been a tragedy for us all.

The presence of Bill's younger sister Marie along with the presentation on behalf of his older sister Sue of his 1966 FIM World Championship silver medal made me feel very proud and humble to have been a family friend of the Ivys for some 45 years.

To have assisted Jim Parker, the New Era Club, Alan Robinson and the TTRA in this memorial event was an honour.

May Bill's memory move on to another chapter.

Roy Francis

Postscript by Gary Swift (Bill Ivy's step-nephew)

My first memory of Bill was when I was playing in the garden when I was around six years old and my dad walked through the back gate carrying a cardboard box with a picture of a motorbike on it. 'Its Bill's bike' I remember him saying, and it was a plastic model kit of one of the Yamahas that Bill rode, though I do not recall which one. I do remember playing with it though and now after all these years I wish I still had it.

When I was growing up, I knew of Bill and that he was a bike racer and that he was my dad's mate. He was also my aunt's brother and I obviously knew that he had been killed in 1969, but that was about it. I never really understood how well known he was in his sport until I was about 12, when I started reading *Motor Cycle News* and other magazines.

They would occasionally mention the late Bill Ivy in various articles and as I read them, I started to realise just how well known he had become in his too brief a life. My Aunt Sue, Bill's sister, lent me the book *No Time to Lose* by Alan Peck, a very interesting biography about Bill, which I read with great interest. It did, however, miss out the relationships that my father John and my stepmother Ann, who was engaged to Bill, had with him for a time.

My Nan (Nell), who sadly died in 1989, would sometimes mention him and I could tell that she had thought a lot about him as she and her neighbour would sometimes remember him while chatting away over the garden fence. Around that time, the pop group Paper Lace had a song in the charts called *Billy Don't be a Hero* and I remember the two of them over the fence almost in tears as they listened to it on the radio and fondly remembered Bill.

I have always been into bikes and even after I had a near-fatal accident in 1980 in which I broke my right leg and both arms, paralysing my right one in the process, I have never lost my love for motorcycles. I now ride a bike one handed, all the controls on the left bar. The throttle is connected up the wrong way round so I can open the bike up as I release the clutch lever. The front brake lever is a converted ISR clutch master cylinder that now acts as a very good front brake. Its much easier to ride the bike than to explain how I do it! When I am riding, I feel as able-bodied as any motorcycle rider does and all thoughts of my disability and pain disappear in the howl of the exhaust noise. I often think of the determination and skill that Bill had as I ride along the same roads that he and my father had raced each other along over 40 years ago. Every time I travel from Maidstone towards Rye in East Sussex, one of the most exciting rides on a Sunday morning, I can imagine them tearing along the A274 as they passed through Langley, past Bill's home at the top of Sutton Valence hill and flat out down the Headcorn straight. Just past the other side of Biddenden at Woolpack corner where it becomes the A262 was where Bill had one of his worst road accidents as he hit a telegraph pole 'long since removed'. That corner always gets my respect as I remember how it nearly killed Bill.

In February 2007 I was thinking about trying to collect some more photographs of Bill after buying a few on Ebay, so I telephoned my Aunt Sue and arranged to go and see her and borrow some pictures and get them copied. After talking to her and David while we looked through scores of old photos I brought some home to scan and save on my PC. It was then that I began to think that there should be another book about Bill as I felt there was a lot more that could be written about him. I had no idea how to go about it, and ever since school I had hated writing and I still am useless at English, but I did have the perfect opportunity to research it seeing as Sue and Marie were Bill's sisters and a lot of his old racing comrades were still living locally around Kent. I started by talking to Sue and David and then went on to see Marie and Sid, her husband. As I progressed it was getting easier all the time to get people to talk to me about Bill as, without exception, they still hold great feelings for him. After talking to Roy Francis, he told me that Mick Walker was writing a book about Bill and put me in touch with him. After talking to Mick he was kind enough to offer a few pages of this book for my own personal words on my research, and I thank him very much for this opportunity. I hope my research has helped in any small part to this book.

Giacomo Agostini

One very good example of the great affection that still exists among Bill's old friends was when I wrote to Giacomo Agostini. I never expected to get much of a response as I knew that he was still heavily involved in bike racing, and with friends like Valentino Rossi and the like why would an ex-multiple World Champion contact a relative of a man he raced with around 40 years ago? Well, I thought any reply would be a bonus. About a month passed when, one Wednesday evening in 2007 while having a few beers, I was watching an England versus Russia Euro 2008 qualifier when the telephone rang. I was not best pleased, as it was a good game – rare at that time for England! And I really did not want yet another cold caller trying to sell me a conservatory or patio for my first-floor flat! As I picked up the phone and said hello the usual long silent pause that accompanied these annoying salespeople started. 'Gary Swift?' said the caller in a foreign accent, 'Yes' I said, and just as I was about to tell him in no uncertain terms to get lost, the voice said, 'Its Agostini'. Well, it is not hard to imagine how surprised I was at hearing the 'salesperson' was in fact probably the most famous ex-motorcycle racer in the world! I was so thrown by this that I had to get my head together and I arranged to call him the following week. The fact that Giacomo Agostini had taken the time to telephone me and be prepared to talk to me about Bill only goes to show how highly he must have thought about him, and I do apologise for mistaking you for a salesperson Ago! Although the years have faded many facts from his memory, Ago had genuine passion in his voice as he recalled how he had a last conversation with Bill at the Sachsenring. With sadness in his voice Ago said: 'He had a very nice character and was friends with everybody, I remember before his crash, we stop because there was some problem with the track, I think there was some oil or something. And we stop and we stick together, sit down on the bike and we waiting about four or five minutes to clean the road. So we talking about something, and after, we have the green flag and everybody go and he crash and he die. I cry for two days when he died because he was a very nice person and very good friend.'

I am very grateful that Ago took the time out to telephone me and as I write down his words, it reminds me of an anecdote told to me by Paul Smart showing again how mischievous Bill was. Paul recalled how Bill would teach Ago some English phrases, one which I doubt he has used for years was 'Well fukka my old boots'.

Pauline Hailwood

Pauline Hailwood was also very helpful and sent me a lovely account of her memories of Bill, some of which I include here:

'I first met Bill Ivy at the Brands Hatch circuit in Kent on 13 August 1967. I was living and working in London at the time and had gone to Brands with a girlfriend of Mike Hailwood's called Erma, and Alan a colleague from the hairdressers where I worked as a receptionist. Erma couldn't drive so asked me to drive her down to see Mike and surprise him. Alan wanted to come too, so eventually we drove down in Alan's car and we enjoyed the day's racing. When the racing had finished, several of the riders including Mike, Bill and their entourages went to the bar to have a drink and relax, and this was when I was introduced to Bill. He was such a bright, bubbly, fun person; you couldn't help but like him immediately.

Bill was a straightforward kind of guy, with no airs and graces, you knew where you stood with him and he didn't suffer fools gladly. Not accustomed to the sophisticated upbringing that Mike had enjoyed, Mike tried to educate him with table etiquette and different foods, but Bill preferred his steak and chips. Mike also taught him a few words of Italian and French, but when Bill tried them out on some poor girl he discovered that they usually got him into trouble because Mike had played a trick on him and taught him something rude.

As a racer, Bill was brilliant and fearless, and was very well respected by his fellow riders. He had the strong determination necessary to be a champion and although small in stature, his upper body was very muscular and strong. This was probably helped by him performing his party trick of doing walking handstands while holding a bottle of coca cola in each hand!

When Mike retired from racing bikes and moved onto cars they didn't spend quite so much time together, but they still got together when they could and remained very close friends. Naturally, when Mike heard the terrible news that Bill had been killed at the Sachsenring circuit he was extremely upset, and it was at Bill's funeral that I saw Mike cry for the first time.

Sadly missed, Bill was one of life's true characters and I still have a photo of him on my dining room wall, and I smile every time I look at it. He was such a talented rider and such a lovely person. A cheeky chappie that you couldn't help but love and I will always remember him that way.'

Michelle 'Mike' Duff

I have spoken to many interesting people and without exception, they all still have great love and respect for Bill's memory. I also contacted Mike Duff, who has now been Michelle Duff for a number of years. She emailed me, and her memories are below:

'Prior to Bill joining the Yamaha Racing Team in 1965 I had little contact with him. At that time he specialized in the short circuits while I was mostly on the Continent. He first rode the Yamahas at Silverstone during a private test session, and that is really where he and I had our first words other than the occasional "Hi" at various race meetings. Both Phil Read and I thought Bill would be best suited to the new 125 Yamaha twin because of his size, but Bill liked the 250 better, and if I remember well, he was faster than me on both the 125 and the 250 during that Silverstone test session. I remember when the mechanics first brought out the little 125 twin and removed the fairing, Bill laughed out loud at the appearance of the engine. Two separate liquid cooled cylinders and heads were bolted to the crankcases and were canted forward slightly from vertical. Even I had to admit the tiny cylinders did look odd, and did seem just stuck onto the top of the crankcase. The design is now not odd but at that time it did seem a departure from what was accepted practice.

Bill only rode the Yamaha 125 and 250 three times before my accident in Japan at the end of the 1965 racing season, where he was flown over to team with Phil Read for the Japanese GP. During the Dutch TT earlier in 1965 there were five of us I think battling for second place with Read out front in first place by some five or six seconds. If I remember correctly, the group included Hugh Anderson (Suzuki), Luigi Taveri (Honda), Katayama (Suzuki) and Bill and myself on Yamahas. Near the end of the second last lap I was leading the group with Bill falling a bit behind (still learning the intricacies of the race course and the bike) and I nearly ran into the back of Read whose bike had slowed with engine problems. So we were now battling for first place. I'm sure I was not the only rider injected with renewed vigour, and managed to hold the lead to the finish. Bill finished a commendable fifth in such elite company. He was learning quickly.

In 1966 Bill had replaced me on the Yamaha racing team and I was relegated to a private runner, although the factory had left me an RD56 to ride, which was still a competitive bike. At the Belgian GP that year, Bill was struggling with the power and precarious handling of the RD05 Yamaha 250-4. He was frequently heard to comment how 'bloody awful' the handling was of the 1966 RD05.

Needless to say, I was a little peeved in 1966 that Bill had replaced me in the squad, seeing as how Yamaha had promised me a spot on the team should I return to form again. We were at Mallory Park for the Race of the Year. Bill's 250 Yamaha RD56 had just been rebuilt by one of the works mechanics and was fitted with short circuit exhaust pipes and had the large front brake from the 250-4. My RD56 had done half a dozen GPs without major engine work, and it had my own home-made disc brake fitted. Bill and I were together during the 250 race battling for second place. Hailwood was in first place on the Honda 6. Each lap coming out of the hairpin Hailwood would look back and wave us on. Sometime Bill was in second, other times I was in second. On the last lap Bill was in second coming out of the 'S' bend accelerating up towards the hairpin. I was determined to show the world, show Yamaha and show myself that I had arrived back and was not going to let Bill, the rider who had taken my place on the team, beat me. I just waited until Bill put on his brakes and then slipped up the outside and into the hairpin to lead him across the line in second place. It was a very satisfying race for me to beat Bill. But I was riding on adrenaline and had few such moments left in my career. Bill was a superior rider but at that time had not fully reached his peak. And, he had yet to experience the wrath of Phil Read. That was to come.

I was very saddened when I heard the news about Bill's death. I no longer raced in Europe in 1969, as 1967 was my last year on the Continental Circus. News of Bill's death came slowly to Canada and details were sparse. His death robbed the sport of a valued member, a great rider and a true hero. Motorcycle racing has little following here in Canada, so none of the national newspapers had any stories about his accident.

The Sachsenring race course was one of my favourite racing circuits but it was also very dangerous, like most of the GP courses at that time. Being public roads the course had all the inherent dangers like curbs, trees, brick walls, corners of buildings sticking out, cobble stone sections, etc. But these dangers tended to sort the men from the boys. A rider gets used to other riders crashing and hurting themselves. It was part of the game. Death was a constant thought, but our passion for the sport was so strong we just thought that an 'accident' was something that would happen to someone else.

The start finish line at Sachsenring back then divided the pit area and any rider who was pitted after the start/finish line could sneak out and get in one more practice lap once the chequered flag was displayed to end the session. I had heard that Bill's helmet had come off when he crashed which contributed greatly to his death. I had assumed that the Jawa pit was after the start/finish line and when the chequered flag was displayed to end the practice session, Bill might have grabbed his helmet, placed it on his head and headed out for a quick lap. He might have been fumbling with the strap of his helmet with his clutch hand when the engine seized. With only one hand on the handlebars he had no option but to crash. This is all pure speculation on my part, but it seemed logical knowing the layout of the Sachsenring race course and the general practise by riders at the time. I always took a pit after the start/finish line and often did as I've described above.'

Other people I talked to also have positive memories of Bill, and I include a few of them here.

Don Godden

I heard about Billy Ivy long before I met him. That was through one of my work colleagues at Drake and Fletchers in Maidstone; his name was George Burniston, commonly called 'Spider'. His friend was Ned Noakes of Noakes Engineering from Ulcombe, for whom Bill Ivy's dad worked. Spider used to come into work at Drake and Fletchers and tell us about this cocky little whippersnapper he knew who used to come into Noakes Engineering and mess about with the bikes that were there and ride around the car park. Bill's dad was a welder for Noakes and repaired the agricultural machinery there.

When Bill left school he went to work for Chisholm's in Maidstone, he was very small for his age and before he had a motorcycle licence he used to ride a bicycle around Maidstone. He would ride around to the motorcycle dealers collecting spare parts. He used to go to Hitches in Knightrider Street, Redhill Motors on the bridge and I used to bump into him at those places.

He ultimately got a motorcycle licence and ended up on a Triumph, or anything else that he could borrow from Chisholm's to get to and from work.

I think it was fairly obvious that he was going to get involved with motorcycle racing, and he did a little bit of grass track racing. I don't know whether he was already racing or not. He obviously had a lot of potential as he was quite fearless.

I got on well with Bill; we were on the same wavelength I think as far as the sport was concerned. All through his life, wherever we met we would chat to each other about what we were doing and how it was going.

I used to meet Bill everywhere to do with motorcycling, I remember meeting him at Brands Hatch in the paddock by the pits where there used to stand an old wooden shed. He was with a very famous lady then, a rock star, Lulu. He left her sitting at a table with a cup of tea and came across to chat to me; she took a very dim view of it. It didn't worry Bill you took him for a friend for what you got out of the friendship and he vice-versa. He obviously had an eye for the ladies, and when he got involved with motorcars he also got an eye for very fast cars. He had a dark blue Maserati, and I remember him overtaking me at the top of Wrotham hill before the motorway was open and there was a sharp right bend and he went round sideways waving his hand at me, but I don't know where he was going at the time.

Once I had to go and visit someone in hospital which meant I had to go up the hill at Boxley to meet someone who I was going with, and there up the hill was a Maserati stuck up to the axles in mud, with the footmarks of

Bill's Italian shoes all around it. I never got to the bottom of that, but obviously he was courting and got stuck in the mud and left it there.

The thing about Bill that always struck you was his spirit. He was a lionheart. He was absolutely fearless; he was having all sorts of motorcycle accidents which I think would have killed a lesser mortal. Somehow or other he managed to survive them.

I knew his family very well and used to go and meet them at their home in Sutton Valence at Captains Close. I knew his sister Marie very well. I was always very well received and it didn't matter when I went round. There was always a cup of tea and a chat.

I progressed through my sport and ultimately went motor racing into Formula 2. Bill was already doing it and he was quite literally setting the place alight. I met him all over the country and in fact all over Europe during that time. I remember one particular incident at Zolder in Belgium. When in practice he went off the track, the car rolled, went back on its wheels and he drove it back into the pits. In the process of the accident he wiped most of the odds and ends off it and so everybody had to rebuild the car overnight to get him racing the following day.

All of the names in Formula 1 drove Formula 2 cars as well. At most F1 meetings there was also an F2 race: you would get Jackie Stewart and all of the stars of the day. I was driving F2 in 1969 and doing my own thing, which was long track racing and rubbing shoulders with the F1 people as well. I have to say that I was making more money out of my longtrack motorcycle racing than the majority of those F1 car drivers! I think Bill was looking to develop more in motor racing because at that time there were not many works motorbike teams. I think if it was not costing him such a fortune Bill would have carried on with F2. There were the works cars like Brabham and Lotus but he was not in any of those seats, had he been in one and thought that financially he would have been as well off, if not better, he would have continued.

Without a doubt, the race cars in those days were more dangerous and there had been a series of fatalities with the open wheel cars. Jim Clarke in particular, was killed in 1968. The bikes in comparison were not as lethal and you had to be unlucky to have a fatal accident, as they had got over previous tyre problems that had affected the sport in previous years. He would not have been riding the Jawa if he could have ridden something else. The Jawa was not a proven race bike, and that is what the Czech factory appreciated in their involvement with Bill. They were lucky to have him as they could take advantage of his experience in developing the bike and the positive publicity which surrounded him.

His funeral was at St Peter's Church in Ditton. I think the whole of the motor racing world both in motorbikes and cars were there. I remember Sir Frank Williams was present, though he was not a 'sir' at the time. Everybody who was on Bill's wavelength attended. I went to the wake, which was also held in Ditton. I felt I couldn't stay very long because I was terribly sad. I'd known Bill virtually ever since he had left school, right through his working life and racing career. We had a bloody good relationship, and I went to his wake and everybody was having a good time. It was too much for me and I had to go.

I had a very good relationship with the Jawa factory. I was there shortly after Bill's death and they were terribly broken up about it. He had given them a lot of very good publicity and they thought a lot of him.

Billy was very straight, he was down the line. You knew where you stood with him. Without a doubt if he had taken life more seriously it might have improved his performance. He did like a good time, and whether that affected his performance or not, who knows?

Tommy Robb

Bill was a cheeky, impish young rider coming on the scene, wanting to get to the top rapidly and equally determined that he would do so. I first met him properly at Brands Hatch when I was riding for the Honda factory. Bill came and asked me to try to get him a ride on the factory team. At that time Bill was riding the Chisholm Honda and was on the lower rung of the success ladder.

Regarding his character, I saw his zest for life. Fun and determination in his own ability were a driving force in his career. He had an outstanding personality and enjoyed a joke. Like me, he was small in stature and took offence at anyone who thought this would reduce his ability to be a great rider.

I remember well the news of Bills death reaching me when I was on holiday with my family in Spain. I was stunned, and saddened to the extent that I had a quiet cry to myself as I had lost a dynamic little friend and motorcycle racing had lost one of its most courageous riders.

How far could Bill have gone in his career? An impossible question to answer, for with 'Little Bill's' determination, anything was possible.

Roy Francis

One of the sayings that Bill used was 'All is fair in love and war' and throughout his life this was adhered to as strictly as his commitment to road racing. Bill would quite often stop at bus stops to see if young women would like a lift! And many of our girlfriends were chatted up.

I do recall another time when he was riding for Frank Sheene, a few of us were going to Cadwell Park circuit and Bill took along the girlfriend he had at the time. We went to pick up the bikes from Frank in Queens Square in London, and when we got there Frank said that his son Barry (who was only about 12 at the time) had to come along with us. Frank supplied us with a tent with some plastic ground sheets but said that Barry was to sleep in the car as it would be more comfortable. Bill and his girlfriend also spent the night in the car. A young Barry Sheene had an unexpectedly early sex education lesson!

Wednesday afternoons we would go up and practice at Brands Hatch. It was our home track and whenever Bill raced on it, he looked unbeatable. He used to live in an old jumper and quite often he would wear it over his leathers while practising.

We would have regular use of the Chisholm bikes or whatever sponsor's bike that he was racing at the time. That was how I got to ride on the Gilera. Bill just asked if I fancied a ride on it.

Monty's, Sheene's and the Chisholms' bikes were all tested around Brands whenever possible. Riding up to four classes in a race meeting meant that Bill always had something to test.

When Bill was picked by Yamaha to race for them I did not get to see him as much, only really when he came home to see his mum or pop into the shop where I was still working. He would always ask me how my racing was going and what I was up too.

Bill and Phil Read both got along quite well together as teammates but did not really socialise in their private lives as much. When it was said that Phil had ignored team orders and won both the 1968 125 and 250 World Championships I can understand that what happened upset their relationship and caused some ill feeling with the motorcycle press and the public.

I was working away on my bikes one Saturday in Geoff Monty's Edenbridge workshop and heard on the radio that Bill had crashed at Sachsenring while practising for the Grand Prix.

For me it just took the wind out of my sails. I had been slowly climbing up the racing ladder myself for the last 10 years following Bill. Riding his old bikes and racing in his old teams, always hoping that I would someday be as good as he was. When Bill was taken, I retired from racing there and then. I told Geoff Monty that I did not want to ride anymore. He did persuade me to ride once more in 1970 but I only completed a couple of laps and decided that was it; I did not want it any more. I have never regretted packing up.

If I had to compare Bill with any of today's riders, I would say that he had the build of Loris Capirossi but with the prospect of a career on four wheels. Personality wise, Bill's relationship with the public and his determination to succeed and will to win reminds me of Valentino Rossi. With his charisma and mischievous nature, he was favoured by the press. In retrospect, he may have needed a damn good PR man like Max Clifford to stop him stepping on a few banana skins.

The Jawa

In 1999 when I went to the tribute at Brands [the 30th, and final, Bill Ivy Memorial meeting] someone in their infinite wisdom had decided that I would ride the infamous Jawa that Bill was killed on. I was glad when it would not run properly! However, on looking at the machine then, it was very well made and when I sat on it it felt like a well put together race bike. It is a misconception that the Jawa was a poorly made death trap. It was no different to the Yamaha race bikes of the same time; two-strokes were prone to seizing. Bill knew exactly what he was riding and with his knowledge, he would not have raced an unsafe machine. It was a freak accident; the bike seized and threw Bill off before he could do anything about it. The same thing could have happened on any of the bikes he rode, Yamahas used to seize with great regularity. Bikes were being developed all the time and things used to happen, it was a tragedy that Bill got killed and it was also a tragedy for Jawa as they were a great band of engineers on the way up in motorcycle racing.

Fans' Memories:

Graham Clutterbuck

I remember being at Brands – it would be 1968 I think (Boxing Day). I had travelled by train with my friend Mark from Guildford. (How times have changed able to catch a train on Boxing Day). We were 13 or 14 at the time. The weather was bloody cold and as we walked along the pit straight behind the stands we spied two 'hippie types'. When they turned around we recognised them as being Ivy and Hailwood. We were awe struck but they knew we had recognised who they were and saw how nervous we were of approaching. They came over asked how we were and then to our amazement and delight took us for a drink and a chat. As you can imagine, 'over the moon' could not describe how we felt about meeting our heroes.

Obviously they were not racing that day but were just out to see the rest of the lads and have a day spectating. My lasting impression was of two great sportsmen who cared for their fans. It is a day I will never forget.

B. Jewitt

Well, many years ago spectating at Cadwell Park I saw Bill Ivy and Phil Read on works Yamahas (125 & 250 fours), plus Mike Hailwood on a works Honda: what a mouth watering proposition!

The weather was really awful, plenty of rain, anyway Hailwood comes round on his 500 four, drops it in the wet, walking along at the trackside then Bill Ivy comes by gesturing to Mike as if to say 'what the hell are you doing walking? Ha-ha!' or something like that. Hailwood's reply was a very quick 'V' sign. Boy, it was hilarious, I think at the time Bill and Mike were flatmates.

I remembered listening to the TT Races on the radio, 125cc race, Bill Ivy being helped from his bike after lapping at 100mph, what a racer. One of the best, sadly missed.

Paul Trayner

He was the Danny Pedrosa of his day. My memories are very hazy, embellished by endless re-telling. I went to Cadwell a few times in the mid-1960s, probably between 1965 and 1968. I have two clear memories. One was stopping a mile or two from the circuit, thinking I had a strange noise from my BSA.

It turned out to be the Honda Six revving at the circuit, what a wail! The same meeting (perhaps) we watched, after the mountain but before the hairpin, all the riders had similar flowing lines through one section, some definitely braking. Bill, however, came through under power and often on just the back wheel! Showboating? It didn't seem so, but the only rider I have seen do anything similar was Foggy through the old Dingle Dell at Brands.

Conclusion

I have enjoyed talking to people about Bill and even now, nearly 40 years after his death, the emotion in people's voices as they recall him shows through strongly. When I look at the men and machines that were around in the 1960s and how fast they were, then I look inside the latest magazines with the road tests of the latest superbikes capable of nearly 200mph. I read various comments of the 2008 Honda Fireblade, for example, saying it is a fantastic bike but boring! It amazes me that we are now so complacent that riding a near double-ton rocket ship can be described in this way. What would Bill have thought? Even now riding a 1000cc sports bike around the Isle of Man you would have to go some to average the 100mph that Bill did on his Yamaha 125. How can any bike be boring?

Above everything else, the passion Bill had for racing bikes and cars and chasing women is so strong that I am sure he would still be doing one or the other if he were alive today.

He has certainly gained my respect for the 'live for the day' attitude that I hope never leaves me.

As I finished writing about Bill, I read that Robert Dunlop had been killed while on the first lap of practice at the 2008 North West 200. His bike seized and he crashed and was hit by another rider and sustained massive chest injuries, proving fatal. It is yet another terrible accident but I am sure Robert will not be the last rider to be killed doing what he loved. Two days after he was killed his son Michael raced in the 250cc class and won! As I watched him on TV after the race he and most of the people around him were so emotional and both happy and sad, it just summed up the spirit of a motorcycle racer. They all know the danger but only the special ones experience the feeling of being a winner, and yet they all give 100 per cent.

Gary Swift
May 2008

Appendices

Bill Ivy Motorcycle Road Racing Results

(RL = Record Lap; FL = Fastest Lap)

1959

Position	Class	Machine	Circuit	Date
3	50cc	Chis Itom	Brands Hatch	27 March
3	50cc	Chis Itom	Brands Hatch	19 April
Retired	50cc	Chis Itom	Brands Hatch	18 May
3	50cc	Chis Itom	Brands Hatch	5 July
Retired	50cc	Chis Itom	Brands Hatch	23 August
3	50cc	Chis Itom	Brands Hatch	20 September
Unplaced	350cc	Velocette	Brands Hatch	20 September
Retired (3rd lap, when leading)	50cc	Chis Itom	Brands Hatch	11 October RL

Bill also rode Don Chisholm's Velocette 350 at one Brands Hatch meeting: date unknown

1960

Position	Class	Machine	Circuit	Date
1	50cc	Chis Itom	Brands Hatch	15 April FL
* 1	50cc Chilton 250-mile Enduro (co-rider Maurice Thomas)	Chis Itom	Snetterton	14 May FL
12	50cc	Chis Itom	Brands Hatch	15 May
Retired	200cc	Gilera 175cc	Brands Hatch	15 May
3	50cc	Chis Itom	Brands Hatch	6 June
Unplaced	200cc	Gilera 175cc	Brands Hatch	6 June
Non-starter	50cc	Chis Itom	Brands Hatch	21 August
Non-starter	200cc	Gilera 175cc	Brands Hatch	21 August

* Disqualified 4 months later

1961

Position	Class	Machine	Circuit	Date
1	50cc	Chis Itom	Brands Hatch	31 March FL
12	200cc	Gilera 190cc	Brands Hatch	31 March
4	50cc Chilton 250-mile Enduro (co-rider Maurice Thomas)	Chis Itom	Snetterton	7 May

Position	Class	Machine	Circuit	Date
5	250cc Heat	Gilera 190cc	Brands Hatch	25 June
4	250cc Final	Gilera 190cc	Brands Hatch	25 June
Unplaced	250cc	Gilera 190cc	Brands Hatch	9 July
3	50cc	Chis Itom	Brands Hatch	20 August
4	125cc	Chis Honda CB92	Brands Hatch	20 August
Retired	50cc	Chis Itom	Brands Hatch	8 October
Unplaced	250cc	Gilera 190cc	Brands Hatch	8 October

1962

Position	Class	Machine	Circuit	Date
1	50cc Heat	Chis Itom	Welwyn Garden City	14 April
3	50cc Semi Final	Chis Itom	Welwyn Garden City	14 April
2	50cc Pursuit Final (partnered by Mike Simmonds)	Chis Itom	Welwyn Garden City	14 April
4	50cc	Chis Itom	Brands Hatch	20 April
8	125cc	Chis Honda CB92	Brands Hatch	20 April
5	125cc	Chis Honda CB92	Brands Hatch	13 May
Retired (engine, 1st lap)	50cc TT	Chis Itom	Isle of Man	8 June
Unplaced	50cc	Chis Itom	Brands Hatch	11 June
Retired (engine failure)	Racing 50 Club 250-mile Enduro (co-rider Roy Francis)	Chis Itom	Snetterton	4 August
Unplaced	50cc	Chis Itom	Brands Hatch	19 August
Unplaced	125cc	Chis Honda CB92	Brands Hatch	19 August
7	50cc	Chis Itom	Brands Hatch	23 September
8	125cc	Chis Honda CB92	Brands Hatch	23 September
Non-starter	50cc	Chis Itom	Brands Hatch	14 October
Retired (crash)	125cc	Chis Honda CB92	Brands Hatch	14 October

1963

Position	Class	Machine	Circuit	Date
2	50cc	Sheene Special	Brands Hatch	12 April
10	125cc	Chis Honda CB92	Brands Hatch	12 April
2	50cc	Sheene Special	Brands Hatch	12 May
2	125cc	Sheene Bultaco	Brands Hatch	12 May
7	50cc TT	Sheene Special	Isle of Man	14 June
Retired (broken carb needle clip)	125cc TT	Sheene Bultaco	Isle of Man	12 June

Position	*Class*	*Machine*	*Circuit*	*Date*
5	50cc	Sheene Special	Brands Hatch	14 July
Unplaced	125cc	Sheene Bultaco	Brands Hatch	14 July
7	125cc	Sheene Bultaco	Snetterton	28 July
7	50cc British Championship	Sheene Special	Oulton Park	5 August
Retired	125cc British Championship	Sheene Bultaco	Oulton Park	5 August
6	50cc	Sheene Special	Brands Hatch	25 August
2	125cc	Sheene Bultaco	Brands Hatch	25 August
2	250cc	Monty Yamaha TD1	Brands Hatch	25 August
8	500cc Redex Trophy	Monty Matchless	Brands Hatch	25 August
5	1000cc	Monty Matchless 496cc	Brands Hatch	25 August
1	125cc	Sheene Bultaco	Snetterton	8 September FL
14	250cc	GMS	Snetterton	8 September
1	500cc	Norton	Snetterton	8 September
Retired	50cc	Sheene Special	Brands Hatch	22 September
6	125cc	Sheene Bultaco	Brands Hatch	22 September
Retired	250cc	Yamaha TD1	Brands Hatch	22 September
Non-starter	500cc	Monty Norton	Brands Hatch	22 September
Retired (crash)	250cc	Monty Yamaha TD1	Madrid, Spain	7 October
Non-starter (over start money)	500cc	Monty Norton	Madrid, Spain	7 October
Non-starter (injured in previous meeting)			Zaragosa, Spain	14 October

1964

Position	*Class*	*Machine*	*Circuit*	*Date*
2	125cc	Chis Honda CR93 (debut)	Mallory Park	22 March
8 (after crash at Druids Hill Hairpin)	125cc	Chis Honda CR93	Brands Hatch	27 March
4	250cc	Yamaha TD1	Brands Hatch	27 March
11	500cc	Monard	Brands Hatch	27 March
Unplaced	1000cc	Monard 650cc	Brands Hatch	27 March
5	125cc	Chis Honda CR93	Snetterton	29 March
3	250cc	Yamaha TD1	Snetterton	29 March
2	125cc	Chis Honda CR93	Oulton Park	30 March
10	500cc	Monard	Oulton Park	30 March
7	250cc	Yamaha TD1	Silverstone	4 April
12	350cc	Monty Norton	Silverstone	4 April

Position	*Class*	*Machine*	*Circuit*	*Date*
14	500cc	Monard	Silverstone	4 April
2	125cc	Chis Honda CR93	Brands Hatch	19 April
3	250cc	Yamaha TD1	Brands Hatch	19 April
Retired (ran out of petrol when leading)	500cc	Monard	Brands Hatch	19 April
5	1000cc	Monard 498cc	Brands Hatch	19 April
4	250cc	Yamaha TD1	Snetterton	26 April
3	1000cc	Monard 649cc	Snetterton	26 April
1	125cc	Chis Honda CR93	Mallory Park	3 May FL
5	250cc	Yamaha TD1	Mallory Park	3 May
2	125cc	Chis Honda CR93	Snetterton	10 May RL
2	250cc	Yamaha TD1	Snetterton	10 May
1	125cc	Chis Honda CR93	Brands Hatch	18 May RL
Retired	250cc	Monty Yamaha	Brands Hatch	18 May
7	500cc	Monard	Brands Hatch	18 May
3	125cc	Chis Honda CR93	Mallory Park	14 June
4	250cc	Yamaha TD1	Mallory Park	14 June
4	125cc	Chis Honda CR93	Brands Hatch	21 June
1	250cc	Yamaha (1963 Works RD56)	Brands Hatch	21 June
5	350cc	AJS	Brands Hatch	21 June
11	500cc	Monard	Brands Hatch	21 June
1	125cc	Chis Honda CR93	Snetterton	26 July FL
4	250cc	Cotton	Snetterton	26 July
6	350cc	Norton	Snetterton	26 July
Retired (valve dropped in practice)	500cc	Monard	Snetterton	26 July
4	125cc	Chis Honda CR93	Oulton Park	3 August
6	350cc	Norton	Oulton Park	3 August
3	Les Graham Memorial	Norton 499cc	Oulton Park	3 August
1	125cc	Chis Honda CR93	Brands Hatch	16 August FL
Retired (holed piston)	250cc	Cotton	Brands Hatch	16 August
7	500cc	Monard	Brands Hatch	16 August
9	1000cc	Monard 650cc	Brands Hatch	16 August
1	125cc	Chis Honda CR93	Aberdare Park	22 August
1	125cc Heat	Chis Honda CR93	Mallory Park	30 August
1	125cc Final	Chis Honda CR93	Mallory Park	30 August FL
1	250cc Heat	Cotton	Mallory Park	30 August
1	250cc Final	Cotton	Mallory Park	30 August FL
1	350cc Heat	Norton	Mallory Park	30 August

Position	Class	Machine	Circuit	Date
6	350cc Final	Norton	Mallory Park	30 August
5	500cc	Monard	Mallory Park	30 August
1	125cc	Chis Honda CR93	Castle Combe	5 September RL
1	125cc	Chis Honda CR93	Snetterton	6 September FL
1	350cc Heat	AJS	Snetterton	6 September
4	350cc Final	AJS	Snetterton	6 September
1	125cc	Chis Honda CR93	Cadwell Park	13 September RL
2	250cc	Cotton	Cadwell Park	13 September FL
2	500cc	Monard	Cadwell Park	13 September
2	1000cc	Monard 650cc	Silverstone	19 September
1	125cc	Chis Honda CR93	Brands Hatch	20 September FL
Retired	250cc	Cotton	Brands Hatch	20 September
5	500cc	Monard	Brands Hatch	20 September
9	1000cc	Monard 650cc	Brands Hatch	20 September
2	125cc	Chis Honda CR93	Mallory Park	27 September
6	250cc	Cotton (Minter's works machine)	Mallory Park	27 September
5	500cc	Monard	Mallory Park	27 September
6	Race of the Year	Monard 498cc	Mallory Park	27 September
1	125cc	Chis Honda CR93	Oulton Park	4 October FL
4	250cc	Cotton	Oulton Park	4 October
3	500cc	Monard	Oulton Park	4 October
1	125cc	Chis Honda CR93	Brands Hatch	11 October FL
2	250cc	Cotton	Brands Hatch	11 October
6	350cc	Norton	Brands Hatch	11 October
6	500cc	Monard	Brands Hatch	11 October
5	1000cc	Monard 649cc	Brands Hatch	11 October
1	Racing 50 Club 250-mile Enduro (co-rider Paul Latham)	Honda CR110	Snetterton	17 October FL

125cc ACU Star Champion

3rd 250cc ACU Star

1965

Position	Class	Machine	Circuit	Date
1	125cc	Chis Honda CR93	Mallory Park	7 March FL
1	250cc Heat	Cotton	Mallory Park	7 March
4	250cc Final	Cotton	Mallory Park	7 March
3	350cc	Norton	Mallory Park	7 March
Retired (broken valve)	500cc	Monard	Mallory Park	7 March

Position	*Class*	*Machine*	*Circuit*	*Date*
1	125cc	Chis Honda CR93	Brands Hatch	21 March FL
4	250cc	Cotton	Brands Hatch	21 March
5	350cc	Norton	Brands Hatch	21 March
3	1000cc	Monard	Brands Hatch	21 March
1	125cc	Chis Honda CR93	Snetterton	28 March FL
1	250cc	Cotton	Snetterton	28 March
4	350cc	Norton	Snetterton	28 March
5	500cc	Norton	Snetterton	28 March
1	50cc	Honda CR110	Brands Hatch	16 April
2	125cc	Chis Honda CR93	Brands Hatch	16 April RL
2	250cc	Cotton	Brands Hatch	16 April
9	350cc	Norton	Brands Hatch	16 April
2	500cc	Monard	Brands Hatch	16 April
Retired (crash)	1000cc	Monard 649cc	Brands Hatch	16 April
1	125cc	Chis Honda CR93	Snetterton	18 April RL
5	250cc	Cotton	Snetterton	18 April
Non-starter	350cc	Monty Norton	Snetterton	18 April
6	500cc	Monard	Snetterton	18 April
2	125cc	Chis Honda CR93	Oulton Park	19 April
2	250cc	Monty Cotton	Oulton Park	19 April
4	350cc	Monty Norton	Oulton Park	19 April
1	125cc	Chis Honda CR93	Mallory Park	20 April FL
2	250cc	Monty Cotton (6-speed)	Mallory Park	20 April
Retired (crash)	350cc Heat	Monty Norton	Mallory Park	20 April
Retired (pulled in)	500cc	Monard	Mallory Park	20 April
1	125cc	Chis Honda CR93	Brands Hatch	9 May
3	250cc	Higley Cotton (4-speed)	Brands Hatch	9 May
3	350cc	Kirby AJS	Brands Hatch	9 May
1	500cc	Kirby Matchless	Brands Hatch	9 May
3	1000cc	Kirby Matchless 496cc	Brands Hatch	9 May
1	125cc	Chis Honda CR93	Snetterton	16 May
4	250cc	Higley Cotton	Snetterton	16 May FL
Non-starter	350cc	Kirby AJS	Snetterton	16 May
1	500cc Heat	Kirby Matchless	Snetterton	16 May
1	500cc Final	Kirby Matchless	Snetterton	16 May
1	125cc	Chis Honda CR93	Mallory Park	23 May FL
1	250cc	Higley Cotton	Mallory Park	23 May FL
3	350cc	Kirby AJS	Mallory Park	23 May
1	500cc	Kirby Matchless	Mallory Park	23 May FL

Position	*Class*	*Machine*	*Circuit*	*Date*
7	125cc Ultra Lightweight TT	Works Yamaha	Isle of Man	16 June
Retired (crash)	250cc Lightweight TT	Works Yamaha	Isle of Man	16 June
Retired (chain)	350cc Junior TT	Kirby AJS	Isle of Man	16 June
Retired (broken con-rod)	500cc Senior TT	Kirby Matchless	Isle of Man	18 June
1	125cc	Chis Honda CR93	Mallory Park	20 June
Retired	250cc	Higley Cotton	Mallory Park	20 June
2	350cc	Kirby AJS	Mallory Park	20 June
2	500cc	Kirby Matchless	Mallory Park	20 June
4	125cc Dutch TT	Works Yamaha	Assen	26 June
1	125cc	Chis Honda CR93	Brands Hatch	27 June FL
2	350cc	Kirby AJS	Brands Hatch	27 June
1	500cc	Kirby Matchless	Brands Hatch	27 June
1	Match Race Team	Kirby Matchless	Brands Hatch	27 June
Retired (engine seizure)	500 Mile Production Race (co-rider Ron Chandler)	Arter Matchless 750cc	Castle Combe	24 July
Retired (when leading)	50cc	Honda	Snetterton	25 July
Retired (broken steering damper)	250cc	Higley Cotton	Snetterton	25 July
1	250cc	Higley Cotton	Thruxton	1 August FL
Retired (crash)	350cc	Kirby AJS	Thruxton	1 August
4	50cc	Honda	Silverstone	14 August
3	125cc	Hannah Honda (debut)	Silverstone	14 August
6	250cc	Higley Cotton	Silverstone	14 August
6	350cc	Kirby AJS	Silverstone	14 August
2	500cc	Kirby Matchless	Silverstone	14 August
1	125cc	Honda	Brands Hatch	15 August RL
7 (plug trouble)	250cc	Works Yamaha	Brands Hatch	15 August RL
3	350cc	Kirby AJS	Brands Hatch	15 August
1	500cc	Kirby Matchless	Brands Hatch	15 August FL
Retired (misfire)	125c	Honda	Oulton Park	30 August
5	250cc	Higley Cotton	Oulton Park	30 August
4	350cc	Kirby AJS	Oulton Park	30 August
1	500cc British Championship	Kirby Matchless	Oulton Park	30 August
4	Les Graham Memorial	Kirby Matchless 496cc	Oulton Park	30 August
1	125cc	Hannah Honda	Snetterton	5 September FL
3	250cc	Higley Cotton	Snetterton	5 September
5	350cc	Kirby AJS	Snetterton	5 September
1	500cc	Kirby Matchless	Snetterton	5 September

Position	*Class*	*Machine*	*Circuit*	*Date*
1	125cc	Hannah Honda	Cadwell Park	12 September FL
Retired (crash)	250cc	Higley Cotton	Cadwell Park	12 September
6	350cc	Kirby AJS	Cadwell Park	12 September
Retired (illness)	500cc	Kirby Matchless	Cadwell Park	12 September
1	125cc	Hannah Honda	Brands Hatch	19 September
Retired (engine)	250cc	Higley Cotton	Brands Hatch	19 September
1	350cc Fred Neville Trophy	Yamaha 254cc	Brands Hatch	19 September FL
5	1000cc	Kirby Matchless 496cc	Brands Hatch	19 September FL
1	125cc	Hannah Honda	Mallory Park	26 September FL
4	250cc	Higley Cotton	Mallory Park	26 September
7	350cc	Kirby AJS	Mallory Park	26 September
2	500cc	Kirby Matchless	Mallory Park	26 September
3	Race of the Year	Kirby Matchless 496cc	Mallory Park	26 September
1	125cc	Hannah Honda	Oulton Park	2 October FL
Retired (broken expansion chamber)	250cc	Works Cotton	Oulton Park	2 October
1	350cc Heat	Kirby AJS	Oulton Park	2 October FL
4	350cc Final	Kirby AJS	Oulton Park	2 October
1	500cc Heat	Kirby Matchless	Oulton Park	2 October FL
1	500cc Final	Kirby Matchless	Oulton Park	2 October FL
1	50cc	Honda	Brands Hatch	10 October FL
2	125cc	Hannah Honda	Brands Hatch	10 October
Retired (engine seizure)	250cc	Works Yamaha	Brands Hatch	10 October FL
Retired (carburation)	350cc	Kirby AJS	Brands Hatch	10 October
1	500cc Redex Trophy	Kirby Matchless	Brands Hatch	10 October FL
2	500cc Race of the South	Kirby Matchless	Brands Hatch	10 October
4	125cc Japanese GP	Works Yamaha	Suzuka	23 October
3	250cc Japanese GP	Works Yamaha	Suzuka	24 October
3	125cc	Hannah Honda	Mallory Park	31 October
1	500cc	Kirby Matchless	Mallory Park	31 October FL

MCN Man of the Year Award

500cc British Champion

125cc ACU Star

500cc ACU Star

1966

Position	*Class*	*Machine*	*Circuit*	*Date*
4	350cc	Kirby Metisse	Mallory Park	6 March
1	500cc Heat	Kirby Metisse	Mallory Park	6 March
1	500cc Final	Kirby Metisse	Mallory Park	6 March FL

Position	*Class*	*Machine*	*Circuit*	*Date*
1	350cc	Kirby Metisse	Brands Hatch	13 March FL
5	500cc	Kirby Metisse	Brands Hatch	13 March
2	1000cc	Kirby Metisse 496cc	Brands Hatch	13 March
Retired (crash)	350cc Heat	Kirby Metisse	Snetterton	20 March
2	350cc	Kirby Metisse	Brands Hatch	8 April
Retired (sticking throttle)	500cc	Kirby Metisse	Brands Hatch	8 April
1	1000cc King of Brands	Kirby Metisse	Brands Hatch	8 April
2	350cc	Kirby Metisse	Snetterton	10 April
2	500cc	Kirby Metisse	Snetterton	10 April
5	350cc	Kirby Metisse	Oulton Park	11 April
5	500cc	Kirby Metisse	Oulton Park	11 April
Retired (ignition)	350cc	Kirby Metisse	Mallory Park	21 April
Retired (suspension)	500cc	Kirby Metisse	Mallory Park	21 April
Retired (engine)	250cc	Works Yamaha twin	Cesenatico	24 April
1	125cc Spanish GP	Works Yamaha twin	Barcelona	8 May
Retired (engine)	250cc	Works Yamaha four	Barcelona	8 May
Retired (clutch)	125cc West German GP	Works Yamaha twin	Hockenheim	22 May
3	250cc West German GP	Works Yamaha four	Hockenheim	22 May
Retired (crash)	250cc French GP	Works Yamaha four	Clermont-Ferrand	29 May
1	250cc	Works Yamaha twin	Brands Hatch	30 May
3	350cc	Works Yamaha 251cc	Brands Hatch	30 May
3	500cc	Kirby Metisse	Brands Hatch	30 May
4	1000cc	Kirby Metisse 496cc	Brands Hatch	30 May
1	125cc	Works Yamaha twin	Mallory Park	19 June FL
2	250cc	Works Yamaha twin	Mallory Park	19 June
1	125cc Dutch TT	Works Yamaha twin	Assen	25 June
Retired (engine)	250cc Dutch TT	Works Yamaha four	Assen	25 June
Retired (crash)	500 mile Production Race (co-rider John Cooper)	Kirby BSA Spitfire 654cc	Brands Hatch	26 June
6	250cc Belgian GP	Works Yamaha four	Spa Francorchamps	3 July
3	125cc East German GP	Works Yamaha twin	Sachsenring	17 July
Retired (carburation)	250cc East German GP	Works Yamaha four	Sachsenring	17 July
3	125cc Czech GP	Works Yamaha twin	Brno	24 July RL
Retired (gearbox)	125cc Finnish GP	Works Yamaha twin	Imatra	31 July
Retired (crash due to broken oil pipe)	350cc	Kirby Metisse AJS	Brands Hatch	14 August
Non-starter (following previous crash)	Ulster GP	Works Yamaha	Dundrod	20 August
Retired (carburation)	250cc Lightweight TT	Works Yamaha four	Isle of Man	28 August
1	125cc Ultra Lightweight TT	Works Yamaha twin	Isle of Man	30 August RL

Position	*Class*	*Machine*	*Circuit*	*Date*
3	125cc Italian GP	Works Yamaha twin	Monza	11 September
1	250cc Heat	Works Yamaha twin	Mallory Park	25 September FL
3	250cc Final	Works Yamaha twin	Mallory Park	25 September
2	Race of the Year	Works Yamaha twin 248cc	Mallory Park	25 September
2	350cc Japanese GP	Works Yamaha twin 251cc	Fisco	14 October
1	125cc Japanese GP	Works Yamaha twin	Fisco	15 October FL
Retired	250cc Japanese GP	Works Yamaha twin	Fisco	15 October

2nd 125cc World Championship

1967

Position	*Class*	*Machine*	*Circuit*	*Date*
1	125cc	Works Yamaha twin	Riccione	5 April FL
2	125cc	Works Yamaha twin	Cervia	12 April FL
Retired (electrical)	250cc	Works Yamaha	Cervia	12 April
1	125cc Spanish GP	Works Yamaha four	Barcelona	3 May RL
Retired (engine)	250cc Spanish GP	Works Yamaha four	Barcelona	3 May
Retired (crash)	125cc West German GP	Works Yamaha four	Hockenheim	10 May RL
Retired (gearbox)	250cc West German GP	Works Yamaha four	Hockenheim	10 May RL
1	125cc French GP	Works Yamaha four	Clermont-Ferrand	24 May RL
1	250cc French GP	Works Yamaha four	Clermont-Ferrand	24 May
1	125cc	Works Yamaha twin	Brands Hatch	1 June FL
Retired (engine)	250cc Lightweight TT	Works Yamaha four	Isle of Man	15 June
Retired (at pits on first lap)	125cc Ultra Lightweight TT	Works Yamaha four	Isle of Man	17 June
1	125cc	Works Yamaha twin	Mallory Park	21 June RL
2	125cc Dutch TT	Works Yamaha four	Assen	28 June
2	250cc Dutch TT	Works Yamaha four	Assen	28 June
1	250cc Belgian GP	Works Yamaha four	Spa Francorchamps	5 July FL
1	125cc East German GP	Works Yamaha four	Sachsenring	16 July RL
2	150cc East German GP	Works Yamaha four	Sachsenring	16 July
1	125cc Czech GP	Works Yamaha four	Brno	23 July RL
2	250cc Czech GP	Works Yamaha four	Brno	23 July
2	125cc Finnish GP	Works Yamaha four	Imatra	6 August RL
2	250cc Finnish GP	Works Yamaha four	Imatra	6 August
1	125cc Hutchinson 100	Works Yamaha twin	Brands Hatch (reverse direction)	13 August RL
1	125cc Ulster GP	Works Yamaha four	Dundrod	19 August RL
3	250cc Ulster GP	Works Yamaha four	Dundrod	19 August
1	125cc	Works Yamaha twin	Snetterton	27 August RL
1	125cc Italian GP	Works Yamaha four	Monza	3 September FL

Position	Class	Machine	Circuit	Date
2	250cc Italian GP	Works Yamaha four	Monza	3 September RL
1	125cc	Works Yamaha twin	Cadwell Park	10 September RL
2	250cc	Works Yamaha twin	Cadwell Park	10 September
2	750cc Invitation	Works Yamaha twin 249cc	Cadwell Park	10 September
Retired (engine)	125cc	Works Yamaha twin	Mallory Park	17 September
5	Race of the Year	Works Yamaha twin 251cc	Mallory Park	17 September
1	125cc Canadian GP	Works Yamaha four	Mosport	30 September RL
Retired (engine)	250cc Canadian GP	Works Yamaha four	Mosport	30 September
1	125cc	Works Yamaha twin	Brands Hatch	1 October FL
1	125cc Japanese GP	Works Yamaha four	Fuji	15 October RL
Retired (broken crankshaft)	250cc Japanese GP	Works Yamaha four	Fuji	15 October

125cc World Champion

3rd 250cc World Championship

1968

Position	Class	Machine	Circuit	Date
1	125cc	Works Yamaha twin	Alicante	4 February FL
1	250cc	Works Yamaha	Alicante	4 February FL
Retired (engine)	125cc West German GP	Works Yamaha four	Nürburgring	20 April RL
1	250cc West German GP	Works Yamaha four	Nürburgring	21 April RL
1	125cc	Works Yamaha	Cervia	21 April FL
1	250cc	Works Yamaha	Cervia	21 April FL
Retired (broken crankshaft)	125cc Spanish GP	Works Yamaha four	Barcelona	5 May FL
Retired	250cc Spanish GP	Works Yamaha four	Barcelona	5 May
1	125cc	Works Yamaha four	Cadwell Park	19 May RL
Retired (misfiring)	250cc	Works Yamaha four	Cadwell Park	19 May
1	250cc Lightweight TT	Works Yamaha four	Isle of Man	10 June RL
2	125cc Ultra Lightweight TT	Works Yamaha four	Isle of Man	14 June RL
Retied (engine)	125cc	Works Yamaha four	Mallory Park	12 June
1	250cc	Works Yamaha four	Mallory Park	12 June FL
Retired (injury)	125cc Dutch TT	Works Yamaha four	Assen	29 June FL
1	250cc Dutch TT	Works Yamaha four	Assen	29 June RL
Retired	250cc Belgian GP	Works Yamaha four	Spa Francorchamps	7 July FL
2	125cc East German GP	Works Yamaha four	Sachsenring	14 July RL
1	250cc East German GP	Works Yamaha four	Sachsenring	14 July
Retired (crash)	125cc Czech GP	Works Yamaha four	Brno	21 July FL
2	250cc Czech GP	Works Yamaha four	Brno	21 July
2	125cc Finnish GP	Works Yamaha four	Imatra	4 August RL

Position	Class	Machine	Circuit	Date
Retired (crash)	250cc Finnish GP	Works Yamaha four	Imatra	4 August
Retired (misfiring)	250cc	Works Yamaha four	Brands Hatch	11 August RL
4	1st leg 1000cc	Works Yamaha four 248cc	Brands Hatch	11 August
3	2nd leg 1000cc	Works Yamaha four 248cc	Brands Hatch	11 August
3	Overall 1000cc	Works Yamaha four 248cc	Brands Hatch	11 August
1	125cc Ulster GP	Works Yamaha four	Dundrod	17 August
1	250cc Ulster GP	Works Yamaha four	Dundrod	17 August FL
5	125cc	Works Yamaha four	Snetterton	31 August
3	250cc	Works Yamaha four	Snetterton	31 August
Retired (non-starter)	1000cc	Works Yamaha four 248cc	Snetterton	31 August
Retired (engine seized)	125cc	Works Yamaha four	Oulton Park	1 September
1	250cc	Works Yamaha four	Oulton Park	1 September FL
1	125cc Italian GP	Works Yamaha four	Monza	15 September FL
2	250cc Italian GP	Works Yamaha four	Monza	15 September
1	125cc	Works Yamaha four	Mallory Park	22 September FL
1	250cc Heat	Works Yamaha four	Mallory Park	22 September
2	250cc Final	Works Yamaha four	Mallory Park	22 September
Retired (crash)	1000cc Race of the Year	Works Yamaha four 248cc	Mallory Park	22 September
1	125cc	Works Yamaha four	Riccione	29 September FL
2	250cc	Works Yamaha four	Riccione	29 September
Retired	350cc	Works Yamaha four 251cc	Riccione	29 September
1	125cc	Works Yamaha four	Brands Hatch	6 October RL
2	250cc	Works Yamaha four	Brands Hatch	6 October
Retired (plug trouble)	1000cc	Works Yamaha four 248cc	Brands Hatch	6 October
4	500cc Redex Trophy	Seeley 496cc	Brands Hatch	6 October

2nd 125cc World Championship

2nd 250cc World Championship

1969

Position	Class	Machine	Circuit	Date
Retired (seized)	350cc	Jawa four	Cesenatico	13 April
Retired (seized)	350cc Spanish GP	Jawa four	Barcelona	4 May
2	350cc West German GP	Jawa four	Hockenheim	11 May
1	350cc Heat	Yamaha TR2	Brands Hatch	26 May
Retired (ignition)	350cc Final	Yamaha TR2	Brands Hatch	26 May
2	350cc Dutch TT	Jawa four	Assen	28 June
Fatally injured during practice	350cc East German GP	Jawa	Sachsenring	11 July

Index